Matchmoving:
The Invisible Art of
Camera Tracking

Tim Dobbert

SYBEX® San Francisco • London

Publisher: DAN BRODNITZ
Acquisitions Editor: WILLEM KNIBBE
Developmental Editor: PETE GAUGHAN
Production Editor: ELIZABETH CAMPBELL
Technical Editor: TIM TURNER
Copyeditor: ANAMARY EHLEN
Compositor: CHRIS GILLESPIE, HAPPENSTANCE TYPE-O-RAMA
Graphic Illustrator: HAPPENSTANCE TYPE-O-RAMA
CD Coordinator: DAN MUMMERT
CD Technician: KEVIN LY
Proofreaders: NANCY RIDDIOUGH, CANDACE ENGLISH
Indexer: TED LAUX
Book Designer: FRANZ BAUMHACKL
Cover Design and Illustration: JOHN NEDWIDEK, EMDESIGN

Software License Agreement: Terms and Conditions

For Desiree, without whom this book would not have been possible.

 # Acknowledgments

I'd like to send out a thanks to everyone at Sybex who was involved with this book, especially Willem Knibbe, Pete Gaughan, Elizabeth Campbell, Tim Turner, and Anamary Ehlen. You helped bring focus to my ideas, and your encouragement was greatly appreciated.

I'd also like to thank Sean Wagstaff for his early support and for kicking me in the pants a little to help get this book off the ground. Thanks to the folks at 2d3 and Realviz, especially Ed Bolton, Steve Hill, Christian Ristedt, and Temis Nunez for their support. Thanks also to Jeff Salzman, Joe Stevenson, and Brian Cantwell at ILM; Luke O'Byrne, John Benson, and David Dranitzke at The Orphanage; as well as Mark Siew, Russ Andersson, and Tony Rizo for all of their feedback and suggestions.

I'd particularly like to thank everyone who contributed some of the fantastic images and sequences used in this book: Greg Downing, Alex Lindsay of dvGarage, Jorge Mendoza of Litigation Animation, Quan Tran, and Trevor Tuttle.

Special thanks to my wife Desiree, whose patience and support never flagged for a moment during the writing of this book. I can't express how much I appreciate everything you've done. And special thanks, too, for my daughter Sabina, who gave up a lot of her "daddy-time" so that this book could happen.

Contents

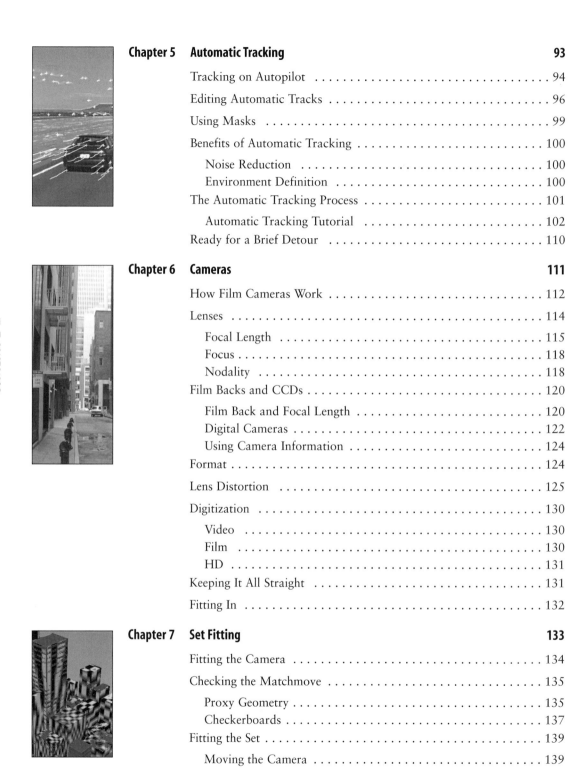

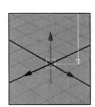

Chapter 8 Being on Set   161

Chapter 9 Matchamation   175

Chapter 12 Multipurposing Matchmove Data   **237**

Appendix A Resources   **253**

Appendix B Matchmoving Software and Useful Links   **255**

Appendix C Film Formats   **259**

Introduction

I remember getting my first glimpses of the sequences in *Hellboy* that my team of matchmovers was about to work on. One that stood out in particular was the opening sequence in the movie, in which the villains were attempting to open the gates of Hell with a special machine. The sequence had all the elements of a great action film: a driving rainstorm, lightning, explosions, people running everywhere, and a lot of fast-moving camerawork. I realized immediately that this would be an incredible sequence, but also a very difficult one from the vantage point of a matchmover.

Experienced matchmovers look at effects shots with a different eye than other visual effects artists because their job is unique. Their main goal is to decipher the clues in the live-action footage and create a 3D scene that animators can use to place their effects in the shot. It is an important job, even though it is not readily visible in the final shot. Actually, the only time a matchmove is visible in the shot is if it is a *bad* matchmove. I often tell my students, "If you've done your job right, no one should ever know you've done your job at all."

In a lot of ways matchmoving—or camera tracking as it's sometimes called—is really just like solving a puzzle. Sometimes they can be fairly straightforward, and other times they can be extremely difficult. But it is this problem-solving aspect of matchmoving that has kept me working in this specialized area of visual effects for so long.

Many visual effects artists understand the need for matchmoving, but very few know what's really happening "under the hood," and that is part of the reason for this book. There is a strong technical aspect to matchmoving, but there is an art to getting a tough matchmove to work. The art of matchmoving becomes easier the more you do it, but there are always interesting technical challenges around every corner.

Who Should Read This Book

I've written *Matchmoving* for two types of people. The first are visual effects artists who are not matchmovers by trade but are occasionally tasked with matchmoving in addition to their other duties as animators or technical directors. Generally, these folks are given some matchmoving software and a few tutorials and sent off to matchmove the shot. Being highly talented visual effects artists, they quickly figure out how the software works and throw their shot at it. If they're lucky, it's an easy shot and they achieve satisfactory results. But often, they find that their footage is considerably more difficult than the tutorial footage, and they are only able to arrive at a solution through a lengthy trial-and-error process. Much of the pain of matchmoving can be eliminated by knowing how the matchmoving software achieves its results. Relatively simple techniques can speed up the process, eliminate the guesswork, and help the matchmover to deliver a quality solution to artists further down the production pipeline.

The second type of person is the 3D animation or compositing student. There are the obvious benefits to knowing how to accurately track 3D elements into your footage, but there are other, more compelling reasons. I firmly believe that matchmoving is a great way to break into the visual effects industry. This industry is a highly competitive one, and with little or no production experience, many students must bang their heads tirelessly on the doors of studios in search of their first job.

Many of my own students have landed their first jobs in the matchmove departments of high-profile visual effects companies. There is one simple reason for this: *Most visual effects artists don't want to be matchmovers!* They'd much rather be character animators, effects technical directors, or compositors. And who can blame them? It's nice to be able to point to a cool character or explosion and say, "I did that!" But no one ever says, "Did you notice the brilliant matchmoves on that show? I didn't see one single slip." Matchmoving may not be the most glamorous job in visual effects, but there will always be a strong demand for knowledgeable matchmovers.

I've written *Matchmoving* to give visual effects artists the tools and techniques to help make their encounters with matchmoving as easy and pain-free and possible. And if you're one of the few who decide to make a career of matchmoving, this book will be a great starting point for your studies. This book won't tell you what every button and menu does for each matchmoving program—I'll leave that to the user's guides. It will, however, show you how those programs work and even walk you through the process.

I've designed this book to be as non–program specific as possible, apart from the obvious need for matchmove-specific software. It was really tough to decide which matchmoving programs to use for the tutorials, because there are so many great options for matchmovers these days. Since space was limited, I decided to pare it down to Realviz's MatchMover Pro and 2d3's boujou. But for the most part, the techniques I describe here are compatible with all 3D animation and matchmove software packages and do not require special knowledge of any particular programs.

What's Inside

Matchmoving: The Invisible Art of Camera Tracking is broken up into 12 chapters:

Chapter 1, "The Basics of Matchmoving" A basic overview of what matchmoving is and how it fits into a typical visual effects pipeline. There's also a tutorial for matching the perspective of a still image.

Chapter 2, "Matchmoving Software" Chapters 2 through 5 all deal with matchmoving programs and how they work. This chapter lays the groundwork by explaining the processes used in photogrammetry and how they are implemented in these programs.

Chapter 3, "2D Tracking" As one of the first steps in a matchmove, 2D tracking can make or break a solution. This chapter breaks down 2D tracking and shows ways to make yourself a more effective tracker.

Chapter 4, "3D Calibration" Calibrating, or solving, can be one of the more frustrating parts of getting a good matchmove. In Chapter 4, I shed light on this sometimes mysterious process and provide ways to help you get the best solution possible.

Chapter 5, "Automatic Tracking" Most matchmoving programs these days have automatic 2D tracking capabilities. In this chapter, I show how automatic tracking is used and how it differs from other forms of 2D tracking.

Chapter 6, "Cameras" This chapter is entirely devoted to real-world cameras since that is a primary concern for matchmovers. It covers everything about cameras that is important to a matchmover and how they are similar or different from their virtual counterparts in animation programs.

Chapter 7, "Set Fitting" Getting the right camera is only half the battle with a typical matchmove because you still must fit the camera into any existing scenes you may have. This chapter shows you how to quickly and accurately place your cameras into your 3D scene.

Chapter 8, "Being On Set" If you're ever asked to prep a set for matchmoving, this is an important chapter for you to read. I cover the roles and responsibilities of a matchmover on a film shoot as well as how to get the best information possible.

Chapter 9, "Matchamation" Matchmovers sometimes have to match more than just cameras. This chapter shows you how to match computer-generated (CG) objects to moving objects in the plate.

Chapter 10, "Troubleshooting and Advanced Techniques" This chapter covers ways to help solve difficult shots or shots that are just giving you problems. It includes a trouble-shooting checklist and tips to coaxing a good solution out of mediocre data.

Chapter 11, "Modeling from Matchmoves and Image-Based Modeling" This chapter covers how to model through a matchmoved camera. It also highlights a related technique known as image-based modeling and how it can be used to create CG objects from photographs.

Chapter 12, "Multipurposing Matchmove Data" There are lots of ways to use matchmove data besides calculating cameras. This chapter shows you some of the possibilities.

Appendix A describes the sample reports and checklists I've provided on the companion CD. I've included a list of current matchmoving programs in Appendix B for those interested in knowing more about them. Appendix C contains key information about various movie cameras that will help your matchmoving efforts. Also, matchmoving comes with its fair share of jargon, so I've defined some key words in a glossary at the back of the book.

As more and more directors add CG elements to their projects, there will be a greater need for matchmovers. Although matchmoving is truly an invisible art, I hope that this book will help bring to light many of the techniques that have languished in anonymity for so long.

How to Contact the Author

If you'd like to contact me with feedback or questions, write to ectokon@hotmail.com.

The Basics of Matchmoving

Anytime a computer-generated (CG) element needs to be placed into a live-action sequence or vice versa, a matchmove is required. But what exactly is matchmoving?

Matchmoving is the process of matching CG elements into live-action footage. As a result, it's a crucial part of many visual effects shots. Despite its importance, it is completely invisible in the final shot—that is, if it's done right.

In this chapter, I explain the key steps involved in a matchmove and how matchmovers work with the rest of the visual effects team. I've also included a tutorial that is designed to help you get comfortable working with cameras and perspective.

1

1

Chapter Contents

A Typical Matchmove

In order to better understand what matchmovers do, let's consider a typical visual effects shot. The director has called for a CG creature to crash out of window of a building and run across the street and into an alley. Because the monster will need to interact with the window, the visual effects supervisor decides that in addition to the monster, the window-shattering effect should also be done in the computer.

On the day of shooting, the director makes artistic decisions as to how he wants to shoot the scene and eventually decides on a camera position that he likes. There is an opening on the building where the window should be, although the panes of glass are missing. The director and the cameraman practice the camera move a few times and watch the video playback to see how it looks. When they are filming, they move the camera as though it were following the monster crashing through the window and running across the street, even though the monster isn't there. Extras react to the imaginary beast, and props around the window are rigged with monofilament string (fishing line) to be pulled down on cue as though they were knocked over. Once the director is happy with the shot, the film is sent off to be digitized and then given to the visual effects artists to add the monster.

When the visual effects studio receives the digitized sequence (known as a *plate*), they decide that they will need an animator to animate the creature and a technical director (TD) to do the glass-shattering effect. And, of course, they'll need a matchmover to matchmove the plate.

The visual effects artists' goals are to make their 3D elements look as realistic as the scene that was filmed. The animator will need to make the creature move as though it were really crashing through a window, and the TD will need to make the window shatter like a real window. The matchmover needs to figure out where the camera was and how it was moving when the scene was filmed.

Matchmovers play an important role in this case, because in order for the creature and window to appear matched realistically with the scene, they need to make sure that the CG objects are "filmed" the same way with their CG camera as the real set was filmed with the real camera. Consider the window that needs to shatter—if the perspective of the window doesn't match the perspective in the plate, it will look out of place. Furthermore, if the real camera moves to the left and the CG window stays put, everyone will know it's a fake.

In our example effects shot, the visual effects supervisor measures key items on the set. For example, she measures the size of the opening of the window as well as its height off the ground. She measures the distance across the street and the size of the opening to the alleyway. She draws a rough picture of the set and makes notes about positions of certain props and lights that might be useful to know. She also measures how high the camera is off the ground, what lens is used, and how far it is from the window.

Typically the animator, TD, and matchmover all start at the same time. Since there are some measurements of the set, the animator knows how high the creature needs to jump to get through the window and how far to make it run across the street. The TD knows the size of the window that needs to shatter and how high it is off the ground. This is enough information to allow them to start setting up their scenes.

While they're doing that, the matchmover starts by first examining the footage to get an idea of how the camera was moving during the shot. He brings the footage into his matchmoving software and begins to track the 2D features in the scene as they move around the screen. 2D tracking usually involves identifying things in the scene that don't move (such as the corner of a building) and then letting the software follow that feature as the footage plays.

Once the matchmover has tracked a number of 2D tracks, the software analyzes these tracks and computes the position of the camera in relation to the items in the scene. At the end of this process, the matchmover exports a scene to his 3D-animation package that includes an animated camera and the 3D positions for all of the features he tracked.

Once the matchmover is happy with the camera he has generated, he goes about fitting that camera into a CG scene that is the same size as the one the animator and TD are using. When he's finished, he is able to look through his CG camera at the CG window and creature, and they appear in the right perspective and scale when compared to the original live-action footage.

Finally, he saves the scene with the matchmove camera in it. The animator and TD both use this camera to render their animations. If they've placed their window and creature in the right place in the environment, then they don't need to worry about whether the perspective matches or whether movement of the camera is the same. As long as they've rendered it using the matchmove camera, it will appear matched into the footage (Figure 1.1).

 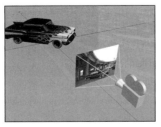 

Figure 1.1 In the original "clean" plate (left) we see the image before the CG elements are placed in the shot. In the 3D-animation software, a CG camera is positioned in the environment (middle) in such a way that when the CG vehicle is viewed through it (right), the perspective matches that of the plate.

From 3D to 2D and Back Again

No discussion of matchmoving would be complete without discussing cameras. For match-movers, it is important to understand how real-world cameras work and how they make the images we see on the screen. I'll discuss cameras more in-depth in Chapter 6, "Cameras," but for now there are a few basic concepts about real-world cameras that are important to know before getting started.

When a real camera films a scene, it is basically doing one thing: capturing the three-dimensional world as a two-dimensional image. That is, it gathers light from the 3D world around us and records it in a 2D form, such as a piece of film or a digital image. Let's consider for a moment exactly how this happens.

The light from the scene passes through the camera lens and is focused onto film that rests in the *film gate* on the back of the camera's inner chamber. The shutter closes, the film advances, the shutter opens again, and the process repeats. In the case of digital cameras, the film and film gate are replaced by a *CCD* (Charge-Coupled Device) that electronically captures the light information and records it to some sort of memory device.

The cameras in a 3D-animation program are based on real cameras, but they are represented in a slightly different manner. 3D-animation cameras represent a mathematically perfect model of the optics and construction of a real camera. Like real-world cameras, they have a focal length and a *film back* (the equivalent of a film gate). But rather than capturing light from the real world, they are simply capturing information of the synthetic, computer-generated environment in which they have been placed.

Whether you're dealing with exposed film or a 3D render, the resulting image is a *projection*. That is, the three-dimensional scene is flattened out into a two-dimensional representation of that scene. We have become so accustomed to these flattened images that we hardly notice them anymore, but every time we watch TV or a film, we are watching a flat recording of a three-dimensional scene (Figure 1.2).

Figure 1.2 When a camera captures an image of the three-dimensional world, it is really capturing the light from the scene that is projected across its image plane.

The Matchmoving Process

So if a camera's purpose is to take the three-dimensional world and make a two-dimensional image, a matchmover's job is the exact opposite. A matchmover must take a two-dimensional image and create a three-dimensional world. The portal between these two halves is the camera. If information about the camera can be reconstructed, it will go a long way toward figuring out how the 3D environment must have been at the time of filming. This information—the 3D environment and the camera—is what a matchmover will ultimately deliver to the animators to work with.

A matchmover's workflow (Figure 1.3) generally follows the same pattern for each shot, although there are a variety of ways to complete each task. The figure shows a typical matchmove *pipeline*. In the following sections, we'll examine each of these steps more closely.

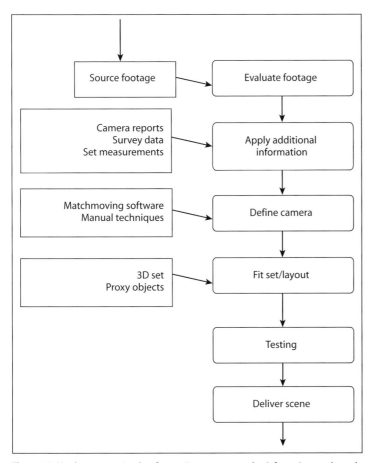

Figure 1.3 Matchmovers receive data from various sources, use that information to solve and set up the scene, and then deliver a scene with a matchmoved camera.

Evaluate the Footage

This is perhaps the most important step in the matchmoving process, and unfortunately it is often overlooked. There are many ways to solve a matchmove, and careful scrutiny of the plate can help decide the appropriate tool to use, what pitfalls to watch out for, and how long it might take. This last item is particularly important, since clients and supervisors often put it at the top of their list of questions.

One reason the evaluation process is so often glossed over is that many of the things that determine the difficulty of matchmove require some experience to judge. Some typical questions asked during the evaluation of a shot could include:

- What does the camera seem to be doing? Is it moving, and if so, how? Is it locked off or panning? How fast is it moving?

- What is visible in the shot? Are there tracking markers? Is anything blocking the markers?

- What format is the plate? Was it shot on film? DV? HD? Is there excessive compression, grain, or noise on the images?

- What needs to be placed in the shot? How accurate does it have to be?

- Who will be using the matchmove, and how will they be using it?

Of course, these only scratch the surface, but the more questions you ask, the more you will know what you need to do. The tutorials in this book are designed to help you learn what these key questions are and how to deal with their implications. A more thorough list of questions are included in Appendix A. The Evaluation Checklist there can be used as a guideline to help determine the difficulty of a matchmove.

Applying Information

As I've said, solving a matchmove can be like solving a puzzle (it's no coincidence that it's referred to as "solving" a matchmove). And as such, the more information there is, the easier it should be to achieve good results.

The amount of information given to matchmovers can run the gamut. There might only be an image sequence and nothing else, or perhaps someone was allowed on set to record all the camera information and take measurements. Usually it's somewhere in between. But the good news is that a surprisingly small amount of data can go a long way toward solving the matchmove.

The following are typical data a matchmover might include:

Camera information Such as focal length, aperture, and film type.

Set measurements Including camera height, focus distance, and measurements of various items in the shot.

Survey data This is very detailed measuring of the set, usually done by a professional surveyor.

Define the Camera

As stated before, the matchmover's job is to define all of the internal and external parameters of the camera, and there are many ways to do that. Knowing which method to use and under what circumstances comes with experience, but sometimes the only way to solve the matchmove is to experiment and see what works best. In broad terms, there are two major ways of solving for the camera: manual and automatic.

The manual methods harken back to the days before software existed to help matchmovers. This category would include perspective matching (matching the perspective of a single background image, rather than an image sequence, which is covered later in this chapter) and old-fashioned hand-tracking. This method of tracking a sequence involves making a speculation as to the camera's position and then refining it over many iterations until a match is achieved. Tracking a camera by hand is no small feat. It can often take weeks to truly figure out what is happening, because the process is nothing more than making educated guesses and tweaking them until they work.

In the past five or six years, software has emerged that allows a matchmover to track cameras somewhat automatically using a sophisticated technology known as *photogrammetry*. These software packages (which are covered in the next chapter) usually have a similar workflow to them. First, features in the image such as props in the scene or tape markers (commonly used on blue screen footage to mark points on the wall) are "tracked" as they move around the image in 2D. Then the software performs a *calibration* (or *solve*) for the camera by mathematically analyzing the movements of the 2D tracking markers. These packages usually generate an animated camera and 3D markers or nulls that represent the three-dimensional location of features that have been tracked in 2D. Matchmovers use this method most often since it is the easiest way to achieve a solution.

Some methods borrow from both manual and automatic techniques. Oftentimes, these are customized solutions that revolve around both types of workflows. For example, the 2D tracking information from matchmoving software could be used with a custom script that allows the matchmover to solve for pan shots.

Set Fitting

While cameras are the primary concern, they are only half of the process of matchmoving. Matchmovers must not only uncover all the facts about the camera, but they must also reconstruct the spatial layout of the environment on the live-action plate.

Figure 1.4 shows why this information is important. The first image shows an incorrect camera and building placement—what a mess. The second image has the correct camera, but the building is too close to the camera; therefore it doesn't match.

But notice the third image. In this case, the building is in the correct position and distance from the camera, but since the camera isn't correct, the building still doesn't line up. The last image shows how it should be matched up with the correct camera and building placement. These images illustrate how matchmoving is not just solving cameras, and not just solving environments, but also figuring out the relationship between the two.

Wrong camera, wrong building

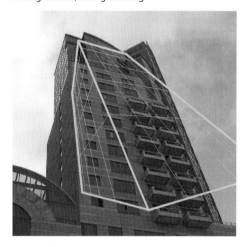

Right camera, wrong building

Wrong camera, right building

Right camera, right building

Figure 1.4 These images show the relationship between solving correctly for the camera and correctly placing the set.

How much of the environment does the matchmover need to reproduce? That depends on what is being placed into the footage. If it is simply a character walking by, the animators and TDs might only need a simple ground plane. Other scenes might need rough geometry in order to cast 3D shadows. In some cases, such as digital set extensions, the matchmove might require an extremely accurate camera, detailed geometry, and spot-on positioning. Before beginning a matchmove, it is important to find out what type of 3D object is going into the scene and exactly where it will be placed.

3D environments might come from a variety of sources. Oftentimes, matchmovers create the rough geometry themselves or are provided a set to "fit" into the plate. And in some situations, the matchmover may provide a rough set from which a more detailed set is later constructed by a modeler. Many times, matchmovers use 3D markers they've calculated during the matchmove to provide information about the spatial relationships of the scene. But regardless of where the information comes from, it is often the matchmover's responsibility to establish the environment and set up the scene so that other artists further down the production pipeline don't need to worry about it.

Testing the Matchmove

Once the matchmove is solved, it needs to be tested for accuracy. A bad matchmove usually shows up as an obvious disconnect between the live-action plate and the CG elements. For example, the CG element seems to follow the motion and rotation of the live-action scene, but then suddenly the CG element pops to another location or gradually drifts away from the feature it's supposed to be resting on. Testing the matchmove consists of compositing the 3D objects over the image sequence and watching as the sequence moves to see if there are any unusual pops, drifts, or jitter.

Most often, matchmovers will have low-resolution objects, or *proxy objects*, in the scene to help them determine the quality of their matchmove. One of the best ways to see if an object is slipping is to place a checkerboard texture on it and render it out. This will help highlight slippage in 3D space.

A thorough testing is crucial, because a bad matchmove conceivably could work its way all the way through the pipeline and not be noticed until the end. And by this time there is usually a lot less time to deal with the problem and a lot more pressure.

Delivering the Scene

Last but not least, the final scene is delivered to other artists down the line. This step will vary greatly depending on whether the scene goes to a single artist working alone, or the scene is being turned over in a large production pipeline.

Certain items will need to be considered, such as:

- Orientation and scale of scene
- Objects that need to be included such as sets, characters, etc.
- Naming conventions, formats, etc.

A well-organized and clearly laid-out scene will make other artists' jobs easier and also make it less likely that you will have to explain the scene to someone after the fact.

 Note: I've included a sample Scene Delivery Checklist in Appendix A. This checklist represents items I've found helpful in making my final matchmove scenes as foolproof as possible. I also cover this in more detail in Chapter 7, "Integrating Matchmoves with the Scene."

Matchmoving in the Production Pipeline

So how does matchmoving fit into the production pipeline? It really depends on the size of the production and the people who are being asked to provide the matchmoves. On larger-scale productions, there is often a department that deals specifically with matchmoving the shots. Of course, matchmoving is only necessary if you are trying to fit CG elements into live-action plates.

Matchmoving usually happens early in a production. This is because the animators and TDs need to know exactly where to place their characters, explosions, etc., and they need a camera from which to look at and render their objects. For tight deadlines, matchmovers might also be asked to set up temporary cameras that approximate the move, so that the TDs and animators can start their preliminary work and testing while the matchmove is finished.

Figure 1.5 shows a fairly common production pipeline and where matchmoving fits in. The matchmover takes the original footage at full resolution, solves the matchmove, and then delivers a 3D scene to an animator or TD. In some studios, matchmove data might be useful to other departments such as roto, paint, or compositing. (See Chapter 12, "Multipurposing Matchmove Data," for more on this.)

Perspective Matching Tutorial

Now that you know how matchmoving fits into the big picture, we're ready to get down to actually working on a shot. In this tutorial, you'll create a simple matchmove scene that solves a problem many CG artists have faced at one time or another: perspective matching.

Perhaps the simplest form of matchmoving is matching the perspective of a single still image. Oftentimes, these are used as backdrops for 3D elements. Since the camera is not moving, all that needs to be done is to position the camera relative to the object so that the perspective of the model looks appropriate. Even so, it can be frustrating to try and line things up.

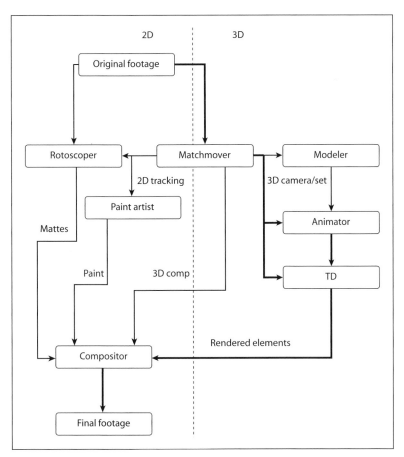

Figure 1.5 The normal pipeline has a matchmover delivering a scene to an animator or TD, but the matchmove data can also be used by other departments.

A few simple pieces of information can help make this process easier and less time-consuming:

- The focal length of the camera used to take the photo
- The height of the camera when the photo was shot
- The distance from the camera to an object in the real scene
- The scale of the object in the scene

Ideally, the person who took the image would provide all of the above information, but in most cases this is wishful thinking. For this tutorial, you'll need the image called f0106.tif (shown in Figure 1.6). For the purposes of this tutorial, let's assume a worst-case scenario: there isn't any information about the camera or environment for this image. The best way to deal with these situations is to approach the problem methodically. By making careful estimations and maintaining a 3D scene that is similar to the "real world" scene, we can zero in on a solution.

Figure 1.6 Our task is to create a camera so that 3D objects can be placed between the two buildings on the right.

Gathering the Data

Let's take a look at the image in Figure 1.6, in which we are asked to provide a camera and scene for the animators to work with. Consider what information we have and what we can do with it:

Focal length The focal length of the camera is a little bit tricky to figure out. For a still image, it's probably not necessary that it be exact, but simply in the ballpark. Until the building is in the right place, there's no way to play with this value, so it'll be necessary to make an initial guess and then try and zero in on a useable value later.

Measurements There aren't any measurements of the scene, but perhaps the strongest assumption that can be made about this image is that it was taken by a person standing at street level. Therefore, it's reasonable to assume that the camera is a little less than 2 meters off the ground.

> **Note:** This book uses metric measurements, because that is the standard practice in most studios.

Distance We don't have any idea of the distance to the buildings or the scale of the buildings themselves. If we were given a model that was based on the blueprints of the building, we would have some solid data to work with, but since we don't, we'll have to make a guess at this as well.

Setting Up the Camera

As is often the case with a matchmove, the process is not a linear one. Usually, it is an iterative one, where we do one or two things to get a rough result and then make a few more passes to refine it and build on known facts, until at some point we have matched it to the required level of accuracy. This example is no exception. Below, I show the steps to get the building matched.

1. **Evaluate the scene.** Since we're not dealing with images in motion, the key thing to figure out when matching the perspective of an image is where your 3D models need to go. Let's say that we want a spaceship to fly in between these two buildings and cast shadows on them as it goes by. That means we need to know the camera's position as well as the position of each of the buildings.

2. **Make a camera and create an image plane or background image using the still image.** First we need a camera to work with. This should be a freely moving camera (as opposed to a targeted or aimed camera). Since the ultimate goal is to align the objects with the plate, we will need to set up the camera or environment so that the image is seen as a backdrop behind the 3D objects when we look through the camera.

3. **Estimate focal length and aperture on the camera.** The two main things we'll need to know for the camera setup are the focal length and the film back. As we've already covered, we don't know the exact value for this lens, so we'll have to guess. I took a guess of 35mm for this lens as a starting point.

4. **Estimate the film back value.** In this case, I don't know the specific value for the film back. If I knew the brand of camera, I could look up the specs for it on the Internet and plug in those values. If you don't know the film back, it's

best to go with a standard value of 0.980″ × 0.735″ or use the default settings in your animation program. The reasons for these values are a bit complicated, so I'll save the explanation for Chapter 6, but for now this will give us something to work with.

5.   **Set the height of the camera.** Since this is the strongest assumption we can make about the camera, we'll enter it in first. We'll assume an average height for the camera of about 1.75 meters off the ground, so place the camera at 1.75m up on the Y-axis.

Not All Film Backs Are the Same

Don't worry if you find yourself a little bit confused by all of this film back business. It can bewilder even the most seasoned visual effects pros. Oftentimes, 3D artists just guess at the value or use preset values in the software.

To make matters even more confusing, every 3D animation and matchmove program uses different terminology and has different ways of entering the information. Matchmove programs use the term "film back," whereas most 3D animation programs call this the "aperture." For example, 3D Studio Max calls it the Horizontal Aperture and only allows you to enter the horizontal measurement in millimeters. Lightwave uses the Vertical Aperture only, and Maya allows you to enter both Horizontal and Vertical Aperture measurements, but only in inches! You should consult the documentation for your software to see where you need to enter this information and how.

Adding Rough Geometry and Refining the Camera

Now that we have a camera set up, we need to start fleshing out the geometry in the scene. When the animators get ready to put the UFO in between the buildings, they'll need to know where the buildings are. The task of identifying the location of objects in the scene often falls on the shoulders of matchmovers. This geometry needs to be accurate to the image so that any additional objects that are added to the scene will appear to be in the correct location. You usually don't need to build geometry for the entire scene, just the portions that will interact directly with the CG objects.

I've found that creating geometry for a scene can be done in conjunction with the initial camera setup. Often you'll need to make continual refinements to the camera and geometry until you've zeroed in on the correct placement for both. The good news is, once you've built one or two objects, the rest become much simpler to build. Also, once you've built objects to work with, you'll find it much easier to find the camera's exact position.

1. **Create a building of an estimated height.** This is where it starts to get tricky, since we really have little to go on here. I estimated the size by looking at the windows. I figured that each floor of the building was about 4 meters tall. So I counted the number of floors and multiplied it by 4m. I guessed that the building was a little under 14 floors, so 55 meters seemed about right. Likewise, I tried to use visual clues to estimate the width and depth of the building. After my initial guess, I came up with values for my building of X = 16.5m, Y = 55m, and Z = 20m.

2. **Move the building to an estimated distance.** This is likely to be the most difficult value to estimate. There aren't too many clues as to how far the photographer was away from the building, so I needed to guess how far away the building should be. I chose 78 meters by comparing the scale of my building as I moved it away from the camera. This, of course, assumes that the size of my CG building is correct. If not, we can always adjust this later (Figure 1.7).

Figure 1.7 For this image, the camera is at its correct height, and the building is approximately the same scale as the building on the right.

3. **Adjust the camera angle until the corner of your object is lined up with the corner of the building in the image.** Now that our camera is roughly positioned and set up, we can start the business of lining up the object. Rather than try and randomly match the entire object at once, it's easier to try and line up just one point on the

model to "lock down" one feature. This creates a connection or common point between the 3D scene and the 2D scene and creates a foundation on which to build a better match (Figure 1.8).

Figure 1.8 By rotating the camera, we can get the upper-right corner of our 3D building to match up with the image.

For now, don't concern yourself if the perspective or scale of the object is off, just focus on getting one corner of the 3D building to match with the corner of the building on the image. The idea here is to find one common point between the CG object and the real-world scene. If we can get one corner of each aligned properly, then we can use that as the basis for aligning the rest of the scene. For now we can assume that the camera height and distance are correct, so we don't want to translate (move) the model. In my scene, I simply rotated the camera until the upper-right corners lined up.

Creating a Camera Rig

Throughout this book, we'll be creating camera rigs in our 3D software. A *camera rig* is similar in concept to a real-life camera rig such as a boom. It simply is another way to move the camera around more conveniently in the scene. How these rigs are built will vary between the different software packages, but they generally consist of grouping or parenting the camera under one or more nulls (or similar nonrenderable objects) so that the camera can be moved around a different pivot point.

In this case, we have aligned the corners of the CG building and the building in the image, thereby establishing a link between the two. We want to be able to move the camera while maintaining that alignment, so we'll create a rig that does exactly that. Here are the steps to create and position a camera rig:

1. **Make a parent object for the rig.** Create a null object in the scene and name it CameraRig. Snap the null to the upper-right corner of the 3D building that we lined up in the preceding section.

> **Note:** Null objects go by various names in different 3D packages. For example, in Maya they're referred to as "locators," and in 3D Studio Max they're called "Dummy Objects." Basically, whenever I use the term "null," I mean a 3D object that doesn't render and can be used in a parenting structure or to mark a 3D location.

2. **Parent the camera to the CameraRig null** (Figure 1.9). Take care that it stays in its position during the parenting (as opposed to snapping to position of the null).

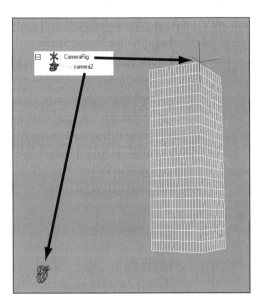

Figure 1.9 The camera rig is created by creating a null that is positioned on the upper-right corner of the image (the object that looks like a crosshair). Then the camera is parented to it.

3. **Use the camera rig to rotate the camera into position.** We can now rotate the CameraRig null to reposition the camera and try to match the perspective. We rotate it on the Y only because our strongest data suggests that the photo was shot at street level, and therefore we want to maintain that relationship. If the rig were rotated on the other axes, it would raise or lower the camera off the ground, and that would be one less piece of information we could take for granted.

If after rotating the camera rig on the Y the building still doesn't line up, you may have to adjust the rotation of the camera a bit more. This will cause the building's corner to come away from the building on the image, so you'll have to reposition it. You might have to go back and forth a few times between rotating the rig on the Y and rotating the camera to get the perspective working better (Figure 1.10).

Camera rigs give you more freedom and control over how you can position the camera. You'll use them quite often in the matchmoving process, and they can really help make it less frustrating.

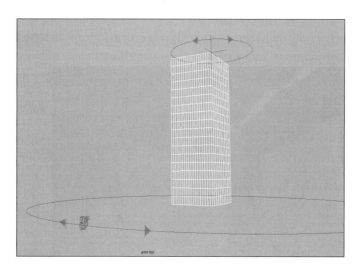

Figure 1.10 Note how the rig allows you to adjust the position of the camera simply by rotating the null. When you rotate the null on the Y-axis, the camera moves around the null on the X- and Z-axes. This keeps the corner of your 3D building on the corner of the building in the image while you adjust the perspective.

Evaluating and Adjusting the Camera

Up until this point, we've been working with approximations for our camera and building. Now we have everything we need to "tighten" up the matchmove and find the exact settings for the camera and the right size and shape for the building. In this phase, we are trying to bring the scene into perfect alignment.

1. **Is focal length right? Experiment.** Now that the camera is roughly positioned, we can do some experimenting to see if the focal length seems right. It looks pretty close, but it can't hurt to poke around some more. I tried different focal length values but ultimately decided that my original guess looked the best, so I stuck with that.

    The focal length can be a little tough to guess, but wider lenses (smaller focal lengths) tend to look more distorted, while longer lenses (higher focal lengths) look flatter. You may also need to do some adjustments to the building's position at this point as well. It's good to do this in tandem with adjusting the focal length, because both produce a similar result, making the building look larger or smaller in the frame (Figure 1.11).

Figure 1.11 Moving the building closer to the camera has made the building too tall and a little bit too narrow. A focal length of 35mm worked better.

2. **Make adjustments to building scale if necessary.** Now it's becoming obvious that the building's scale isn't too accurate, so we adjust it to fit better by scaling it to fit.

When you scale the building, you should scale it from one of the bottom corners. If you scale the building from the center, it will be more difficult to control. In most software packages, you can scale by moving the object's pivot point to the bottom corner of the object (Figure 1.12).

Figure 1.12 Rescaling the building from its bottom finishes off the matchmove.

3. **Continue adjusting the camera rotation, group rotation, and object placement until a fit is achieved.** From here, it's just a matter of tweaking the camera and/or building if necessary. One of the benefits of having created the camera rig is that it gives you several more degrees of freedom without losing accuracy. The CameraRig null allows you to spin the camera to different locations around the building (on the Y-axis only). If you need to adjust the distance of the camera, you can move the camera itself along the X- and Z-axes and rotate it on all three axes.

4. **Place a second building.** Once we've figured out the camera and the position of the first building, the second building's placement is easy. From the looks of it, they are both aligned at their fronts, so we can simply duplicate the existing building and slide it down the X-axis until the right edge of the 3D object lines up with the right edge of the building in the image. Next, we'll slide the model up until the corners are aligned and then scale the building to match (Figure 1.13).

With both buildings in place, you've provided a scene with the correct camera and enough information to show animators or TDs (or even yourself) where the CG object needs to go. If we were adding a UFO between the two buildings, as in Figure 1.14, our rough geometry would show us where to put it. These objects can also serve as geometry for reflections, shadows, or other effects.

Figure 1.13 The second building can be placed simply by duplicating the original and sliding it over on the X-axis.

Figure 1.14 Now we're ready to have our UFO do some fancy flying between the buildings.

Moving Toward Moving Pictures

So as you can see, matchmoving doesn't have to be a completely blind process of random guesses. By building on the information at hand, you can infer the information you don't have. Although we are working on a still image here, the same techniques can be applied to a moving sequence as well.

This method works well for these relatively simple still image situations, but for more complicated shots, it is useful to enlist the help of matchmoving software. Starting with the next chapter, I cover how these programs work, and how they can be used effectively to help solve even the toughest shots.

Matchmoving Software

In Chapter 1, you learned how to place a camera into the scene by matching the perspective of a still image. Perspective matching is helpful in getting a camera set up for a single frame, but what if you had to repeat that process for 100 frames—or 200 or 1000? This is exactly what matchmovers did in the early days of CG. If you've ever tried matchmoving "by hand," you probably found yourself thinking, "There has to be an easier way to do this!"

Thankfully, we now have specialized matchmove programs that help us re-create the cameras quickly and accurately. These programs were created specifically to take the guesswork out of matchmoving and to make matchmovers' lives a whole lot easier.

Chapter Contents

Using Matchmove Programs

Matchmoving programs are arguably the most important tools in a matchmover's arsenal. They give the matchmover the ability to take nearly any image sequence and generate a "solution" for the camera's movement and the positions of features seen in the images.

In Chapter 1, I briefly outlined the overall matchmove process, and in the following chapters I'll talk more about how to use matchmoving programs, but before we get into specifics, it's helpful to know how these programs work.

Matchmoving programs convert 2D information (such as features in images) into 3D information about the camera and scene. The exact procedures vary from program to program, but they generally follow these specific steps:

- Identify 2D features in the image sequence
- Follow those features as the sequence progresses (called *2D tracking*)
- Calculate the 3D camera position
- Calculate the 3D position of the features seen in the image sequence
- Export the resulting camera and nulls to a 3D animation package

As I mentioned in the preceding chapter, matchmoving programs use a sophisticated technique known as *photogrammetry*, which literally means "measuring from photos." Photogrammetry has been around since the advent of photography but hasn't come into widespread use, except in the field of surveying, until recently, when computers became fast enough to perform the complex calculations.

Researchers in the field of robotic vision, in particular, have fueled a renewed interest in photogrammetry. Scientists needed a way for a robot to autonomously navigate a 3D environment using only standard 2D cameras. The fruits of this labor can be seen in the Mars rovers Spirit and Opportunity. They use photogrammetry to help navigate their way around the rocky surface of Mars with a minimal amount of human intervention. Call me a geek, but I get a kick out of knowing that the technology I use every day is the same technology being used to explore other planets.

Photogrammetry 101

Photogrammetry is not an easy thing to research, let alone describe. Look up anything on the subject, and you're likely to run across impossibly dense white papers full of puzzling formulas and Greek symbols. What I hope to accomplish here is to give you a little bit of background on the subject while avoiding the math and minimizing the technical jargon.

Calibration

Matchmoving programs are designed to help you take 2D information from an image sequence and derive a 3D camera move from it. This involves a somewhat mysterious process known as *calibration*. More specifically, you are calibrating the camera in order to reproduce the exact camera movement that created the image seen in the live-action plate.

Calibrating a camera means finding out all the information possible about it. In order to accurately match a camera, you usually need to discover the following about it:

- Position (also known as *translation*)
- Rotation
- Focal length

There are other data you can calculate that can prove useful in some circumstances. These data would include the amount of lens distortion and the optical center of the image. More often than not, however, you can get by without calculating these values.

For our purposes, cameras fall into one of two categories: calibrated or uncalibrated. *Calibrated* cameras are cameras about which all information is known, including position, rotation, and focal length. You often find calibrated cameras in *stereoscopic* systems, in which two cameras are mounted in a specially constructed rig. The position and rotation of each camera relative to the other is known. Perfect examples of this are NASA's Mars rovers. One camera is mounted slightly to the left of another camera, whose position is a known distance to the right. The rover uses these stereoscopic cameras to navigate around the surface of Mars without human intervention. Because the cameras are calibrated, scientists can use photogrammetry to calculate the 3D topology around the rover, which in turn allows the rover to avoid obstacles autonomously.

In visual effects, the most common type of calibrated camera is used in a motion control camera setup. Motion control cameras are mounted to robotic rigs that are controlled by motors and servos. The motion of the camera can be either preprogrammed in a computer or recorded as the camera operator moves the camera. The camera's position, rotation, and focal length are recorded on the computer and can then be repeated as many times as necessary with a high level of precision.

Matchmovers more commonly deal with *uncalibrated* cameras. That is, they don't have any exact information about the cameras. Sometimes, matchmovers are given the image sequence and nothing else. More often, though, they have some information about the camera, such as its focal length or the camera's height, and in such cases the camera could be considered at least partially calibrated.

The good news is that matchmoving software excels at solving partially or completely uncalibrated cameras. In order to do that, the software applies the principles of photogrammetry.

The Optics of Photography

Photogrammetry exploits certain known facts about light and photography in order to calculate the 3D space. So in order to understand how photogrammetry works, we need to know a bit about how photography works.

Light radiates from every surface point of every object in an environment. As light from the environment strikes an object, it excites the object's atoms and they in turn emit light. The amount of light they reflect and its color depend on the surface properties of the object (Figure 2.1).

When an object (such as our eyes or a camera lens) captures the light from the environment, it is really capturing the rays of light from the environment that converge on its location. What this means is that a lens gathers light that happens to be aimed in its direction and, in essence, is sampling a particular cone-shaped region of light (Figure 2.2). Any light emitted from a surface that does not fall within this cone is not seen by the camera.

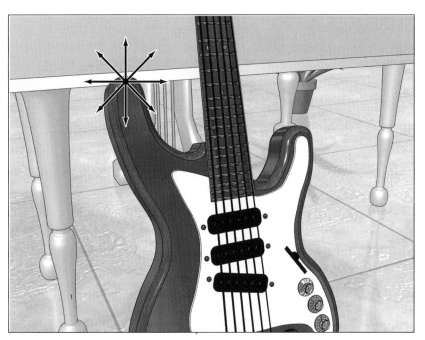

Figure 2.1 Light is reflected from an object in all directions.

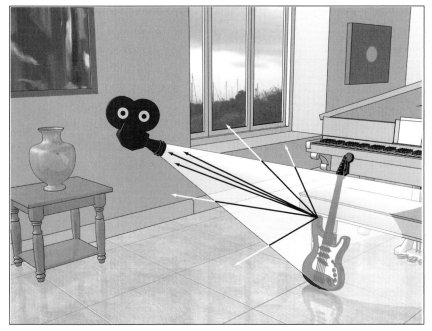

Figure 2.2 Only light that is reflected from an object and heads directly toward the camera can be seen.

The light from the scene is gathered by the lens and focused onto the film plane at the back of the camera where the film sits. Since the image plane is a 2D plane, it represents a 2D slice of the cone-shaped region of light. Since the light in the cone represents the same light in the scene, you could slice the cone of light anywhere along its length and get the same image. By focusing the light, the lens creates a sharp image at the film plane (that is, when the camera is focused properly).

The key thing to remember about photography is that light from a 3D scene is flattened out or projected onto a 2D surface. In matchmoving, we need to take the 2D image and figure out the 3D scene. In order to do that, we also need to understand a thing or two about how projection works.

Projection

When we talk about cameras in photogrammetry, it's useful to think about them in terms of projections against a flat surface (such as the film plane). In a real camera, an image is projected from the *nodal point* (at the center of the lens, or more specifically, the iris) onto the image plane or *film back* (where the film or CCD lies).

When the 3D environment is projected onto the 2D image plane, it does so in a predictable way. Centuries ago, mathematicians developed methods to transform 3D (or Euclidian) space into 2D (or projective) space. In doing so, they created a branch of mathematics known as projective geometry. This field deals with what happens when you project 3D space onto a 2D plane—the exact same thing that happens during photography. Not too bad, considering photography hadn't been invented yet!

One of the most obvious differences between 2D space and 3D space is the extra dimension. You only need two numbers to describe an object's position in 2D space. In 3D space, you need three numbers to describe an object's position. In 2D images, X generally represents the left/right position, and Y represents the up/down position. For 3D space, you need three values: X (left/right), Y (up/down), and Z (in/out).

Note: While it is true that X and Y values describe 2D space, and X, Y, and Z values describe 3D space, there's not much consensus on which letter should represent which axis—particularly in 3D. For example, Maya uses the Y-axis to describe the up/down direction, but 3ds max uses the Z-axis to represent the same direction. To prevent confusion, I use the Y-axis to represent the up-axis in this book.

In digital images, we often describe a certain position on the image in pixels using the (X,Y) values. For example, in Figure 2.3, a point on the piano bench lies 434 pixels from the left of the image, therefore its X value is 434. The feature is 1068 pixels from the top of the image and that makes its Y value 1068.

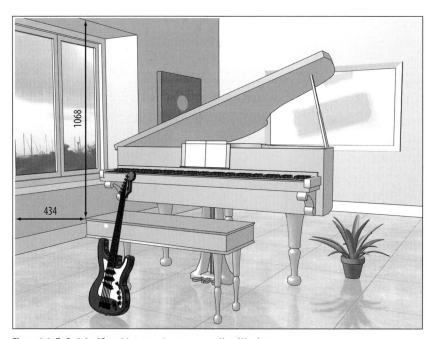

Figure 2.3 To find the 2D position on an image, you use X and Y values.

When we start talking about 3D space, things get a lot more complicated. The object now needs three values to describe where it is in 3D space—X, Y, and Z. But if we say an object is located at the 3D coordinates (0,0,0), where is that exactly? The place where all three coordinates are zero is called the *origin* of the scene. The origin can pretty much lie wherever you want. It simply represents the point where you want to start counting from.

Another problem is that the X- and Y-coordinates in 3D space don't usually correspond to the X- and Y-coordinates in 2D space (Figure 2.4). In order to convert the (X,Y,Z) position of a feature in 3D space to an (X,Y) position in 2D space, the feature needs to be projected, and that's what the rules of projective geometry were made for.

Among other things, projective geometry defines how various types of shapes behave when they are flattened out onto a 2D plane. For example, take a look at Figure 2.5. In the actual environment, the lines of the railroad tracks are parallel and never meet.

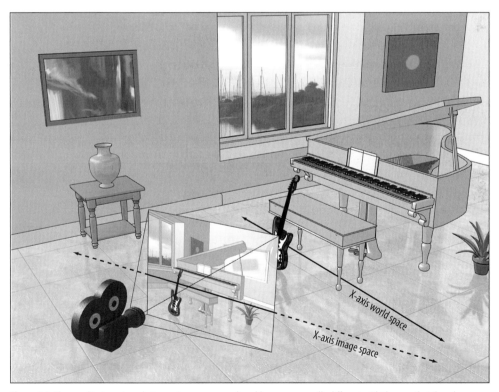

Figure 2.4 The coordinate systems between image space and world space are usually different with the axes that they share.

Figure 2.5 Parallel lines converge at the horizon when projected as an image.

Notice how in the image the parallel lines seem to converge. This is a predictable side effect of projection, and it is responsible for what we perceive as *perspective*. Projective geometry dictates that lines that are parallel in 3D space will never meet, but parallel lines in projective (2D) space can meet and will.

Projective geometry gave mathematicians a way to accurately show how 3D space can be projected as 2D images. Photogrammetry, on the other hand, shows us how 2D images are used to calculate 3D space.

Building a Better Camera

Photogrammetry is nothing more than a lot of math, particularly the type of math you never study unless you're a mathematician or an engineer—namely trigonometry, linear algebra, and projective geometry. But this math provides a precise way to analyze features in two or more images in order to figure out the 3D positions of the objects in the scene as well as the position of the cameras.

So how do you go about figuring out 3D space from a 2D image? A handy way would be to reverse the direction of the projection. If we could take the 2D position of a point on the image and project it out into 3D space, we might be able to find out its correct position. But we need to do it correctly and in accordance with the laws of optics.

If we simply project lines through our points out into 3D space, directly away from the image plane as in Figure 2.6, we end up with points that are technically in 3D space, but they are all still parallel to each other and therefore still pretty much two-dimensional.

In order to more accurately reproduce what happens in a camera, we need to change how our lines are projected. Remember that in a camera, the light from the scene passes through the center of the lens and then projects onto the film. Likewise, our *projection lines* need to pass through an optical center as they are projected. In a real camera, the optical center (center of the lens) is in front of the image plane. To more easily visualize things here, imagine the optical center behind the image plane. Notice in Figure 2.7 how the lines are projecting from the optical center and through the 2D feature on the image plane, causing the projection lines to radiate outward away from the optical center. This is a better representation of what happens in a real camera.

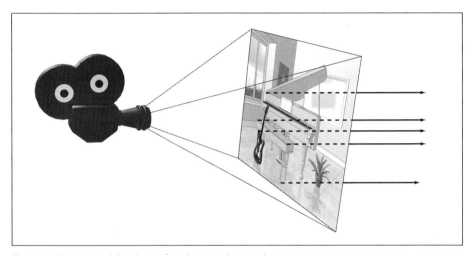

Figure 2.6 Lines projected directly away from the camera's image plane

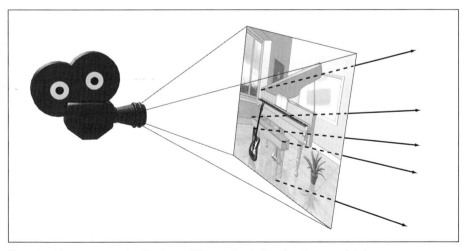

Figure 2.7 A better representation of optics would be to project the lines from the center of the lens.

A Slice of Light

There is a good explanation why in discussions of optics/photogrammetry, the image plane can be represented as both in front of and behind the optical center of the camera. The light that is reaching the lens is the same all along the length of the cone of light. That means we could take a slice out of the cone anywhere along its length, and we would have the same rays of light. The rays of light converge and are inverted at the lens' center, and then they continue toward the film plane. After passing through the center of the lens, the light rays no longer converge but diverge, and they become a diverging cone of light behind the lens. This is the mirror image of the converging cone of light in front of the lens. Therefore, if we sampled a slice of this light cone at the exact same distance in front of the lens as the film plane is behind the lens, we would see the exact same image, only inverted.

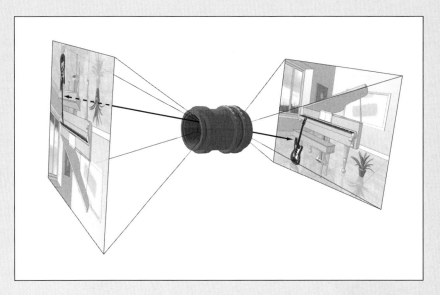

Those of you who already know a bit about cameras may know that the distance from the center of the lens to the film is known as the *focal length*. The image that we sample a focal length's distance from the front of the lens is the same as the image that is projected on the film. For example, a 50mm lens means that the film sits 50mm behind the center of the lens. An image sampled 50mm from the front of the lens will be the same image that shows up on the film.

Now that we know how to correctly project lines from our 2D image plane, let's see how photogrammetry uses those lines to help find the position of the camera. Imagine that we have a camera, and we've taken a picture of a scene. We start by identifying some features in the image that correspond to features in the real scene. For example, we can mark a point on the piano bench. This mark on the image has only a 2D position (X,Y), but it corresponds to a 3D position in the scene somewhere. The problem is, we don't know where.

There is one thing we do know, however. We know that the point on the piano bench emitted a ray of light that passed through the center of the lens and onto the film (Figure 2.8). By projecting a line from the center of the lens through the point on the image and out into 3D space, we can at least know that this part of the bench lies somewhere along that line. It's not much, but it's better than nothing.

We do not yet know the exact position of the camera because we don't know how far away from the camera that feature is; we will make that determination later. If you imagine that our projection line is a skewer, you can see that it is possible to rotate the camera around this axis and the feature will remain in place (Figure 2.9). In a sense here, what we've done is constrained one axis of the camera. Even so, we can still rotate the camera around in pretty much any direction.

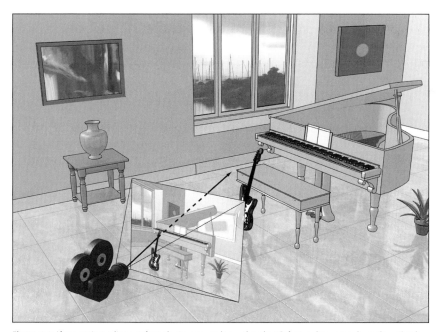

Figure 2.8 If you project a line out from the image, you know that the 3D feature lies somewhere along that line.

If we choose another feature in the scene, such as in Figure 2.10, we will have two anchor points for our rotation. In this example, we have a feature that is next to the first point, so we can only move the camera up and down (more or less around the X-axis).

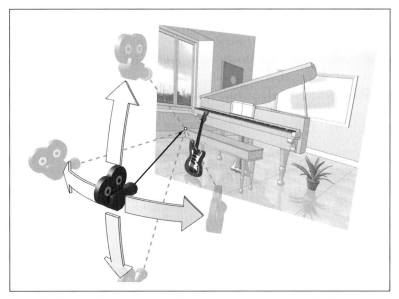

Figure 2.9 With one point selected, we can still move the camera in virtually any direction.

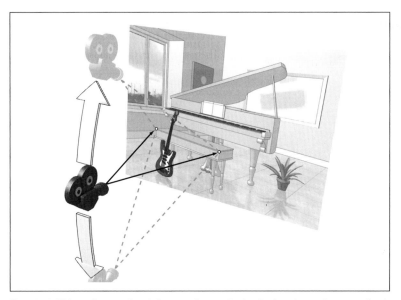

Figure 2.10 With two features selected, the camera is constrained so that it can't rotate in as many directions.

Figure 2.11 With three features, we can lock all three rotational axes, but we still don't know where the camera is in space.

If we add a third point, we can lock all three rotational axes for the camera (Figure 2.11).

This is a good start. We now know the rotational aspects of the camera, but we are still missing quite a bit of information about where the camera is, and we still don't know exactly where those points lie along the projection lines. Therefore, we could still manage to move the camera by sliding the points along their respective projection lines. But that's where having other cameras comes in handy.

Let's say we have another image of the scene that was taken from another point of view. The features in that image look different because the image was taken from another perspective. Things that are closer to the camera appear to move in the image much farther than things that are far away from the camera. This phenomenon is known as *parallax*, and I'll talk more about that later in this chapter.

If each of our cameras had the same features marked on the images, then they too would have their respective rotational axes locked. To find the positions of the two cameras, we need to find out which position in the scene will allow the 3D point to intersect with the projection lines of both cameras.

Note: This is where the really tough math comes into play for matchmove programs. To do this computationally is very difficult and is beyond the scope of this book. If you're interested in knowing more, brush up on your matrix notation and then read *The Geometry of Multiple Images* by Olivier Faugeras and Quang-Tuan Luong (MIT Press, 2001).

To get some idea of how this works, let's add just one feature to our second image—the corner of the piano bench. As you can see in Figure 2.12, if we mark the location of the piano bench (A) in the second image and project a line out into space, we know that the corner of the bench needs to lie somewhere along that line. We also know that it needs to lie along the projection line from the first camera, so logically the corner of the bench lies where those two lines intersect. Therefore, we can move the second camera until its projection line intersects with the first camera's projection line.

If we choose a second and third point, as in Figure 2.13, we can do the same process. After these features are placed, we have increased how much our cameras are constrained. As we add points, the cameras become increasingly constrained until they are close to the right positions. You can also start to see how this process eventually will define not only the camera's position, but the 3D position of the features seen in the images as well.

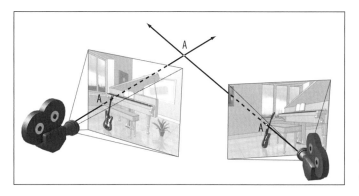

Figure 2.12 By projecting through multiple images, we can find the 3D position of the feature.

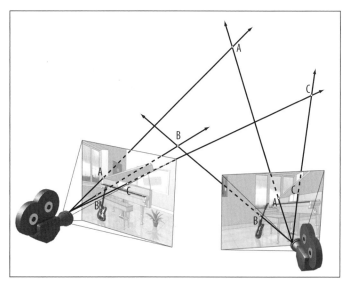

Figure 2.13 With multiple features identified, we can simultaneously calculate the 3D position of the features and the positions of the cameras.

The more cameras you can do this with, the more accurately you can determine the position of the cameras and the locators. It is important to note that the positions of both the cameras and the object features are completely relative at this point. It is only when we define certain distances in the scene that they become more in line with measurements in the real scene.

In the tutorial from the last chapter, we zeroed in on the correct camera placement by analyzing various things in the image and 3D scene. In many ways, this is exactly what the photogrammetry calculations do. The matchmove program analyzes the 2D points on the image and feeds that information into a special formula that gradually constrains the cameras and 3D points in the scene until they are approximately correct. The program then refines those camera positions until it comes up with the most probable solution.

In Figure 2.13, I used just two separate cameras instead of a movie sequence, but the idea is virtually the same. If you are using a sequence of images, the calibration process usually begins with a selection of two or three images that serve as the starting point for the calibration. The program solves for those initial frames, then one-by-one adds new frames to the solution. At the end of the process, you have a single camera that moves to each position the program has solved (Figure 2.14).

Figure 2.14 A movie sequence can be thought of as a series of individual images and camera positions.

In the example above, I've shown how the position and rotation of the camera is calculated, but I haven't really addressed the other parameters, such as focal length. During the process of calibration, the formulas can also calculate the focal length and the amount of lens distortion. The formulas that do this are complicated and beyond the scope of this book, so I've intentionally left them out. If you're interested in knowing more, check the resource listings in Appendix B.

Parallax: A Matchmover's Best Friend

Okay, let's review what we've covered so far: matchmoving programs use photogrammetry to analyze image sequences and calibrate cameras. But what are these programs analyzing? How does this fit in the matchmoving process?

Matchmoving programs analyze parallax in the image sequence and use that information to generate a 3D camera and scene. To understand what parallax is, we need to first examine perspective.

Whenever you take a 3D scene and project it onto a 2D image plane, the 2D image is said to contain perspective. Perspective is dependent on the viewer's position within the scene. If the viewer moves to another position, the perspective changes. This change in perspective is called a *parallax shift*. It is this change in parallax that matchmoving software analyzes to reconstruct the scene.

Note: The word *parallax* technically refers to the visible evidence of perspective in an image, while *parallax shift* refers to the change of perspective caused by changing the viewer's point of view. In this book, I've shortened the term *parallax shift* to just *parallax*, since that is how it is more commonly used.

Whether you know it or not, you are already familiar with parallax. In fact, our brains use it every day to help us navigate around our environment. It's no coincidence that we have two eyes, slightly offset in our heads. Each eye represents a slightly different perspective on the world, and because of this, parallax is present. Our brains automatically decipher the parallax in order to determine the 3D positions of the things around us and how far away they are.

You don't need any images to see parallax. To test this, hold up your index finger in front of your face, slightly in front of your nose. Look at your finger while alternately closing one eye and opening the other. You'll see that the apparent position of your finger jumps significantly, while the other things in the background change very little. This effect is known as *stereopsis,* and it is instrumental in our sense of depth perception.

Parallax is evident in photographic images in much the same way. Objects that are closer to the camera change their position more noticeably than objects farther away. In order to determine if parallax is present, you simply need to check whether the foreground objects are moving more than the background.

Take a look at the images in Figure 2.15. If you compare the foreground building on the very left to the fence behind it, you can see that the apparent position of both objects has changed relative to one another. This means that there is parallax in the images. Notice how the tree a little bit farther back does not change its position very much relative to the building behind it.

Parallax is present when the camera is moving, and thus a lack of parallax means the camera is not moving. If there is no parallax, the camera is simply panning.

Figure 2.15 An example of parallax

How Matchmove Programs Use Photogrammetry

Matchmoving programs harness the power of photogrammetry and apply it to solving the camera for a movie sequence. Each program does this in a slightly different way, but the similarity is enough that if you know one program moderately well, you should be able to use the others. In this section, I'll show you briefly how the programs use the concepts we've just covered to solve real-world problems.

In most matchmoving programs, the solving process is broken up into two distinct phases: 2D tracking and calibration. During the 2D tracking phase, the user selects features on the images to use during calibration. For an image sequence, it is necessary to identify the feature not only in one image but also for the duration that feature is visible in the image. Most matchmoving programs allow the user to place the 2D track in one frame, and then the program attempts to track the remaining frames. Once the software has a certain number of 2D tracks, the user can begin the calibration process.

How many tracks you need to calibrate varies widely depending on the software you are using, the type of camera move, and how much additional information you have about the scene. In general, though, most programs need seven to 12 tracks visible at any given frame in order to achieve a solid calibration.

In some matchmove programs, you need to place the 2D tracks one-by-one. Others can automatically choose the 2D features to track without much user intervention. Some programs can do both. We'll cover both types of 2D tracking in more detail in the next few chapters.

Calibration in matchmoving programs is pretty much a one-button process. You tell the program that you want to calibrate with the 2D tracks you've defined, and it starts crunching the numbers. Sometimes, however, you may have information about the cameras, such as focal length or height, that you will want to enter to help the process as much as possible. Some programs also offer the ability to use previous calibrations to help solve scenes in which changes have been made. Still others allow you to specify the type of camera move (such as a dolly or pan) to restrict the types of camera moves the software can solve for.

The greatest thing about these matchmove programs is that you don't need to fully understand the complicated math that the software uses to solve for the cameras. You only need to feed it the right information, and the program will generate a camera for you—well, at least most of the time. Sometimes you will need to "coax" a solution out of the software. It may give you a solution that is close, but to really lock in the exact camera move, you have to know how to make adjustments to bad or partial solutions.

Requirements for Matchmove Programs

Perhaps the most amazing thing about matchmove programs is how little information they really need. Often, you'll find yourself in a situation where you know nothing about the camera or scene, and yet the software can give you a solution that works.

Now that you know a little bit about how matchmove programs perform their magic, you are in a better position to find out what they need to achieve a calibration. The exact details will vary depending on the program you're using, but in general they all have similar needs.

Parallax Matchmoving programs use photogrammetry to get their solutions, and photogrammetry relies on parallax to work. Therefore, matchmoving programs need parallax to get a good solution. Actually, that's not entirely true. As you'll see later in the book, most matchmoving programs can also achieve a solution for shots that contain no parallax. But in order to use the photogrammetry part of the program, you need to use a shot taken by a camera moving through the scene. As a general rule of thumb, a shot that contains a lot of parallax is easier to solve than one with just a little bit of parallax.

Adequate 2D tracks If you don't have good 2D tracks or don't have any at all, the program has nothing to input into its algorithms, therefore, it can't give you a solution. Most matchmove programs require a minimum number of tracks at any given frame, and if there are not enough, the solution will either completely or partially fail.

The right 2D tracks Choosing 2D tracks is not a completely random process. The solutions you get from your matchmoving program rely on the 2D tracks to try and decipher the true 3D space of the scene. If the features you are tracking are not well chosen, you may have difficulty achieving a solution. For example, if you place all of your tracks in the center of the image, the program will have no way of knowing what the 3D space is like anywhere except in the center of the scene. We'll talk about this more in the next chapter, but for now it's good to know that your 2D tracks need to reflect as much spatial information about the environment as possible.

Laying Down Your First Tracks

Matchmove programs are fantastic time-savers, but they can sometimes use a little bit of guidance. A knowledgeable operator can get a scene to solve faster than someone without such knowledge—especially if the shot is more difficult.

Over the next several chapters, I break down the process of solving a camera in matchmoving software in more detail. The goal is not to tell you what buttons to push, but rather to help you understand how the process works globally, which will then help guide your decisions as you work.

2D Tracking

The first step in creating a matchmove involves identifying important features in the image with special markers or tracks in a process known as 2D tracking. These markers are used to calculate the camera's motion and the overall three-dimensional layout of the scene.

2D tracks are how matchmoving programs know what's going on in the scene. They serve as the two-dimensional clues that help us to re-create the three-dimensional scene. In this chapter, I'll show you how 2D tracking works, how to create accurate tracks, and what effect tracking has on calibration.

3

Chapter Contents

The 2D Tracking Process

Matchmovers occupy a unique place in the world of visual effects. They begin with 2D images and then transform that information into 3D scenes. But before they can re-create the 3D scene, they need to gather accurate information from the 2D image.

As you can probably tell from the preceding chapter, it is impractical (at least with today's computer speeds) to apply the complex techniques involved in photogrammetry to every pixel in an image. Out of necessity, we need a way to let the matchmove software know what is going on in the scene, without bogging down the calculations with too much information. That's where 2D tracking comes in.

2D tracking allows matchmovers to identify and follow important features in the image, like the one shown in Figure 3.1. This process is similar to 2D tracking used for compositing or rotoscoping. The main difference is that matchmovers use the tracking to help determine the 3D space of the scene.

Figure 3.1 A 2D track is nothing more than a marker for the position of an important feature in the image. In this image, the track has been placed on the lower-right corner of the sign.

Selecting a feature in a still image is easy, but when you are dealing with an image sequence, you must follow the feature as it moves around the screen. In most matchmoving programs, the user places the 2D track on a feature on one frame and instructs the matchmoving program to follow the feature throughout the rest of the sequence. The program starts with the frame where the user placed a track and then scans the next frame to determine where the feature might have gone. Once it finds the feature, the program searches the next frame and so on.

The Anatomy of a 2D Track

A 2D track identifies a position on the image with X- and Y-coordinates. This location is usually expressed in pixels. For example, if I place a track on the lower corner of the sign in my image, the track would have a position of 543 on the X-axis and 665 on the Y (Figure 3.2). Generally, X-values are measured from the left side of the image and Y-values are measured from the top. Of course, the values in the figure show fractional pixels; I'll explain this later in this chapter.

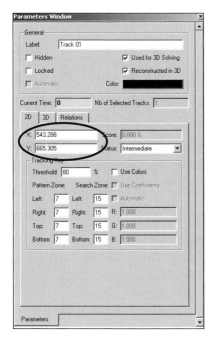

Figure 3.2 2D tracks represent the position on the image. This position is expressed in pixels. This property panel for a 2D track shows that the track's position is 543 pixels from the left of the image and 665 pixels from the top.

A track has three components: the centerpoint, the pattern area, and the search area. The centerpoint is generally a small crosshair at the center of the tracker and represents the exact center of the pattern you are tracking. The pattern area and search area appear on the screen as one square nested inside another (Figure 3.3). The inner square is the pattern that the software will search for. The outer square is the search area and represents the area in the next frame where the software will search.

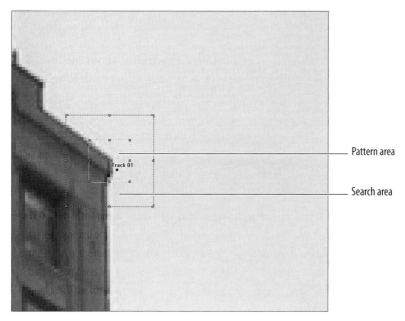

Track 01

Pattern area

Search area

Figure 3.3 A track is composed of three main parts: The centerpoint (the crosshairs at the center of the track), the pattern area (inner square), and the search area (outer square). During 2D tracking, the program looks for the pattern in the next frame in an area as big as the search area.

During tracking, the user places a track on a feature and then lets the software track the feature. The software examines the part of the image inside the pattern area and begins searching for a similar pattern in the subsequent frames. If the pattern changes too significantly (for example, it gets brighter suddenly, or the feature moves behind another object), it will either stop tracking or jump to another feature. If the pattern moves beyond the search area, the tracker will likewise stop.

Whenever we look at an image sequence, we instantly recognize the features of the scene. For example, we can see the brown building hydrant in front of the blue sky. But matchmoving software only sees a bunch of pixels. By placing tracks in the image sequence, we help the program identify important features in the image. But even the best 2D trackers will occasionally fail. In those situations, we need to help the tracking along with keyframing.

2D tracks can be keyframed to guide the software during tracking by identifying where the tracker is located during specific frames. To do this, the user goes to a frame where the tracker has either stopped or slipped off of its mark and moves the track to its proper position. The program then retracks the frames in between the user's keyframes.

Track Placement: Making Every Track Count

When performing 2D tracking, matchmovers must be very selective about the features they track. Calculating the camera's position involves some heavy-duty math, and that math relies upon the 2D tracking. The purpose of 2D tracking for matchmoving is to help the software understand the 3D space of the scene that was filmed. As such, tracking markers should be placed in a way that give the software the most information possible with as little work as possible. When performing 2D tracking, you should keep the following in mind:

- Sample the 3D space.
- Maintain the minimum number of tracks.
- Track stationary objects.
- Track "true" 3D positions.

Sample the 3D Space

Think of the 2D tracks as sampling points of the scene that was filmed. You should track things at various depths, heights, and widths as much as possible. Each track you select should help give the software a clearer picture of the 3D environment (Figure 3.4).

For example, you wouldn't want to group all your tracks in the center of the image, because the software would only be able to define the space of that center area of the scene. Likewise, don't track only features on a wall while ignoring the rest of the scene. This would result in a solution that works great for the area near the wall but is not as accurate closer to the camera.

A good thing to keep in the back of your mind is that you will only be able to know the 3D space of areas in which you track. Everything else will be inferred from these tracks. If you don't place any tracking markers in a particular area, the software will have no way of accurately reproducing that portion of the 3D scene.

Figure 3.4 Notice how the tracks are spread throughout the scene. They are placed at various heights, depths, and widths in order to get a complete picture of the 3D layout of the scene.

Maintain the Minimum Number of Tracks

Most matchmoving programs need a minimum number of tracks in order to provide a solution. The number will vary from one program to another, but it generally is from seven to 12 tracks per frame. Whatever the minimum number of tracks is, you must maintain that number at all times during the shot. For example, if you have the eight tracks you require on frame 10, and then one of the tracks moves off-screen at frame 20, you must replace it with another track, preferably before the first one exits.

A 2D track does not need to remain on-screen for the duration of the shot. If the feature you are tracking leaves the frame, the track needs to be replaced by another one. If you don't replace the track in a staggered manner, you can cause problems such as harsh discontinuities in the camera's motion. It's important to introduce new 2D tracks as gradually as possible in order to avoid these types of problems. For example, having eight tracks that all end on the same frame and eight new markers that replace them in the very next frame will usually cause a harsh "jump" in the camera, where it suddenly moves to another position at that frame.

The best way to avoid these jumps is by "stair-stepping" the tracks as they enter or leave the image. *Stair-stepping* is the gradual introduction of new tracks as the image sequence progresses. It is best to have a new track already in the shot before the track it is replacing leaves and vice versa. If multiple tracks leave at the same time, you should shorten one of them and then introduce two new ones at staggered intervals (Figure 3.5).

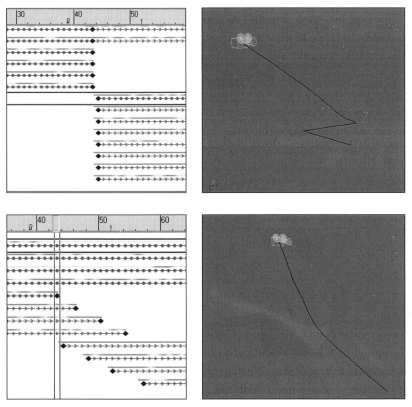

Figure 3.5 Multiple tracks that end or start on the same frame can cause breaks in the camera's motion path.

Track Stationary Objects

Matchmoving programs use the 2D tracks you provide to examine the spatial relationship of objects in the images. The calculations that re-create the 3D scene run under the assumption that everything being tracked is stationary. Therefore, you should only track objects that do not move for the duration of the shot.

This might seem like a fairly straightforward thing to do, but it can sometimes give you problems when you least expect it to. Trees, for instance, often seem like ideal items to track since they're rich in detail, but in fact they might be subtly moving in the wind. Matchmove software is extremely sensitive to even the smallest movement, since most software evaluates the 2D data on a subpixel level. Therefore, you should be reasonably sure that the features you are tracking are indeed static. You may encounter shots in which an object is stationary for part of the shot and then begins moving. In cases like this, you can track the object during the frames it is stationary, but you should stop tracking it before it starts moving.

Track "True" 3D Positions

Is there such a thing as an object not having a "true" 3D position? In a sense, yes. What I'm talking about here are features that are easy to track but don't represent a static 3D position in the scene, such as lens flares, reflections, specular highlights, and features that seem to intersect but in fact do not. These types of features don't make good tracking markers because their position and shape change as the camera moves. This problem is a little bit harder to recognize, but it's important to avoid. For example, don't track the apparent overlap between a foreground building and a background building, because it is not an actual position that remains stationary (see Figure 3.6). When the camera moves, the buildings change their relationship to one another, and therefore the intersection between the two buildings changes its position.

Getting Tracks to Stick

The name of the game with 2D tracking for matchmoving is accuracy. And as such the tracks that you choose should be as accurate as possible. The features you track will vary depending on what was shot. In wide, outdoor shots or highly detailed interiors, you can track virtually anything in the shot, from bushes and lines on the road to furniture and window frames. Other times, you might track an actor on blue screen (such as in the tutorial later in this chapter) and only have markers on the walls or floor. Here's what you can do to help make the process easier:

Track the corners of objects where possible. Corners of square objects are the best features to track because most 2D trackers can easily hang on to them. They're also less likely to cause track slippage as the camera moves.

Figure 3.6 Avoid tracking the apparent overlap between foreground and background objects such as the one indicated here. Although you could track this feature easily enough, the apparent 3D space of this marker would change position as the camera moves.

Avoid tracking edges. It's often tempting to track the edge of an object, such as a long edge of a building. But avoid this. The reason is that the tracker is looking only for the pattern inside the pattern area, and along an edge, the pattern would look nearly identical along the length of the edge. This causes the track to slide up and down the edge during tracking, as demonstrated in Figure 3.7.

Use care with circular markers or features. Small dot-like features make excellent tracking markers, but large circular features can mean trouble. There are no corners on a circle, so the track will be potentially less accurate. In addition, if the camera changes angle too much, the circle becomes more oval-shaped (as demonstrated in Figure 3.8), which again introduces inaccuracies. Some matchmove programs have a 2D tracking feature called *symmetrical centering,* which examines the circular area and centers the track across it, even if it becomes oval-shaped. If the software you are using does not have this feature, you should scrutinize such tracks to make sure they're not slipping.

Figure 3.7 When you track an edge rather than a corner, the pattern looks nearly identical to the matchmoving program. This causes the track to slide up and down the edge as the track proceeds through the frames.

Figure 3.8 A circular marker can become oval-shaped as it is viewed at an angle. This can reduce a track's accuracy.

Hints for Effective 2D Tracking

In my experience, most problems with calibration can be traced back to the 2D tracking. Matchmoving software is very sensitive to the smallest deviations in the 2D data so accurate tracking is key.

It is not uncommon for a single track that has slipped for a few frames to cause an entire *solution* to fail. With this in mind, it makes sense to take a little extra time making solid and accurate 2D tracks. Rushing through the sometimes tedious task of 2D tracking often comes back to haunt you during the calibration phase of the matchmove.

> **Note:** Many matchmoving programs are accurate to 1/32 of a pixel. The accuracy requirement for a good matchmove is generally less than 1 pixel. Subpixel accuracy helps the matchmove programs accurately solve all of the markers with the utmost accuracy globally and helps to achieve the best solution possible.

Here are a few things to remember as you're tracking that can help improve your efficiency and speed:

Keep your eyes on the tracks. It's helpful to track one feature at a time and then examine the tracking results before continuing to the next track. Most matchmoving programs will show you the motion path of the tracker as it makes its way across the image (Figure 3.9). The motion path often appears irregular and jagged. This is acceptable to a point, since camera motion will always have some degree of "natural" jitter, but you should watch for any sudden jumps or spikes in the motion that indicate the track has slipped off the feature.

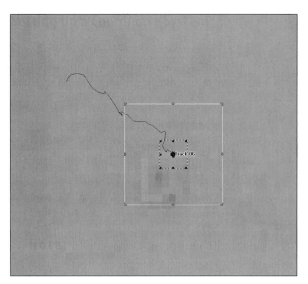

Figure 3.9 Tracks will have a certain amount of "natural" jitter to their motion. This is normal, but if the jitter is too severe, it may find its way into the camera's motion path after calibration.

Watch tracks as they approach the edge of frame. Tracks have a tendency to slip off as they exit the frame. Most programs include a small, zoomed-in view of your tracking pattern as it tracks. It's a good idea to keep your eye on this close-up view as the program tracks to spot any signs of slipping as they happen. This would also apply to features that pass behind other objects.

Add as few tracks as possible. Deciding how many tracks you'll need can be a little bit challenging, because the ultimate goal is to track enough tracks to achieve a solution but not so many that it becomes difficult to troubleshoot if something goes wrong. It's best to use the minimum number of tracks and continue tracking them as long as possible before adding any new ones. I always look at it this way: it's far easier to troubleshoot eight tracks rather than a hundred.

Use the right size tracker. Most software packages have a tracking marker of a certain default size. These sizes are usually geared for video resolution images and may not be big enough for film or HD resolutions. If you find your tracks are not sticking very well and you're working at a higher resolution, you may want to double the default size of your pattern and search areas. This can usually be done in the software's preferences or by dragging the edges of the tracker's pattern and search areas (Figure 3.10).

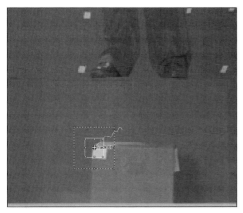 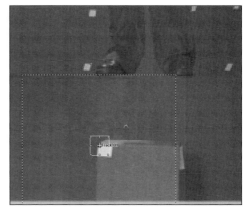

Figure 3.10 You can change the search area size by dragging the outer square. If you are tracking high-resolution plates, you could even set this in your preferences as the default size.

Think about resolution. The final thing to keep in mind on track placement has to do with resolution. You should always perform your 2D tracking on full-resolution plates. High-resolution plates (such as HD or film resolution) can be difficult to work with and greatly slow down the process of 2D tracking, but they are a necessary evil. Tracking on a plate with a lower resolution than the final output can result in jitter and drift in the final matchmove. Low resolution reduces the effective sampling rate for the 2D tracking and therefore translates into an inaccurate camera motion.

Plate Issues

Of course, some problems that always plague 2D tracking have to do with the image sequence itself. While these can't be avoided, there are some strategies you can use to minimize their effect on your solution. In this section, I'll cover a few such problems and how best to deal with them. These plate problems include:

- Motion blur
- Soft focus or rack focus
- Occlusion
- Noise
- Low-contrast features
- Lack of trackable features
- Interlacing

Motion Blur

Motion blur occurs when the camera or objects being filmed move quickly. Objects in motion (or the entire image if it's the camera that's moving) appear blurred along their axis of motion. This can make 2D tracking difficult since the feature not only becomes elongated and distorted, but it also becomes less distinct and has less contrast. As objects get motion blurred, other objects behind them tend to start "poking through," becoming more visible and more likely to cause tracks to slip (Figure 3.11). Matchmoving programs can usually do a decent job at tracking through moderate motion blur, but when the blur becomes excessive, it can cause the trackers to stop or fail.

In cases of heavy motion blur, there are a few things you can try:

- Expand the search area. The extreme motion of the camera might be causing the pattern you are trying to track to move beyond the default search area, and this will cause the tracker to stop or slip. Expanding the search area allows the tracking engine to look further during its search for the pattern.

- Expand the pattern size. This gives the software more information to work with (although it slows the tracking down significantly) and might help it to continue through the motion blur.

- If you still can't get the track to stick, you may have to keyframe the track by hand through the motion-blurred area. This can be difficult because the blur causes the feature to become so elongated that it's sometimes hard to tell where the track needs to be placed. Examine the other tracks if possible and try to determine how the software deals with the problem. If the software places the track at the leading edge of the blurred object, or places it in the middle, you should do the same. You should keep in mind, though, that your keyframes will be inherently inaccurate, but at least you may be able to get a solution out of it.

Figure 3.11 Motion blur is caused when either the camera or objects are moving very fast. Notice how the sign post gets heavily blurred, to the point where the seagull behind it is visible

Soft Focus or Rack Focus

When an image is out of focus, the features are softer and more diffuse. Often when tracking a soft feature, the 2D tracker tends to slide around the feature as it tries to decipher the pattern, or else it just slips off. One reason for this is that when features are significantly out of focus, the film grain often becomes more noticeable.

Just from the fact of being out of focus, you can almost guarantee that any 2D tracks will be inaccurate. That being said, you can try a couple of things that might at least make it easier to get a good track:

- Use a bigger pattern size. Bigger pattern sizes can sometimes compensate for the noise in soft focus features because the program is sampling more pixels. This causes a sort of averaging effect on the track.
- Slightly blur the image. It seems to go against common sense to blur the plate when blurriness is the problem you're trying to solve. But this technique is sometimes effective because it can help get rid of the graininess and help produce smoother tracks.

Another type of problem involving blurriness is rack focus. A *rack focus* is when the camera changes focus from one object to another. Rack focus shots are at least partially trackable while the object you are tracking is in focus. With this type of shot, it is best to start the track while the image is in focus and then track into the out-of-focus area.

Occlusion

A fairly common occurrence during 2D tracking is that the feature you are tracking moves behind another object. In matchmoving parlance, this is known as *occlusion*. If the feature doesn't reemerge, there isn't much you can do, but if it comes out the other side, you can usually pick the track back up. There are times when you may really need to have the track's information during the area of occlusion. This most often happens when you are having trouble finding features to track. Different programs have different ways of dealing with this issue, but here are a few things to try:

- Use "gap-filling" tools in the matchmove software. Some programs allow you to fill the gap in the track by assuming that the track maintains a linear path as it passes behind the occluding object (Figure 3.12). This is a handy feature but should be used with caution. If the camera is particularly shaky or has an irregular motion, the feature may not, in fact, move in a straight line while it is occluded, and therefore your 2D track would be incorrect.

- Keyframe through the occlusion. If the occlusion is short enough—say, less than a few frames—you may be able to keyframe through it by making an educated guess as to the position of the feature.
- Add more tracks. The only other option is to add a track on another feature that takes the place of the occluded track while it is occluded.

Figure 3.12 These three images show the track during an occlusion by a passing lightpole. Notice how the motion path is missing in the middle. The path in the second image shows the results of "gap filling," and the third image shows the path as it exists behind the pole.

Noise

If enough of your 2D tracks are jittery or noisy, they may not make your solution fail, but they can cause the resulting camera motion to be jittery. The most common culprit for noise in 2D trackers is film grain or compression. There are a variety of ways of combating this problem:

- Remove the grain before tracking. The simplest solution would be to use uncompressed images and, if necessary, remove the grain in a compositing package.

- Only track one channel. With film grain, you might check to see if the grain is less severe in one channel and then only track that channel. Often film grain is heaviest in the blue channel.

- Edit the camera's motion curves after calibration. It might be easier to edit the camera's animation curves after calibration. Most matchmoving software packages have a tool to smooth out the camera's curves, but you could also use the curve-smoothing capabilities of your 3D animation software with similar results.

N o t e : Some matchmoving programs allow you to track individual color channels. If your program doesn't support this, you could isolate the channel in a compositing program ahead of time. See the later section, "Optimizing the Plate for 2D Tracking."

Low-Contrast Features

Matchmoving programs can have difficulty sticking to low-contrast features. This is because they generally track the luminance values by default. To deal with this, try the following:

- Track by colors. Many matchmoving software trackers allow you to switch over to tracking by colors instead, as illustrated in Figure 3.13. This can really improve a track on a low-contrast or similar colored feature. The only downside is that it may take longer to track.

- Pretreat the plate to make the features more visible. If your matchmoving software lacks the ability to track by colors, you can try pretreating the plate ahead of time in a way that makes it more "legible" to the tracker. I'll discuss how to do this in the next section.

Composite Red channel

Green channel Blue channel

Image sequence courtesy Quan Tran

Figure 3.13 Sometimes tracking can be made easier by tracking the individual channels. Shown here are the original image and the red, green, and blue channels.

Lack of Trackable Features

There are times when you simply don't have enough things visible in the shot to track. This happens more often on blue screen shots since you usually can only track markers intentionally placed on the screen. If no one on-set had the forethought to place them or didn't place enough of them, you may have trouble finding anything to track. Unfortunately, this problem has few solutions, at least in matchmoving software. You might be able to crowd tracking markers onto the existing markers (Figure 3.14). For example, sometimes they create Xs on the blue screen with gaffer's tape. You could try tracking not only the center of the X, but the four legs of the X as well—and if the X is close enough to the camera, the two corners on the edge of the X. It's not an ideal situation, but at least it might give the matchmoving software something to work with.

Interlacing

Interlacing is the process of breaking up an image sequence into two fields and is used with video images for television broadcast. Each field represents every other row of pixels. The top row of pixels is the odd field or upper field, while the second field is the even or lower field. All upper fields are grouped into one image, while all lower fields are grouped into another. What this means is that for each frame of video, there are two frames in the form of fields, and since each of these frames represents only half of the fields, the image is half as tall vertically. Also, since each frame is broken up into two images, there are twice as many images as usual. For example, a 30 frame-per-second (fps) video, when interlaced, is 60fps (this is often referred to as 60i footage).

Interlacing can affect matchmoving because of the visual difference present in an interlaced plate. Diagonal edges often appear like steps, or vertical edges have a "ladder" effect (see Figure 3.15). These edges can wreak havoc on a 2D track. As the track tries to follow the feature, it is constantly jumping back and forth on the edge. The result is a very noisy 2D track and consequently a noisy camera motion.

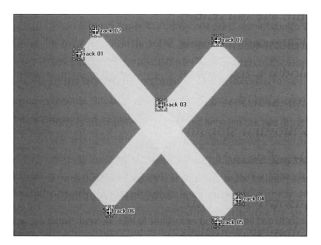

Figure 3.14 Crowding multiple tracks onto a single mark on a blue screen

Figure 3.15 An example of interlacing. Notice how the vertical edges of the lightpole exhibit a "ladder" effect

The easiest way to deal with this problem is to de-interlace the image before you begin the 2D tracking. This can be done in most compositing programs. There are times, however, when the rest of the production is working on interlaced images, and you will be forced to do so as well. In these cases, the matchmoving programs have you covered. When you import a clip into the matchmoving program, you will have the option to set the "interpretation" of the image sequence. That is, you will be able to choose whether the sequence is interlaced or not. By choosing the interlaced option, you instruct the program to provide smooth edges on which you can place your 2D tracks.

 Note: This interpretation option does not actually alter the image. It simply affects how it is displayed and used internally for tracking purposes.

Optimizing the Plate for 2D Tracking

Sometimes it is helpful to create an altered version of the plate to help ease the tracking process. This can be done in any compositing software and is fairly straightforward to do. Some common alterations to a plate include changing the colors or contrast, removing grain, isolating color channels, etc. These changes are made to a copy of the plate and not the original, in most cases. The matchmover uses them for their tracking purposes in the matchmoving program, and later on, once the plate is matchmoved, the unaltered plate can be switched back in.

When altering the plate, you should confine your editing to those effects that change the value of the pixels but not their spatial relationship. For example, you could drop out the blue channel and add some contrast, but you wouldn't want to rubber stamp or clone out an annoying feature. The reason is, when you clone a portion of an image, you are scrambling its pixels (ever so slightly), and this could lead to calibration problems down the line. Other things to avoid are resizing the image, offsetting the image, and changing the speed of the sequence.

Acceptable Plate Changes	Potentially Bad Plate Changes
Adjusting contrast	Resizing
Adjusting color	Cropping
Isolating color channels	Offsetting
Flopping the plate	Distorting effects
Inverting the frame order	Speed changes (retiming)

You'll often run across the speed change issue, because a director may want to change the timing of the shot without reshooting. This is usually done with some sort of time-remapping method in a compositing or editing program. This process adds or removes frames (thereby slowing down or speeding up the footage), either by blending adjacent frames or by computing in-between frames based on the existing frames. Either way, it pushes around pixels in a way that can be difficult for matchmoving software to interpret. Where possible, it is better to matchmove the plate *before* retiming and then alter the keys of the camera in the 3D program to match the retime speeds. Another option is to retime the final rendered footage with the same settings as the plate.

2D Tracking Tutorial

Now that we've examined all of the issues with 2D tracking, it's time to start putting that information to good use. In this tutorial, we'll use Realviz's MatchMover Pro 3.0 to place 2D tracks manually. MatchMover has an excellent 2D tracking engine that is both fast and accurate. In this section, we'll track some blue screen footage. We'll then use this tracking to calibrate our cameras in the next chapter.

1. For this tutorial, you'll need the `bluescreen.####.jpg` image sequence from the Chapter 3 folder on the companion CD. In MatchMover Pro, begin by loading the sequence into the program (File > Load Sequence). This brings up the Load Sequence dialog box (Figure 3.16).

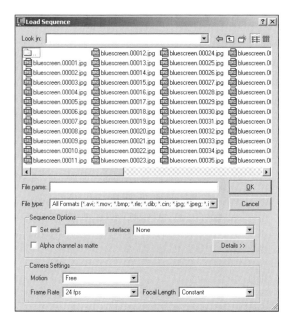

Figure 3.16 Loading the image sequence

2. Navigate to the image sequence and select the first frame. The end of the sequence is automatically listed as the end frame, and there are various options for importing the clip. This particular clip was shot on film, so the Interlace option should be set to None. Under Camera Settings, the motion of this sequence is Free and the frame rate is 24fps. For now, leave the Focal Length as Constant. Don't worry if you forgot to set something in this panel. You can always change the settings later. The file bluescreen_01_Start.mmf on the CD shows the proper setup before tracking.

Evaluating the Shot

Before we get started, we need to evaluate the sequence. This shot is of an actor filmed in front of a blue screen. Perhaps the most basic question you should consider is, what is the nature of the camera move? Is the shot panning, translating, or some combination of the two?

In order to determine this, you need to check for parallax. If there is parallax in the shot, then the camera is moving. The easiest way to check for parallax is to compare a foreground object with a background one.

In Figure 3.17, look at the shot on frame 1. Notice the markers on the wall to the left of the man's leg. If you advance to frame 70, you'll see that they move away from his leg to the left more. Some markers move behind him altogether. This means that there is parallax in the shot, and therefore the camera is moving.

The fact that there is parallax in the shot means that the matchmoving software should have no problem solving it.

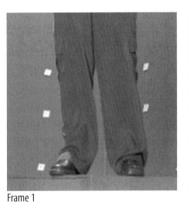
Frame 1

Frame 70

Figure 3.17 The background markers move away from the man's leg. This is an indication of parallax.

Note: There's a minor detail worth noting here: the black strips at the sides and top of the image are camera hoods. These are black cards taped to the camera to prevent the lights from flaring into the lens. Since they are moving with the camera, we will not track these.

Placing First Tracks in MatchMover Pro

Before getting started, let's take a look at the MatchMover interface (Figure 3.18). When you start the program, there are four main sections: the Project View (top left), the Video Window (center), the Properties Window (right), and the Timeline (bottom).

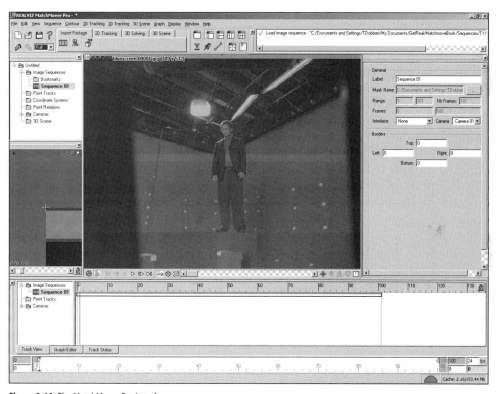

Figure 3.18 The MatchMover Pro interface

The Project View lets you see all of the components of your matchmoving project such as 2D tracks, cameras, and 3D objects. The Video Window shows the image sequence you are working on. The Video Window is where you'll do most of your 2D tracking work, and it also converts to a 3D perspective view once you have a 3D calibration. The Properties Window shows all the information about the currently selected item. The Timeline shows your 2D tracks and where they start or stop. It also can show a motion graph of the camera as well as graphs of the quality of various 2D tracks.

The first thing is to place your 2D tracks. To do this, follow these steps:

1. Make sure you are on frame 1 before you place the track. In MatchMover, you place tracks by right-clicking in the Video Window and choosing New Track, or you can go to the 2D tracking menu and choose New Track. Your cursor will turn to a crosshair, which means that you are ready to place the track on the image. You'll place your first tracking marker on the corner of one of the small markers on the foreground center box. To place it, just click and hold it until you have the track positioned exactly on the corner of the marker. As you do this, the small magnifier window on the side shows a close-up view of the track to help get a better placement. Make sure to place it on the corner and not on the sides of the marker.

   When you place this first track, you'll notice that it shows up in the Timeline below, and it has a black diamond on the first frame (Figure 3.19). This black diamond is a keyframe. It lets you know that you placed the 2D track on that frame.

2. Tracking the marker throughout the shot is simple; just choose 2D Tracking > Track Forward or hit the F3 key. You'll see the 2D track begin following the marker from one frame to the next. Since this marker stays in frame for the entire sequence (Figure 3.20), the track will probably run all the way to the end of the shot.

3. If you zoom in on the end of the track, you'll notice that the track strays a bit from the corner of the marker. To fix this, you'll need to place a keyframe. You can do this one of two ways: you can go to the end frame and choose 2D Tracking > Set Key > Intermediate (F6), or you can just drag the track to the correct position. When you do this, the intermediate tracking may disappear because it needs to be retracked for those frames. To retrack, choose 2D Tracking > Track Bi-directional. The file bluescreen_02_1stTrack.mmf shows how the project should look after you've place your first track.

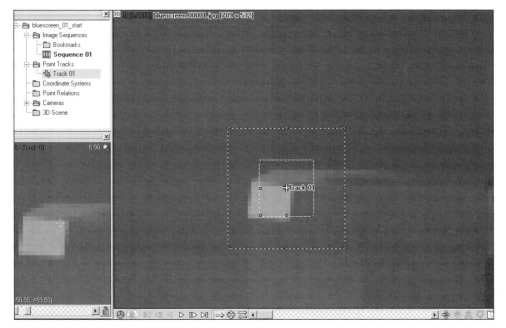

Figure 3.19 The first 2D track in position

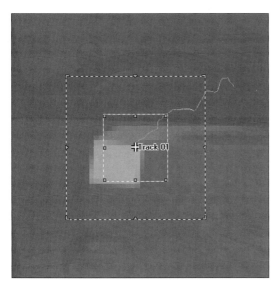

Figure 3.20 The tracker's path after 2D tracking the entire sequence

Note: *Bidirectional tracking* means that the program will first track the feature in one direction (either forward or backward) and then make a second tracking pass in the opposite direction. What's nice about this feature is that when it makes its second pass, it references the first pass. This has the general effect of tightening up the tracking and making it smoother.

Choosing Your Tracks

Before we place more markers, we should examine our tracking requirements as they apply to this shot:

Sampling the 3D scene In this shot there are a lot of things to track at various places in the environment. To help get a solid solution, we should give MatchMover a good idea of the spatial make-up of the scene. We'll need to track markers on the wall (on the left and right sides) as well as various depths such as the foreground boxes, the midground pole, and the background wall. We should also give the program an idea of the height of objects in the scene by tracking both markers down low and up high.

Minimum number of tracks MatchMover Pro needs a minimum of eight tracks to achieve a solution—that's eight tracks at any given frame. Since there are plenty of features to track here, you shouldn't have a problem.

Stationary objects Nearly everything in this scene is static except for the actor, so of course we can track everything but him. There is a sneaky problem, though, that you should watch out for. Notice the marker on the right side of the small foreground box in the center. It's blowing around because of an off-screen fan. We don't want to track that marker because it is not static relative to the other markers and therefore might spoil the solution.

Trackable features This shot contains lots of things to track. But can you imagine if no one had bothered to place markers on the walls?

Adding the Remaining Tracks

From here we need to add more tracks until we have at least eight tracks. Keep the guidelines listed above in mind as you add them.

1. For your next track, try placing it on the marker on the foreground box to the left. This track doesn't quite run to the end of the clip, so you'll need to make sure to add an extra track before you finish tracking. Pay particular attention to the track as it approaches the edge of the frame. It might just stop tracking, but it also could slide around the image as it tries to match the pattern (Figure 3.21).

2. Continue adding tracks in this fashion until you have the minimum number of tracks you need. In order to get the smoothest possible tracks, I like to place a keyframe at the end of the sequence and track each track bidirectionally. Figure 3.22 shows the tracks I selected.

3. The lines for each track that run between the keyframes are quality indicators and give you some feedback as to the quality of the track. It's not necessary to have the line entirely green in order to achieve a good solution. You should, however, investigate any large patches of red.

That's about it for the 2D tracking. In the next chapter, we'll use this project to do the calibration. The final results of my tracking are in the file bluescreen_03_2DTrackDone.mmf.

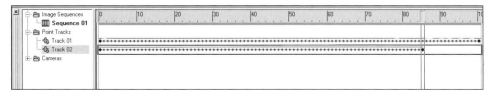

Figure 3.21 The second track exits the frame before the end of the sequence.

Figure 3.22 For this shot, I ended up using a total of nine tracks positioned as shown.

From 2D to 3D

Of course, 2D tracking is just the first step in the process. The 2D tracking capability of matchmoving programs is pretty amazing, but the real magic starts when we calibrate the 3D scene. In the next chapter, we'll dive into this mysterious process and see what it takes to create a 3D environment from 2D images.

3D Calibration

2D tracking provides the clues, but 3D calibration provides the solution. Calibrating or solving, the camera is a fancy way of saying that we're determining all of the camera's attributes—position, rotation, focal length, etc. Now that we've given the matchmove program some 2D information, it's time to start solving.

Calibration can be one of the most difficult and frustrating parts of matchmoving to newcomers. Much of this is due to the "black box" nature of matchmoving software and the occasionally perplexing results. In this chapter, I'll try to clarify some of the murkier aspects of 3D calibration and provide some tips to getting good results.

Chapter Contents

What Is a "Good" Calibration?

To answer this question, you need to consider the goals of matchmoving:

- Reproduce a 3D camera that matches the one used to film the scene
- Find the 3D locations of features in the scene that was filmed

Consider for a moment what is necessary to completely define a camera. We need to know its 3D position and rotation as well as its focal length, film back, principal point, and the amount of lens distortion. When you consider that the matchmoving program must do this for every frame in the sequence, it's no wonder it gets a little fussy when we try to solve a difficult shot!

Note: Throughout this book I use the terms *calibration* and *solution* somewhat interchangeably because they mean virtually the same thing. Technically speaking however, "achieving a calibration" refers only to cameras, whereas "achieving a solution" generally refers to the entire 3D scene.

In most matchmoving programs, the calibration is a one-button operation. You simply instruct the program that you want to solve the shot. The program analyzes the 2D tracking you have provided and (hopefully) generates a camera that matches the real-world camera. It also creates markers that represent the 3D locations of the features you tracked in 2D tracking. But how do you determine whether the camera calibration is good or bad?

Residuals

When a matchmove is solved correctly, the 3D camera matches the real-world camera exactly. The best way to tell whether or not the two cameras are identical is to look through them. The view afforded by the real-world camera is the image itself. The view from the new 3D camera is the 3D scene. If our calibration is correct, then the 3D markers should line up with the feature they represent in the image (Figure 4.1).

For example, let's say we placed a 2D track on the corner of a building. After calibration, that 2D track is converted to a 3D marker that represents the 3D position of the corner of that building. When we look at the 3D marker through the calibrated 3D camera, it should appear to line up with the original 2D track on the image. Therefore, a good calibration could be defined as the perfect (or near-perfect) alignment between the 2D track and the 3D marker when viewed through the 3D camera.

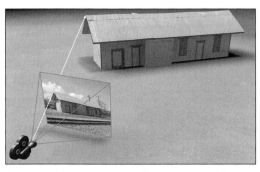

Figure 4.1 When the camera is correctly calibrated, you can draw a straight line between the lens center, the track on the 2D image, and the 3D marker in the 3D scene. The image on the right shows how the scene looks when viewed through the 3D camera.

The alignment of the 2D track and 3D marker is almost never perfect. The difference between them is called a residual (Figure 4.2). Residual values are usually expressed in pixels. For example, if the 3D track is reprojected onto the 2D image plane and ends up being 3 pixels away from the original 2D track, it is said to have a residual of 3. If the residual of the majority of the tracks is less than 1 pixel for the duration of the shot, it is considered a good calibration. Why 1 pixel? If the shot is tracked at full resolution, any track that slips by less than a pixel shouldn't be noticeable.

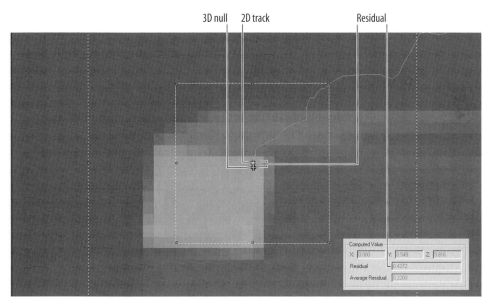

3D null   2D track   Residual

Computed Value		
X: 0.000	Y: 0.549	Z: 5.816
Residual	0.4272	
Average Residual:	0.2200	

Figure 4.2 A residual is the difference between the 2D track and the 3D marker as seen through the camera. The top crosshair represents the 2D track and the bottom one the 3D marker. The difference between them in pixels is the residual—in this case, about a 0.4 pixel difference.

Calibrating Your Cameras

I've heard that there's not much room for aesthetics in matchmoving because the solution either works or it doesn't. Perhaps it's technical nature of this discipline or a lack of understanding of the process of matchmoving that gives people this impression. But there is an art to getting the right solution, especially the difficult ones. Whatever the reason, knowing how a calibration happens can be a great asset to a matchmover.

A matchmove doesn't simply pop into existence. Like many other aspects of 3D effects, such as animation or lighting, matchmoving can be an iterative process where a solution must be zeroed in on rather than solved the first try. Many times, you will have a partial solution or a "weak" (inaccurate) solution that must be improved. Sometimes you'll fight the nature of the footage (pans, zooms, etc.), and other times you'll deal with your own bad 2D tracking. But whatever the cause, you can take heart in knowing that most matchmoves need a little extra "love" before they're ready to deliver.

In order to understand why matchmoves can fail, we need to look at how matchmoves are solved by the matchmoving program. No, I won't bombard you with matrix notation and trigonometry. I simply mean we're going to look at how the software goes about doing its job. A lot of what happens during calibration is invisible to the user. In this section, we'll look at what happens "under the hood" while the matchmove program is solving the scene.

Finding the Right Fit

When beginning a calibration, the task at hand is rather enormous. There are an infinite number of possible camera/track/null configurations but only a few that will produce the desired results—a perfect alignment of all three elements during the entire shot. Matchmoving software tackles this problem by breaking the task up into smaller, more manageable subtasks.

The program usually begins its calibration by scanning the 2D tracks available and making a very cursory examination to decide on the frames that will be used as a starting point. These frames, which I'll call the "initial frames," are calibrated by themselves and used to generate a camera and nulls (Figure 4.3). This minicalibration becomes the baseline for the full calibration. The software starts adding more and more frames throughout the shot to its initial calibration and makes slight adjustments to the overall solution as it does so. As a final step, the software adds in all of the in-between frames to the solution. In this manner, the software can start with a rough calibration and refine it until it achieves a single solution that works for all frames.

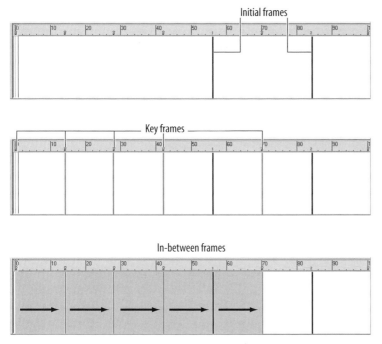

Figure 4.3 The matchmoving program begins by calibrating just a small number of frames, then it adds more frames to the solution and adjusts as necessary. Finally, the program adds in all of the in-between frames to the solution and creates a single solution that works for all frames.

The matchmove program uses an iterative process for determining the camera location, and it's a good reason to approach your calibration the same way. For example, if you find problems in a certain area of the shot, it would make sense to start troubleshooting in that area. We'll discuss troubleshooting later in this chapter and again in Chapter 10, "Troubleshooting and Advanced Techniques," but suffice it to say that you should expect to work *toward* a solution rather than instantly arriving at one. Consequently, the first skill you must master is how to evaluate the matchmove as you work.

Calibration Tutorial

To illustrate how a basic calibration works, we'll use the tutorial from the previous chapter. We'll continue using MatchMover Pro 3.0 for this calibration, but the techniques are similar in other matchmove programs. If you haven't saved your scene, you can use the project named `bluescreen_03_2DTrackDone.mmf` that is included in the Chapter 3 folder on the CD.

Normally, before we run the calibration, we would give MatchMover Pro any information that we have. For now, let's assume we don't have any information on the scene. We don't, for example, know anything about the camera or what focal length was used. There are, however, a few assumptions we can make about these values.

It seems fairly obvious that the camera is not doing any zooming during the shot, and this is one important piece of information we can use during calibration. Match-Mover Pro doesn't necessarily need to know the exact focal length in order to achieve a solution; it merely needs to know what type of lens was used.

1. It's always a good idea to check your camera settings before you begin calibration. To do this, click the plus sign on the Cameras folder in the Project View on the left side of the interface, then click again on the Camera. This opens up the Properties Window for the camera on the right (Figure 4.4).

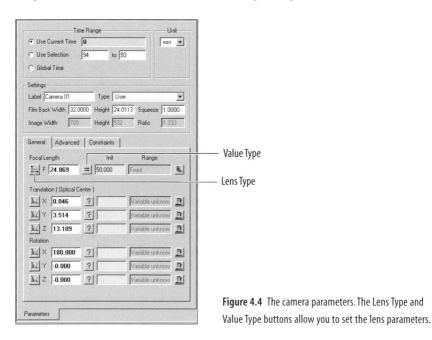

Figure 4.4 The camera parameters. The Lens Type and Value Type buttons allow you to set the lens parameters.

The two fields you will be most concerned with are the focal length field and the film back. We don't know anything about this camera, and therefore we don't know the film back. So for now, we'll let the program use the default film back size, which is approximately 32.00mm × 24.00mm.

2. As for the focal length, there are two considerations: the lens type and the value type. The Lens Type button sets what type of lens was used: choose Constant.

Clicking the first button in the Focal Length row toggles the setting between Constant or Variable:

Constant The lens doesn't zoom or change focal length during the shot.

Variable The lens zooms during the shot or is a variable lens.

> **Note:** The film back and the focal length work together to show the proper view of the scene. When the precise value of the focal length is required, you must also know the precise film back size. We can ignore the film back measurements in this case because we are not trying to solve for a specific focal length. The program will automatically compensate for any film back differences by changing the value of the focal length to a value that will work.

3. The next field is where you would set the focal length if you knew it, as well as where any solved focal lengths would appear. After that is another small button that sets the Value Type. It toggles between two types, Fixed or Initialized; choose Initialized.

    Fixed You know the exact value and will set that value in the Init field (to the right of the button). You generally want to use this type if you know the exact value of the focal length.

    Initialized You do not know the exact value. When you are using this value type, you can enter the approximate value in the Init field if you have any idea what it might be. The program then uses that value as its starting point for the calibration but may change the value if it needs to.

    In our tutorial, we'll need to use the Constant/Initialized setting. This is because we don't know what the focal length is, but we do know that it's constant.

    Once you've set the camera's parameters, you're ready to run the calibration—the moment of truth!

4. Under 3D Tracking, choose Solve for Camera or hit the F9 key. MatchMover Pro begins working through the calibration process. How fast this goes depends on your processor speed, but it shouldn't take more than a minute or so. As the program works, I like to keep my eye on the status bar at the lower-right side of the frame. This lists the residual values of the tracks as they are solved. When a calibration is going well, these values will generally stay under 1.0, and when a solution is more difficult, these values may creep up over 1.0. If the values are under 10 or so, you may have problems but probably correctable ones. If the values get up into the hundreds or even thousands, you may want to hit Escape to stop the tracking process, because something is obviously wrong.

After the calibration is complete, MatchMover Pro will give you some initial clues as to how well the cameras are calibrated. The most important indicator is visible at the very top of the Timeline (Figure 4.5). You'll see a colored bar beneath the frame numbers, with key icons along the top of it. This shows you how well the camera has solved. If it has solved correctly, it will be all green. Any yellow or red here is an indication that the camera wasn't solved well.

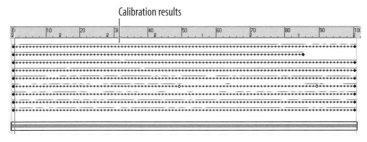

Figure 4.5 The very top of the Timeline serves as an indicator of the quality of the solution.

Note: In the preceding chapter, I said it was usually not a problem if the track's individual colors contained some red or yellow. This is not the same for the colored bar at the top of the Timeline, which indicates the status of the matchmove. The individual track's color has to do with the tracker's confidence in how well the pattern compares from one frame to the next. The bar at the top of the Timeline is the average of all the track's residuals. If the bar is red, that means that enough tracks are misaligned and the matchmove is bad during those frames.

If everything in your Timeline and Project View looks green, then you probably have a good solution. I say *probably* because sometimes MatchMover Pro indicates it has a good solution, but in fact it may not. The program may have found a solution that works mathematically, but not in a sense that is useful to us. In the next section, we'll evaluate the solution a little more thoroughly to make sure we have a good solution.

Evaluating the Solution

As you work on a matchmove and generate solutions, you will need to verify that they are, in fact, valid solutions. One common beginner's mistake is to create a solution and immediately export the solution to the 3D scene. The problem is, if the matchmove isn't right, you'll have to go back to the matchmoving program and fix the solution.

A more efficient way to work is to use a step-by-step analysis during each stage of the process. While performing your final checks in the matchmoving program, you should evaluate:

- 3D nulls
- 3D space
- The rendered movie

Evaluating the 3D Nulls

The first stage of evaluation is to examine the results in the matchmoving software. The first test I like to perform is to compare the 2D and 3D markers. To do this, you need to look at the nulls through the camera by clicking the small 3D button in the upper-left corner of the Video Window, then right-clicking and choosing Lock to Camera. This allows you to see the nulls directly over the features they represent (Figure 4.6). The nulls should appear to match up with the features that were originally tracked.

Figure 4.6 The first item to check is whether or not the 3D markers seem to line up with the correct features on the image.

The 3D markers can also help you determine the quality of the solution in another way. If your solution is accurate, then the size of the nulls should reflect this. For example, nulls that are closer to the camera should appear larger, while nulls that are farther away will be smaller. Notice in Figure 4.6 how the nulls on the back wall seem much smaller than the ones on the foreground boxes. This is what we would expect to see for any objects placed in the scene.

If this seems to be the opposite of what you're seeing through your camera, you may have a problem with the solution. It is fairly common to have one or two points that do not seem to be quite the right size, but if the discrepancy is happening globally, investigate further.

Evaluating the 3D Space

If the 2D/3D track comparison looks good, then proceed to the 3D perspective view and look at the camera and nulls. Does the camera move as you would expect it to? Are there any obvious spikes in the movement? Is there an excessive amount of jitter or noise in the camera path? Are the 3D nulls where you would expect them to be? Are any markers missing? Common signs of a failed solution (Figure 4.7) would include:

- Camera path appears random or erratic.

- Camera path works for one portion of the sequence then jumps to another location before finishing its move.

- Camera is not visible at all.

- Nulls are in the wrong position (i.e., nulls that should be far away from the camera are close to it and vice versa).

- Nulls are all in a line, on a single plane, all crammed into a single point, or even behind the camera.

- Nulls are not visible at all.

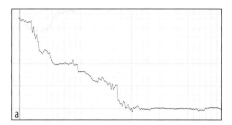
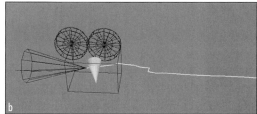

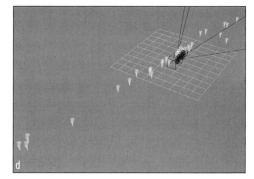

Figure 4.7 Some common signs of a failed solution: (a) erratic motion or motion curves, (b) broken motion path, (c) 3D markers are not appropriate scale, and (d) 3D markers are in a line or behind the camera.

When you are looking at your 3D scene and any of these situations is present, it's possible that your solution is not perfect. That's not to say it's hopeless. In the case of certain difficult shots, an imperfect solution may be better than no solution at all. You might get one-half of the shot to solve correctly, or maybe the nulls aren't spaced properly, but perhaps the camera moves more or less the right way.

> **Note:** In Chapter 7, "Integrating Matchmoves with the Scene," I discuss ways to manipulate imperfect solutions in the 3D application, but there are plenty of things you can do in the matchmove software to help fix or improve bad solutions. I discuss ways of doing this more in an upcoming section on troubleshooting, "When Good Solutions Go Bad."

Rendering the Matchmove

Before you export your final solution, it's a good idea to do one final check in the match-moving program. So far we've examined the 3D space in the perspective view and looked at the markers over the image. But there are some problems you might only notice when the image sequence is playing, such as:

- High-frequency noise

- Subtle drift

- Sudden pops in the camera's rotation

Most matchmoving programs include a way to render a test movie to see whether the markers are in fact sticking throughout the sequence. It basically amounts to render-ing the matchmove tracks as seen in the 3D view.

To illustrate how this works, let's render out a test of our calibration for this shot:

1. Make sure you are in the 3D view in MatchMover Pro. If you aren't, click the small 3D button in the upper-left corner of the Video Window. You also need to be "locked" to the camera, that is, the view of the markers is the same as if you were looking through the calibrated cameras. To do this, right-click in the Video Window and choose Lock on Camera. This should give you a view of the plate with the 3D markers on top of it.

2. Choose 3D Scene > Render Setup (Figure 4.8). This is where you set up all the parameters for your render from MatchMover Pro. You will probably want to render the full length of the clip at 100% size. You can choose a file type and use a compressor if you'd like, but don't compress it so much as to make it visu-ally difficult to see the markers. You should also render out the markers as Anti-Aliased, which will make them smoother.

Figure 4.8 The Render Setup panel

3. Click the Render button. You'll see MatchMover Pro start working its way through the render. When it's finished, it will play the video back and provide a way for you to scrub the footage to check for problems.

When Good Solutions Go Bad

It's entirely possible that your calibration may not have turned out well. Fortunately, with this type of shot, there are only a few things that could go wrong. I cover trouble-shooting in detail in Chapter 10, but here are a few things that could conceivably derail your calibration in this shot:

Slipping tracks I've found that most problems with a calibration lead back to the 2D tracking. In this particular shot, the features should be easy to track, and there are plenty of markers on the wall in various areas throughout the shot. Make sure that none of your tracks are slipping, especially as they approach the edge of the frame. An easy way to do this is to select a track and then right-click in the Video Window and choose Lock on Track. This keeps the track always centered in the window. You can then scrub the video by holding down the Ctrl key and dragging back and forth in either the Video Window or the Timeline.

Tracks not properly spaced Make sure that your tracks are well spaced throughout the environment and not all bunched up in one area or only on the walls. Remember, you're trying to sample the 3D space. You need to help MatchMover Pro understand where the walls, cubes, and ceiling are through 2D tracking.

Not enough tracks MatchMover Pro requires that you have at least eight tracks on the screen at any given time. If one of your tracks leaves the screen, make sure another replaces it before the departing one exits the frame.

Tracking a moving object All the features you track should be static. In this shot, that's pretty easy. The only things you should *not* track are the man, that little moving marker on the foreground cube, and the hood on the camera.

Calibrations and Camera Moves

One thing to consider during the calibration phase is what type of camera move seems to be present in the shot. This is not always clear just by viewing the footage. For example, a subtle zoom can look like a subtle camera dolly and vice versa.

It's important to determine, or at least guess, the type of camera move, since different moves require different tactics. To better understand how the camera's movement can affect the solution, we'll cover six basic types of camera moves:

- Dolly/crane
- Pan
- Slight dolly
- Lock-off
- Zoom
- Handheld/shaky footage

Dolly/Crane/Moving Camera

These are the types of shots that matchmoving software excels at. With these camera moves, the objects that are closer to the camera move faster than those far away, and that means they'll exhibit more parallax. You'll often see these referred to in the various matchmoving programs as Free Move or Free cameras, since their movement is not restricted. These types of shots are usually easier to solve with matchmove software, but they can be more difficult to place correctly into the 3D environment because the amount of camera movement must correspond to the scale of the scene.

Pan Shots

In a pan shot, the camera simply rotates on its tripod or mount. By definition, pan shots have no parallax, but the matchmoving programs can adjust their solving engines to generate a solution that is not completely a 3D solve. Rather, it is a "2.5D" solution, which results in a 3D camera with the nulls arranged around it as though they were stuck to the inside of an large sphere (Figure 4.9). The scenes that these programs export can be great for computing the camera, but the nulls they generate cannot be used to accurately determine the spatial position of features within the scene.

Slight Dollies/Translation

While matchmove programs can usually make quick work of either dolly shots or pan shots, a subtle camera move can make it surprisingly difficult to get a good solution. The reason is that these shots fall in a gray area within the solving capabilities of the software. They have too much parallax to solve as pans and not enough parallax to solve as straight dolly shots.

Unfortunately, there is no quick and easy way to deal with them. It often means manually editing some of the animation channels. For example, you may have to let the matchmove software calculate the translation the best it can, and then manually adjust the rotation. Or conversely, allow the software to solve it as a nodal pan and then reintroduce some translation by hand.

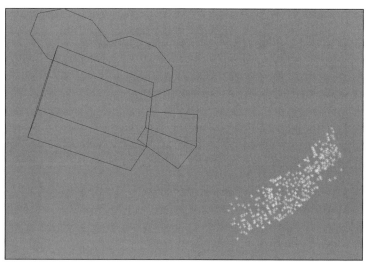

Figure 4.9 The 3D markers for a pan shot. Notice how they curve around the camera as though they were on the inside of a sphere.

Lock-offs

I had a visual effects supervisor who used to say, "There's no such thing as a lock-off." A lock-off is a camera that supposedly doesn't move during filming, but in reality there is some camera movement in all shots, even if it's only a few pixels. This small amount of movement can show up in the final renders, especially when you're working at high resolutions. If accuracy is an issue, you may want to run locked-off shots through the matchmove process. This helps stabilize the subtle jitter that can be present in the plate—jitter that may not show up until it gets to the compositor. By then there is usually a lot of time and work invested in the shot, and it might need to be redone—under a much tighter deadline.

There are a couple of ways to work with locked-off shots. First, you could stabilize the plate in a 2D compositing program and then simply set up the camera in the appropriate place. There may be times, however, when this is not practical—for example, if you need to use the whole image and can't have the edges of the image pulling away (a side effect of 2D stabilization). You could also track the plate for stabilization and then apply the offset to the rendered 3D elements. But again, you will need some extra rendered image or "padding" so that when the element is repositioned, it doesn't tear away from the edge of frame.

The second option is to matchmove the lock-off as a nodal pan (this essentially amounts to a 3D stabilization). This gives you a virtual camera that follows the almost imperceptible changes in the real camera's rotation.

Zoom Shots

When the focal length changes during a shot, it is called a zoom shot. These can be tricky to solve for two reasons. First, matchmoving programs vary in their capabilities. Not all programs can track zoom lenses, and those that do may not be able to for certain types of camera moves.

Second, it is more difficult to get accurate focal length values during a zoom. This loss in accuracy is partially due to the fact that zooming a camera and dollying a camera are similar but not identical. Depending on the camera move, this can potentially confuse the program and produce mixed results. When you are calibrating a fixed lens, it's usually easier to get an accurate solution when you specify the focal length. But when you calibrate a zoom, the focal length changes every frame. In order to solve a zoom, the matchmove software must be able to define the focal length on its own terms, which might not necessarily be the same focal length as what was actually used during filming. Only you can decide during calibration what is the acceptable amount of deviation and make corrections if necessary.

Shaky Footage/Handheld Footage

Although shaky footage is generally more of a 2D tracking problem, it can also translate into a 3D calibration problem. The areas of the footage where the blur is heavier will cause the 2D tracks to become more inaccurate, which in turn causes the calibration to become more inaccurate in those areas. Perhaps the only way to deal with this is to add more trackers than normal through the motion blurred areas. (Automatic tracking is a useful option for heavily motion blurred sequences.) The more data the solver has, the more likely it can achieve a solution.

Setting Up a Coordinate System

One aspect of the scene that matchmovers must designate is the coordinate system they plan to use in the 3D animation package. In most cases, a coordinate system is a foregone conclusion that the animation software has already imposed on them. But this is not so with matchmoving programs. When the matchmoving program creates the 3D world from the 2D tracks, it has no idea which way is up or how big anything is. When we look at an image, we can see immediately how things are oriented, but the software needs to be shown this information.

In most animation programs, you rarely need to think about the coordinate system. When you want to move an object up, you move it along the Y-axis.

 Note: Different animation programs use different designations for their coordinate systems. For example, Maya uses Y as the up-axis, while 3ds max uses Z as the up-axis. For simplicity's sake, I'll refer to the up-axis as the Y-axis.

In matchmove programs, the definition of the coordinate system is rather flexible, and the Y-axis might not always be the up-axis. That is, it is up to the matchmover to specify the coordinate system. The reason for this is two-fold: (1) matchmove software needs to be flexible enough to export to various animation programs, and (2) matchmove software cannot determine the coordinate system without user intervention.

Coordinate systems are somewhat independent of the calibration in most matchmove programs. Defining the coordinate system can be done either before or after calibration, although in my personal experience, it is most helpful to do it after calibration.

The coordinate system is established by referencing different axes and length measurements based on the various features that were tracked (Figure 4.10). For example, you may have tracked the bottom and the top of a pole during your matchmove. You can tell the software that a line drawn between those two tracks represents the Y-axis. The software would then know which way to orient the scene. Different programs have different ways of specifying this information, such as lines between two points, normal direction to three points, or defining planes. The concept is generally the same: you need to specify tracks that have some relevance to the way the scene is oriented.

The orientation of the exported scene does not need to be perfect because you can adjust this in the 3D animation package quite easily (and I discuss how to do this in Chapter 7). It's more important to correctly set the scale for the matchmove.

Most productions have a predefined scale for 3D models (usually a real-world scale), and the matchmover must deliver a scene that is consistent with that standard. This can be a problem with cameras that are translating, because if the scale isn't set correctly in the matchmoving program, the camera will either move too far or too little, and the matchmove won't work.

Figure 4.10 The coordinate system is set up using the various 3D markers that have been solved. By doing this, you can orient and scale your scene properly. In this scene, I've used the various marks on the wall to help define the coordinate system.

Note: It is very important that the scale of the matchmove camera's movement matches that of the scene. You can waste a lot of work by working in the wrong scale and having to redo it later.

The definition of scale is set in the matchmoving program by specifying the distance between one or more points that you have tracked. For example, suppose you have tracked the left and right corners of a building. You can specify the distance between those tracked corners as 10 meters. When you export the scene, the distance between those two tracks in the 3D scene will be exactly 10 meters.

Note: Changing the coordinate system in the matchmoving program doesn't usually require that you resolve the scene. When you change the coordinate system, you are simply altering the way the information is presented. The relationship between the tracking markers and the camera will remain the same, and as long as this is the case, the matchmove won't break.

Coordinate System Tutorial

Now that the calibration is complete for our tutorial sequence, we can set up a coordinate system. If you don't already have your scene open, do so, or you can load the bluescreen_04_Solved.mmf file from the Chapter 4 folder on the companion CD.

1. Make sure you are looking through the calibrated camera, and it is locked (that is, looking at the 3D markers through the camera). Right-click the Coordinate System folder and choose New Coordinate System. Once you've done this, there are two ways to create the coordinate system: you can drag the manipulators in the Video Window, or you can set it manually through the Properties Window (Figure 4.11).

To set the coordinate system using the manipulators, start by dragging the center of the system to the track that you want to use as your origin. Then drag the ends of the various axes to other tracks for setting them up. Set the scale by dragging either end of the light blue line between two tracks you want to use to determine the scale.

In this shot, I'm going to set the coordinate system manually since the tracks I have are not all set up in a way that I can use the manipulator.

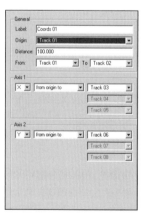

Figure 4.11 The coordinate system parameters

2. To establish a coordinate system, you need to determine four things: the origin, the scale, and two axes. The origin determines at which point in the scene is the 3D origin, that is, which place in the environment will be designated as (0,0,0) in 3D coordinates. You can only specify one point for this value. In our shot, let's set it to a marker on one of the cubes. In my scene, I chose Track 01. (We will change this later, but for now, this will do.)

3. The scale represents how large your environment will be (and how far the camera is moving within that environment). It is generally established by inputting the distance between two tracked features. For example, in our scene, we might select two tracks on the wall, and (assuming they're two feet apart) set our scale to 2 feet. We don't have exact measurements for this scene, but you should be able to make a reasonable estimate based on what you've tracked.

It's important to note that MatchMover Pro uses generic units for scale values. Inside MatchMover Pro they have no specific meaning, but once you open up the scene in your animation program the units will fit with whatever units you are using there. For example, if you set a scale of 10.0 in MatchMover, it could mean 10 meters, 10 centimeters, or 10 feet. In Maya, if your units are set to centimeters, when you open the scene, it will mean 10 centimeters. The same is true for most matchmoving programs.

4. The last thing, and perhaps the most important, is to set two of the axes. In the MatchMover Pro interface, you can choose which axis you are setting (X, Y, or Z), and then there are several options for setting it from there. They do similar things, but with different numbers of tracks:

Origin To This sets the direction of the axis as though a line were run from the origin to the selected track. For example, if you choose Origin to Track 01 for the X-axis, then the X-axis will be defined as running from the origin to Track 01.

Through 2 Points This is the same as the Origin To option, but it allows you to choose any two arbitrary points.

Normal to 3 Points This setting allows you to choose three tracks for the axis definition. If you were to create a polygon from these three tracks, the axis would point in the "normal" direction of that polygon. This is often used to define a ground plane using three tracks on the ground. By selecting them in counterclockwise order, the program assumes that the axis being defined runs in the normal direction to those three tracks. If you are using this method for your up-axis, and your markers end up facing down instead, you simply need to invert the selection order of the tracks.

Note: Why do only two axes need to be chosen? This is in some ways to protect us from ourselves. You choose two axes explicitly, and the third axis is assumed to be orthogonal (perpendicular) to the first. If it wasn't set up this way, you could potentially choose three axes that weren't truly perpendicular and therefore create problems. It's a good habit to explicitly define the up-axis since that's the most important axis to get right. After all, if you delivered a scene that was facing the wrong way, no one would probably care because it would be a minor annoyance. But if you delivered a scene that was upside down, that scene would be very difficult to work with.

For my project, I used two different sets of tracks to define the axes. For the X-axis, I chose "through 2 points" between Tracks 04 and 03. For the Y-axis, I chose "through 2 points" between Tracks 08 and 05. Figure 4.12 shows the scene with the completed coordinate system. The file `bluescreen_05_Coordinate.mmf` in the Chapter 4 folder on the companion CD shows my setup.

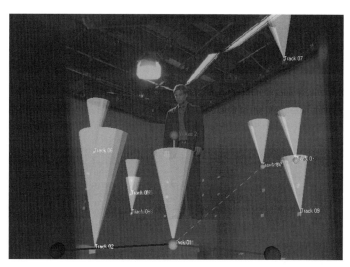

Figure 4.12 The coordinate system after it has been set up

In MatchMover Pro, it is not necessary to recalibrate the camera once you have set up the coordinate system. So at this point we are ready to export the solution—well, almost. There are a few loose ends we should probably clean up before that, so let's tackle that part next.

Prepping for Export

There will be times when you will need to add additional tracks (in order to create a coordinate system, mark important features, etc.). As you get better at matchmoving, you will find better ways to keep the tracks that you use to a minimum, but in certain circumstances (such as automatic tracking), you might not have enough to work with. For example, you might not have two tracks that represent the known scale of an object, and therefore you'll need to add them.

If you add any new 2D tracks after calibration, you will need to recalibrate in order to see them as 3D nulls. Some matchmoving programs allow you to add new tracks without breaking the existing calibration by calculating their position based on previous solutions.

In our tutorial, there is perhaps one shortcoming: we don't really know where the man is standing in the scene. In this shot, we need to re-create that man's position, and in order to do so, we need to track something near where he is standing.

This should be a relatively simple matter, but it requires a few extra steps:

1. Switch back into the 2D mode in MatchMover Pro by clicking the 2D button in the upper-left corner of the interface. Your tracks should become small crosshairs again.

2. Right-click in the Video Window and choose New Track. You should track something on one of the corners of the podium that the man is standing on, so that you can determine his position.

   You may find that the tracker has trouble sticking to the front corner because it is so similar in color to the objects around it. You really only need to track one of the three visible corners on the podium, and I found it easier to track the screen-left corner since it is a little bit darker than the others.

3. Although you've tracked in the new track, it hasn't been computed into the solution yet. It exists in 2D but not in 3D. In order to do this, you need to recalibrate. Choose 3D Tracking > Solve for Camera, or press the F9 key.

4. Any time you recalibrate with new data, you should double-check your solution, since even small changes can potentially alter the solution in big ways. Switch to the 3D view again and look at the tracks. Do they make sense and seem to be in the same place? If so, you are just about ready to export. I would first recommend changing the name of the track on the corner under the man's feet to something descriptive, like LedgeTrack.

Exporting the Scene

Last but not least, if everything seems to be working in MatchMover Pro, you're ready to export the solution to the animation package. This process is pretty self-explanatory, but we'll run through it here using our tutorial footage.

1. Choose File > Export. This brings up the Export dialog (Figure 4.13), which allows you to choose various options for export as well as the type of scene you'd like to export.

2. Select the type of file you'd like to export.

3. Choose the quality of tracks that you'd like to export. With just a few tracks, it probably makes sense to export them all. The only exception to this would be if you had some bad tracks that you'd rather not have in your final scene.

Figure 4.13 The Export dialog

4. You also have two options as to how the data is exported: Camera and Scene. The Camera option (which is the one you want in this case) exports a moving camera with static nulls representing the tracks. The Scene option exports the tracks as moving with a static camera. The Scene option is most often used for object tracking, so we won't use it here.

5. After you've exported, save your project. That way if you have any problems during export, you can reexport it.

At this point you are essentially finished with the matchmove program. The scene that you exported contains a camera and nulls representing the features that were tracked in 2D. The next step in the process will be to fit the camera properly into the 3D scene in your animation program. In Chapter 7, I'll show you how to use the scene we exported to finish the matchmove.

But It Gets Better

That's it! You've calibrated your first shot. Now that you've got the camera and the 3D space calculated, you're ready to drop the camera into your 3D scene in the animation program. But before we do so, I want to point out a particularly useful aspect of matchmoving programs called automatic tracking. This feature has revolutionized the matchmoving business and can really help make matchmoving less of a chore. In the next chapter, I describe how this technology works and how it is used.

Automatic Tracking

When matchmoving software first came on the market, 2D tracking was strictly a manual affair. Matchmovers had to place 2D tracks one at a time (much like we did in the Chapter 2 tutorial). But then automatic 2D tracking came on the scene, and it was a whole new ballgame. This made more shots solvable, and perhaps more importantly, solvable without any special knowledge of how the software worked.

Automatic tracking represents a huge paradigm shift in how matchmoving is approached. Rather than laboring to place tracks in the right position, the artist simply runs the automatic tracker. But there are a few major differences between the two different approaches, and that's what this chapter is all about.

Chapter Contents

Tracking on Autopilot

2D tracking in matchmoving programs is probably not most people's idea of fun. Admittedly, it can be tedious and mind numbing, but it is also one of the more important aspects of the work. The most appealing thing about automatic tracking is that it does make the job a lot more bearable.

Automatic trackers perform their magic through an exhaustive process of analyzing the image, identifying features, and eliminating unwanted features. The matchmove programs with this capability are designed so that these steps can be done entirely without human intervention (although, as you'll see later on, you can and will need to intervene on occasion). There are times when shots will work perfectly the first time through and others where you'll need to give the program a little guidance, but the process, as the name suggests, is mostly automatic.

The first step the software performs in automatic tracking is to go through the sequence and place a track on any feature that is appreciably unique. By unique I mean a bright, high-contrast feature or feature of a different color. This phase is very much a shotgun approach to 2D tracking. The more detail that is present in the image, the more tracks that will be generated. This can sometimes amount to tens of thousands of tracks per sequence!

After the initial tracks have been laid down, the tracks exist only on single frames. The program then examines how the tracks line up frame to frame and tries to join them together into tracks that last across multiple frames. Its ultimate goal is to identify which ones represent features that can be used for more than one frame and which ones can be eliminated.

The last thing an automatic tracker does is analyze the 2D tracks to determine if any of the features are not desirable. The same rules for calibration apply, including the fact that all tracked points should be static relative to one another. During automatic tracking, the program tries to identify any tracks that move significantly differently than most of the tracks around them. By doing this, it can eliminate features on moving objects, specular highlights, reflections, dirt, etc.

Perhaps the most obvious difference between automatic and manual tracking is the large number of final tracks produced during the automatic process. Usually there are significantly more than the matchmover would have tracked manually—all from a relatively easy, hands-off process. How many tracks are produced will depend on the complexity of the scene and length of the shot, but it can number in the hundreds or even thousands (Figure 5.1).

Image sequence courtesy Alex Lindsay/dvGarage

Figure 5.1 Automatic tracks can number in the hundreds or even thousands.

The large amount of data requires some differences in the *calibration engine* as well. The engine refers to the type of algorithms and techniques used, as in manual versus automatic calibration engines. While these two engines produce nearly the same results, their differences in approach can affect how you perform and troubleshoot your calibrations.

When a matchmove program solves a set of manual tracks, it is trying to infer a large amount of spatial information from a small number of tracks. Its calibration engine is fine-tuned to extrapolate a lot of information from small track changes. This can be beneficial when troubleshooting but problematic if the image is difficult to 2D track or susceptible to noise.

Automatic engines, however, analyze the tracks as a group and try to solve the scene in a more statistical manner. They examine the tracks in a global sense so that individual track differences don't affect the overall solution as much. With automatic tracking, it usually takes quite a few bad tracks to spoil the solution. The downside is that the huge number of tracks can make it more difficult to troubleshoot.

To the user, the difference between the two calibration methods is transparent. Solving a set of manual tracks or solving a set of automatic tracks is nearly the same—just press the solve button. But knowing the difference in the way the data is calculated can be of great help while troubleshooting a bad solution.

Editing Automatic Tracks

The good news is that automatic tracking produces a lot of 2D tracks; the bad news is that automatic tracking produces a lot of 2D tracks. Automatic tracking can track things that would have been too difficult or time-consuming to do manually. But if you ever need to edit the tracks, finding the bad track can be like finding a needle in a haystack. In this section, I'll cover a few techniques that can help you edit automatic tracks.

Besides the large number of tracks present after automatic tracking, the brevity of these tracks can make them a headache to edit. Autotracks often double up on certain features, last only a few frames, or fail to track the feature the entire time they are on-screen. Even the task of deleting tracks of such short duration is no simple matter. It often requires not only eliminating the track on a certain frame, but also scanning through the clip to make sure that the track doesn't pop up again later.

The difficulty of editing and deleting automatic tracks is balanced out by the fact that the automatic solving engines aren't as sensitive to individual track deviation as are the manual engines. This means a stray track here or there doesn't usually present a huge problem (Figure 5.2), and that means you will probably need to edit fewer tracks than you would for manual tracking.

Editing automatic tracks is usually a subtractive process. You remove large numbers of tracks to help guide the solving engine. For example, you may find that the program has tracked a lot of features on a moving object, and this is causing the solution to fail (Figure 5.3). By eliminating all the tracks on the moving object, the software can focus on the good tracks and make them work better. This also happens when the software places a lot of tracks in an area that really shouldn't have been tracked, such as areas that are constantly changing or being occluded.

Automatic tracking works in very broad strokes, and because of this, you will from time to time find yourself guiding the program to a solution. The three most common ways of doing this are to (a) emphasize existing automatic tracks, (b) add new manual tracks, or (c) edit or improve tracks.

To be as efficient as possible during troubleshooting, it makes sense to try and make the existing automatic tracks work as they are. One of the main ways to do this is to specify automatic tracks that you feel are especially good. These are tracks that were originally tracked by the automatic engine but that you have identified after the fact as being important tracks to the solution. These tracks are then given a greater statistical weight during calibration. That's just a fancy way of saying that the tracks are deemed more important to the solution than the average automatic track.

Note: Matchmoving programs vary in how they represent this type of weighted track. For example, in boujou bullet you select the automatic track and convert it to a Gold Track. In MatchMover Pro, you convert the automatic track to a manual track, thereby increasing its effect on the solution.

Figure 5.2 There will always be automatic tracks that are not tracking properly, as in this section of the image. Notice the long lines on some of the tracks. These are the motion trails that indicate some of the tracks are slipping.

Image sequence courtesy Litigation Animation

Figure 5.3 Automatic trackers need to figure out which features are in motion (like the car to the left of center) or static. Ultimately, it must remove 2D tracks that are inconsistent with the overall solution for the scene.

Adding a few of these weighted tracks can often help nudge a weak solution into a solid calibration. An ideal candidate for such a track would be one that is solidly tracked, not slipping, and of a fairly long duration. You may have to identify multiple tracks to get coverage for the duration of the sequence, and it doesn't hurt to have a few of them on the screen at the same time.

If none of the existing automatic tracks are sufficient to assign a greater importance, you can usually add manual tracks to the mix in order to help the solution. This also may be necessary if the automatic tracking didn't track a particular feature that you need. The manual track used in this scenario is exactly the same as one used in normal manual tracking. It is not necessary to designate the track as having a greater statistical weight, since the program assumes that if you're taking the time to add a track by hand, it must be important and tracked with extra loving care.

There are also times when an automatic track is almost good enough to use as a particularly important track, but the track could use some extra finessing. The most common reason for tweaking such a track is that it doesn't track for a long enough duration. In many cases, the track goes only a few frames and then stops, but another track picks up the same feature and continues tracking for a few frames, and so on. This break in the continuity of the track can be repaired by combining or merging the two tracks together, provided they are supposed to be tracking the same feature. For example, Track A tracks the corner of a building from frames 1 through 10 and then stops. Track B then tracks the same corner of the building from frames 11 through 20. By merging these two tracks together, you get a single track that goes from frame 1 through frame 20 (Figure 5.4).

Some matchmove programs allow you to convert the automatic track to a manual track. This allows you to manually extend a track that is too short in duration.

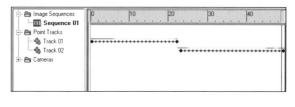

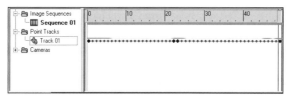

Figure 5.4 Two tracks before merging, then after merging

Using Masks

Of course, the best way to avoid having to edit too many tracks is to control what is tracked from the start. As I said before, automatic trackers track any feature they can without exception. Sometimes it is clear from the beginning that you will not need to track certain features, such as objects or people that fill a large portion of the frame during some or all of the clip. This is where masks come in.

The concept of masks or mattes as used for automatic tracking isn't too different from masks used in compositing. *Masks* are black-and-white images that define which areas of the image can be tracked and which cannot. For example, features in the white part of an image are tracked, and features in the black area are ignored. The masks are normally *articulated mattes*, that is, they are keyframed so that they follow the objects they are masking as those object move around the frame (Figure 5.5).

Figure 5.5 To prevent the moving car from being tracked, a mask was placed on it in the matchmoving program (top). This prevents the program from tracking it (bottom).

Masks used for automatic tracking do not have to be fancy. They are more akin to *garbage mattes* (in compositor-speak). They don't have to hug the curves, just be close enough to ensure that the object stays inside its borders. If your mask is too small, it's possible that the tracker will start tracking objects at the boundaries of the mask, potentially negating its usefulness. In the same sense, though, you want to avoid masking out features around the object, in case they are helpful to the solution.

Benefits of Automatic Tracking

Some special benefits arise when you use automatic tracking. Automatic tracking produces a large set of 2D tracks, and subsequently you have a large amount 3D data to work with. In many cases, matchmovers can take advantage of this data in ways that are not normally available to them.

Noise Reduction

When you are tracking a shot with a lot of noise or film grain, the resulting solution can create a camera motion that is noisy or jittery. This is because the small deviations of each 2D track cause similar small-scale deviations in the solution. Shots that are tracked using automatic tracking don't suffer from this problem as often. This is due to the large number of tracks involved in the solution. Each track has a slightly different pattern of noise, and therefore it is less likely that any one pattern of noise will dominate the solution.

Manual 2D tracking is more susceptible to camera noise, and automatic tracking can help alleviate this problem. In the programs that support both manual and automatic tracking, it can be helpful to run automatic tracking on top of the manual tracking. This has an overall dampening effect on noisy camera motions.

Environment Definition

Another benefit of tracking a lot of features in 2D is that you end up with the multitude of tracks in 3D as well. Depending on the number of features tracked, this can give you a real good idea of the spatial layout of the scene, sometimes to the point where you can model from the 3D positions of the tracks (Figure 5.6).

There are benefits to this in cases such as a landscape of which you want to know the topology. But be aware that the accuracy of the 3D markers may not be 100 percent. 3D markers will work perfectly fine for the matchmove you modeled from, but if you are planning on using them for other scenes, you should remember that the track positions might not work from other points of view.

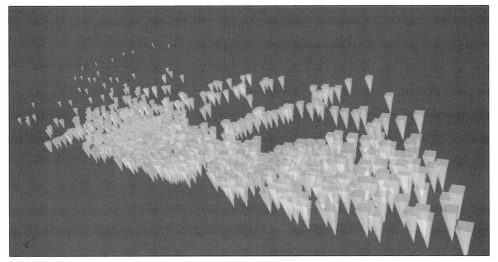

Figure 5.6 These tracks were done using automatic tracking for an aerial shot. The high density of tracking data makes it possible to make out the general shape of the ground. Notice near the top center that you can even see a square that represents two roads.

The Automatic Tracking Process

Automatic tracking is nearly identical in workflow to manually tracking a shot with a few key exceptions. First, and most obviously, the 2D tracking is done automatically. This means that the program, rather than the user, analyzes the clip and selects the appropriate tracks. This is often a double-edged sword, because while it makes the 2D tracking process much easier, it may not always track the feature you want or track enough features. As with any automatic process, the 2D tracking needs to be monitored and, in some cases, manipulated to produce the right results.

The calibration process from the user's perspective is identical. The program takes the 2D tracking data and uses photogrammetry to produce a solved camera. As I've noted before, the calibration engine is slightly different, but the end result is about the same.

One area where you will often find significant differences in approach is during the troubleshooting and refining stages of calibration. During the troubleshooting phase of a manual tracking session, you often must add tracks or edit the motion of individual tracks until the right result is achieved. But during troubleshooting of automatic tracks, you often edit out tracks and remove tracks that aren't necessary. Only then do you start adding back in tracking data to fill in trouble spots or areas with difficulties.

Automatic Tracking Tutorial

To get a better idea of how automatic tracking works, we're going to track a pan shot using 2d3's boujou bullet. boujou bullet has a strong automatic tracking engine, and it can really speed up the process of matchmoving. This tutorial will also introduce you to the slightly different approach that you need to take when matchmoving a pan shot. The Chapter 5 folder on the companion CD contains the sequence called PanShot.####.jpg, which we will use for this tutorial.

1. Begin by opening boujou bullet. When you start the program, a Wizard menu opens, prompting you to load an existing project. Since we're starting from scratch, just hit the Hide button.

2. The first thing you need to do is load the footage. Choose File > Import Sequence and browse to the footage. Select the first frame of the sequence and click the Open button (Figure 5.7). This automatically brings up the Import Sequence panel, which you will use to specify the specifics of the shot.

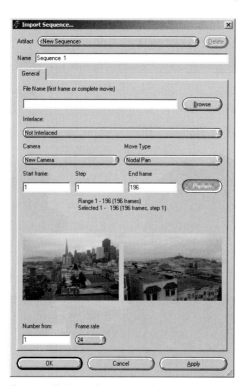

Figure 5.7 The Import Sequence panel

3. At the top of the Import Sequence panel is the footage you've selected. Directly below that is the Interlacing option. This footage was shot as progressive scan (noninterlaced), so you can leave the field at the default Not Interlaced setting.

4. The next field you'll need to look at is the Move Type field. boujou bullet has two options here: Free Move and Nodal Pan. Free Move applies to shots in which the camera moves during the shot, whereas Nodal Pan means the camera simply pans while maintaining a fixed position. This shot is a pan shot and doesn't appear to be moving, so change this field to Nodal Pan.

> **Note:** The term *nodal pan* referred to in this panel is a technical term that means the camera is rotating around its optical axis (usually the center of the lens). Most often, including in this shot, the camera pivots around the tripod head's pivot point near the bottom of the camera. Technically, this means that our shot is not a true nodal pan. But boujou bullet should still be able to calculate it correctly. The only time this really becomes an issue is when there are objects very close to the camera.

5. The start and end frame will default to the first and last frames of the footage, so you shouldn't have to change these values. That leaves the last field at the bottom of the panel. This footage was shot at 24 frames per second, so you can set that in the Frame Rate field. This footage starts on frame 1, so for consistency, you should probably change the Number From field to 1 as well. Once you've change the appropriate fields, click OK to accept them.

6. As soon as you hit OK, boujou bullet automatically brings you to the Cameras panel (Figure 5.8), where you can set the parameters of the camera (if they're known). In this case, again you don't know the measurements of the film back or CCD, so you can leave the default settings in those fields. You also don't know the exact focal length, but it doesn't appear to be changing, so you can leave it as Constant. Due to the size of the footage (720 × 480 pixels), the program has correctly interpreted this footage as DV NTSC. This also sets the Pixel Aspect Ratio to .9, which is also the correct setting. To accept these settings, click Apply, then Close.

Once these settings are complete, you enter the main interface where you will begin working. You might want to click the small arrow key at the top right of the interface to hide the Wizard menu and give yourself more screen real estate to work with.

Let's take a quick look at the interface (Figure 5.9). boujou bullet's interface is very streamlined and designed to follow the logical progression of creating a match-move. The largest part of the interface is the Image window, where the video plays back. You can make the clip framed to the view by choosing View > Fit to View from the main menu.

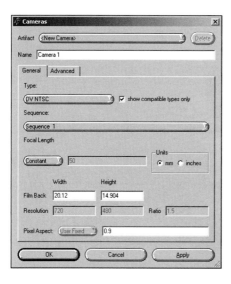

Figure 5.8 The Cameras panel

Figure 5.9 The boujou bullet interface

At the bottom of the interface are some standard shuttle controls for controlling the playback of the clip, including ones for playing forward, backward, etc. The interface also contains buttons that put you in 2D or 3D mode (more about that later).

On the left side of the interface, you'll find Shortcuts that help you work through the various steps of the camera tracking. They are arranged in a logical order and will most often be worked through from top to bottom, although you may not need every shortcut for every shot.

There is also a small History window in the lower-right corner of the interface that lists the steps you've taken and allows you to back up a few steps if necessary. Now that we know a little bit about the interface, let's continue the automatic tracking:

7. The first item in the Shortcuts is for Polygonal Masks. As mentioned earlier, masks are used to indicate to the program which areas of the shot need to be tracked and which don't. This is most often used when an object fills a large portion of the frame and needs to be ignored. At this point, you could mask off parts of the image as needed, but since that isn't the case with this shot, we can skip this step.

8. The next item on the list is Feature Tracking. This is the meat and potatoes of the program. Click on the Feature Tracking button to bring up the Feature Tracking panel (Figure 5.10).

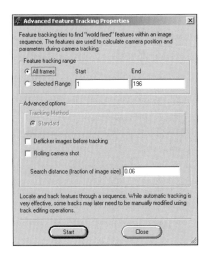

Figure 5.10 The Feature Tracking panel

You should track the entire shot, so you can leave the tracking range alone. You also don't need to bother with the advanced options here. The Deflicker option allows boujou bullet to average adjacent frames' contrast values to help it track through shots where there are flashing lights or sudden changes in brightness values. This, of course, doesn't apply to this shot. The second check box refers to shots in which the camera rolls around the optical center. This also is not the case with this shot, so you can leave them both unchecked.

9.   Save your scene (File > Save) at this point, since you've input all of your information.

10. Once you're ready, click the Start button to begin the 2D tracking process. For now, when the status bar comes up, uncheck the Camera Track on Calibration check box. The screen should instantly fill up with little red crosshairs that represent the 2D tracks that boujou bullet is going to use for its solution. The small yellow trails show you how the individual tracks are moving (Figure 5.11).

After Feature Tracking is complete, the wizard interface will prompt you to begin Camera Tracking. For now, hide the panel by clicking the Hide button.

11. Now that the automatic tracking is complete, you're ready to start calibrating the camera. Click the Camera Tracking Shortcut in the left panel to bring up the Camera Tracking panel (Figure 5.12). At this initial stage, the only option you can change is the Camera Path Smoothing. This option is usually only necessary for noisy or jittery camera paths. Since that's probably not the case here, you can leave this value at 0.

Figure 5.11 Automatic tracks

12. When you're ready to start calibrating, click the Start button. boujou bullet will begin analyzing the 2D tracks and creating a solution based on that data. How long this will take depends on the speed of your computer's processor, but it should take only a couple of minutes on most systems.

After the calibration is complete, the wizard interface again pops up and lets you know whether or not the process was successful (Figure 5.13). If the wizard does not re-appear, click the Wizard button on the right side of the interface to bring it back.

Note: In previous chapters, I've shown the steps you need to take in order to evaluate your matchmove and see whether your tracks are correct or not. The boujou bullet Wizard is a great tool that guides you through this process step-by-step and not only helps you to check the quality of your matchmove, but also shows you steps to correct problems if necessary.

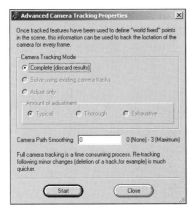

Figure 5.12 The Camera Tracking panel

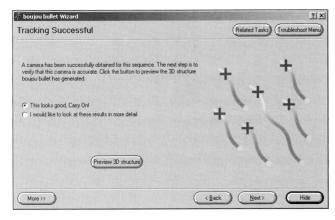

Figure 5.13 Wizard interface

13. Before you go through the wizard, click the button that says Preview 3D Structure. This takes you to the 3D view, where you can examine the camera and markers in 3D space to see what you have. Since this is a nodal pan, the camera won't have a motion trail; it is simply spinning in place. The direction of the camera is represented by the yellow line. The markers (and there are a lot of them) are arranged in front of the camera as though they were mapped on the inside of a sphere (Figure 5.14). This is the desired configuration for a pan shot. If you do not have this type of situation in your scene, then you can solve it through the wizard.

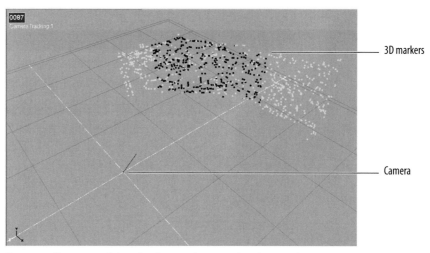

Figure 5.14 The camera and 3D markers for a pan shot. Notice how the 3D markers seem to be wrapped on the inside of a large sphere. No motion trail should be visible for the camera since it is not moving, only panning.

14. Click the check box in the wizard that says, "I would like to look at these results in more detail," and click the Next button. This begins the evaluation portion of the wizard. The wizard consequently takes you through a series of steps to help evaluate the camera:

    a. First the wizard asks you how the camera path looks. Since this is a pan and there is no translation on the camera, we cannot see any path. For now, you can say it is smooth.

    b. Next the wizard asks you about the 3D structure of the markers it generated. Since this is a pan, the markers should be neatly arranged as though they were on the surface of a sphere. If this is the case, choose Good and then Next.

c. Then boujou bullet prompts you to check the predictions by flipping you back to the 2D mode and having you play back the results. The blue and yellow dots are called predictions and they represent the 3D markers in the scene (Figure 5.15). When you are in the 2D mode, you are looking at the predictions through the reconstructed camera. If everything is working with the camera, the predictions should not slip off as the clip plays.

15. The next step asks if you want to place a 3D test object into your scene. Since this shot is a pan and the 2D tracks look good, it isn't totally necessary, but you can add one if you like by following the prompts.

16. Next, the boujou bullet Wizard prompts you to add in scene geometry. This helps define the coordinate system, including origin, axes, and scale. Again, since this is a pan shot, you can put this off until you've exported, but you can add the coordinate system in an arrangement you like for now.

17. The last wizard item allows you to do your final export. Simply select the file type for the 3D animation package you plan to export to and hit Export.

Once you've exported the matchmove, you can open up the scene in your animation program and check the results.

Figure 5.15 The final calibration showing 3D predictions over the image

Ready for a Brief Detour

As you can see, automatic tracking greatly simplifies the process of matchmoving a shot; however, we're not quite finished yet. Now that you've solved two shots using matchmoving programs, you need to incorporate your shots into a final scene in an animation program. But before we do that, we'll take a look in more detail at cameras. We'll learn how they work and what aspects of cameras are most important to a matchmover.

Cameras

A matchmover's primary concern is usually cameras. After all, it's their responsibility to take an image sequence and provide a 3D camera that precisely mimics the camera that filmed that sequence. They must know not only where the camera was positioned and which way it was facing but also what focal length and format were used. In order to make solving matchmoves easier and more precise, it is invaluable to know how real-world cameras work.

Chapter Contents

How Film Cameras Work

Whenever I'm on set, I marvel at the sheer complexity involved with a film shoot. Dozens of crew members, lights, props, the set, producers, and actors all come together to create something amazing. But all of this activity centers on one little machine at the heart of it all—the camera. Despite their central role in movie-making, cameras are still a mystery to many visual effects artists. To help dispel some of the mystery, let's take a look at the basic components of a camera and how they work (Figure 6.1).

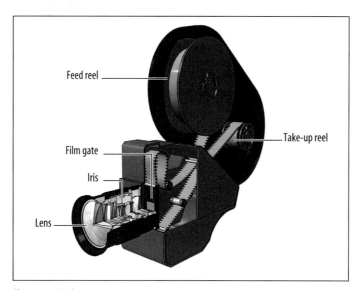

Figure 6.1 Inside a camera

Film cameras are designed to record moving images. At the heart of this process is a lens that focuses light onto some sort of recording media such as film. The unexposed film initially starts on a reel (known as a *feed reel*) that sits inside a lightproof cartridge. As the film comes off the feed reel, it winds its way through various spindles that thread it down into the *film gate*. The film gate consists of two pieces: the *pressure plate* (in the back) and the *aperture plate* (on the side closest to the lens). The aperture plate has an opening called the *film aperture*, and it is through this opening that light from the lens exposes the film.

A small claw grabs the sprocketholes (called perforations) on the edges of the film and pulls the film, one frame at a time, down through the film gate. When a frame is pulled down into alignment with the aperture, it is ready to be exposed to light from the lens.

In front of the aperture is the *shutter*. This is usually composed of two semicircular pieces that can change angle relative to one another (Figure 6.2). As the shutter spins in front of the aperture, it alternately blocks the light and lets light through. First, a frame is pulled down to the aperture while the shutter is blocking the light from the lens. The frame is briefly held in place while the shutter spins around so that light shines through and exposes the frame. Once the shutter is blocking the light again, the claw advances the film another frame, and the cycle repeats. If the shutter didn't intermittently block the film, the resulting image would be blurry. Consequently, the longer the shutter is open, the more light is allowed to expose the film, and thus the more motion blur will appear in the final image.

Note: Digital cameras do not usually have a mechanical shutter; instead, the shutter action is performed electronically.

The exposed film feeds out through the other side of the gate and is taken up on the take-up reel, which is usually housed in the same light-tight cartridge as the feed reel.

This process is repeated rapidly and in perfect synchrony to capture the images at a steady rate. When the images are played back at the same rate, they become a moving recording of the scene. Most film cameras record at 24 frames per second, although they can often record at various other speeds as well. Video cameras usually capture at 30 or 25 frames per second, depending on the format. (I'll discuss video later in this chapter.) Film cameras record at different speeds for many reasons. Cameras are sometimes *over-cranked* to higher frame rates; when played back at normal frame rates, the images appear slower. Conversely, a camera can be *undercranked*, in which case the footage would appear faster than usual when played back at a normal frame rate.

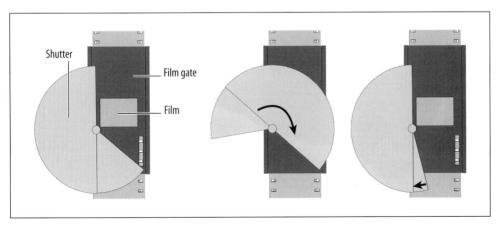

Figure 6.2 The shutter spins around in front of the film gate, alternately blocking the light. The shutter plates can slide past each other to let more or less light through during each rotation.

Note: The terms under- and overcranked harken back to the early days of film, where the frame rate was controlled by the camera operator, who would advance the film through the camera manually by turning a crank.

The two elements of a camera that the matchmover is most concerned with are the lens and the film aperture. In the next few sections, I'll discuss how each of these components works and how they're intimately related to one another.

Lenses

A camera lens is a surprisingly complicated piece of equipment that is manufactured to incredible levels of precision. A camera lens generally contains multiple lenses (called elements) inside the lens body, each with a slightly different purpose (Figure 6.3). Some are primary focusing elements, designed to accurately focus the light onto the film plane; others are auxiliary elements to compensate for imperfections such as distortion and chromatic aberrations in the primary elements. Often these elements are coated with thin films that refract or filter light in a specific way that is beneficial to the overall image quality.

In addition to the elements, the lens also contains the iris or diaphragm, which controls how much light is getting to the film. The iris is composed of interlocking plates that can slide past each other to make the opening larger or smaller, thus adjusting the

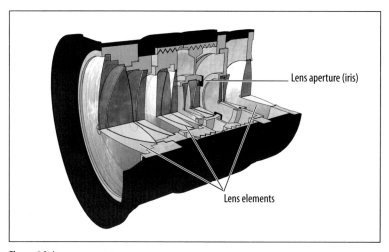

Lens aperture (iris)

Lens elements

Figure 6.3 Lens components

CHAPTER 6: CAMERAS

amount of light getting to the film. The size of the opening is often referred to as the aperture setting, but this should not be confused with the film aperture at the film gate. The word *aperture* really just means an opening, so it is an appropriate term for both components; however, each of these openings serves a different purpose. The iris (lens aperture) controls the amount of light getting into the camera, while the film aperture defines the shape of the image on the film. It's a subtle distinction but, as I'll show later, an important one.

Focal Length

The lens feature that has the most prominent effect on the final image is the focal length. The *focal length* is the distance between the center of the primary lens and the film. A shorter focal length (usually referred to as a "wider" focal length, for reasons I'll explain later) produces a more pronounced perspective, a larger sense of depth, and more of the scene visible in the image (as in the first image in Figure 6.4). A longer focal length produces images that exhibit a flatter look with a less obvious sense of depth and less of the scene visible in the image (as in the second image in Figure 6.4). Extremely long lenses are referred to as telephoto lenses, and extremely wide lenses are called wide-angle lenses.

It is a useful skill to be able to make a good guess about the focal length used to shoot an image. Unfortunately, this only comes with experience. What is considered a long lens and what is considered a wide lens will vary depending on whom you talk to. Generally speaking, though, wide lenses are about 24mm or less, and long lenses are about 50mm or greater.

Figure 6.4 Wider lenses produce a more pronounced perspective and sense of depth, while longer lenses tend to flatten everything out.

Some lenses are fixed lenses (also called prime lenses), which means that their focal length is fixed and does not change. There are also variable lenses (or zoom lenses), named so because the focal length can be changed. Zooming a variable lens from one focal length to another is done by a set of elements inside the lens that move along the length of the lens barrel and increase or decrease the focal length. When a lens is zoomed in (that is, it goes from a shorter focal length to a longer one), objects in the scene appear to get closer and fill the frame more. It looks almost as if the cameraman walked toward the subject with a fixed lens, but there is a subtle difference between zooming in and dollying in. Figure 6.5 shows this difference. Note how the relationships of foreground and background elements change drastically between the two.

Zoomed in

Dollied in

Figure 6.5 The difference between dollying and zooming. The first image shows the baseline image. In the second image, the camera was zoomed in by changing the focal length. The third image was made by dollying forward. Notice the difference in perspective, even though the statue is about the same size in both images.

When analyzing a plate to determine whether a camera is zooming or not, just check out the relationship between foreground and background. If they do not move independently, then chances are that the lens was zoomed. One of the more challenging things to do in matchmoving is to try and calculate the focal length during a zoom. Most matchmoving software is adept at this, but it is extremely difficult to do by hand.

Types of Camera Moves

There are a lot of different ways to describe camera moves, but Hollywood has distilled them down into a relatively short list of interesting jargon. These terms are good to know for several reasons:

- Quickly communicating ideas to other artists

- Deciphering camera reports or storyboards

- Understanding information from camera operators, visual effects supervisors, etc.

Here are some common terms used to describe different camera moves:

Lock-off/locked-off Camera doesn't move at all. The camera is usually mounted to a tripod, and then the camera operator locks all of the mechanisms for moving the camera.

Dolly Camera moves in some direction (for example, "dolly forward"). To perform this type of move, cameras are often mounted on a special cart with wheels called a dolly, hence the name.

Crane Camera is mounted on a crane. This term can refer to a shot that is simply very high above the scene or a camera move in which the camera moves a significant distance up or down (e.g., "crane-up").

Pan Camera rotates. This term can refer to virtually any camera move where the camera rotates, whether it is mounted on a tripod or not. Very fast pans are sometimes called "crash pans" or "whip pans."

Zoom Camera's focal length changes during the shot. Very fast zooms are sometimes called "crash zooms."

Dutch (angle) Camera is tilted along its optical axis. For example, the image appears tilted, as when the left side of the image is higher than the right or vice versa.

Rack focus Camera's focus changes from one object to another. This is often done for dramatic effect or to help the viewer's eye follow the action.

Focus

Besides gathering light and controlling the amount of light that gets into the camera, the lens is also the way the image is focused. In most cases, focus isn't something that a matchmover can solve for, but it can have an indirect effect on the matchmove in two important ways: blur and focal length.

When an image is said to be in focus, it means that the lens is bending the light in such a way that the beams of light converge exactly at the film plane. If the light from an object converges in front of or behind the film plane, the object will be blurry and out of focus. Because the light from closer objects enters the lens at different angles than light from distant objects, it is possible to have some objects in focus while others are out of focus. Often, the director may wish to change the focus from one object to another in the middle of a shot, which is called a *rack focus*. Blurry images can affect how hard a shot is to matchmove: a blurry image is often more difficult to 2D track. Also, when features are blurred out, the tracks become inherently inaccurate and can make it more difficult to achieve an accurate solution.

Sometimes a focus change manifests itself as a small change in focal length. Normally the difference is so slight that it isn't a major problem, and the matchmoving software can adjust its solution to deal with the change. But you may encounter some problems when the camera does a rack focus. If you are having trouble solving a rack focus with a fixed lens, it might help to try changing the settings to solve as a zoom lens.

Nodality

It is also important to note that the optical center of a camera is at the center of the lens. (To be more specific, it is centered on the iris within the lens, which is usually very close to the primary lens.) This optical center-point is known as the nodal point. Why is this important? First, when a camera moves or translates, the resulting image will exhibit parallax, but when a camera pans or rotates, it should generate no parallax—*if the camera is rotating around its nodal point.*

Many times this is not the case. Sometimes the camera is attached to a tripod at its base and rotates around that point. Because the optical center is in the lens and the pivot center is at the base of the camera, the camera's lens actually describes a small arc in space (Figure 6.6), which means that even though the camera is panning, the image could still exhibit a small amount of parallax. Since the 3D cameras are mathematically perfect cameras, they also need to reflect that small amount of parallax. This sometimes presents a bit of a problem for matchmoving software in that there may be too much parallax to solve as a pan and not enough parallax to solve as a dolly. One other reason that the nodal point is important is that camera operators typically measure their focal distances and distances to the subject from the nodal point of the lens.

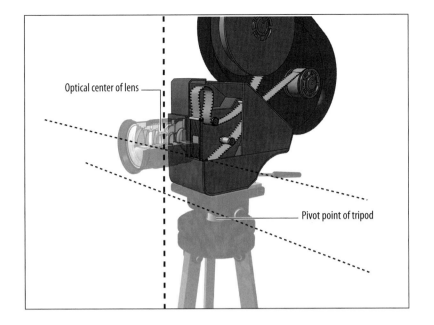

Optical center of lens

Pivot point of tripod

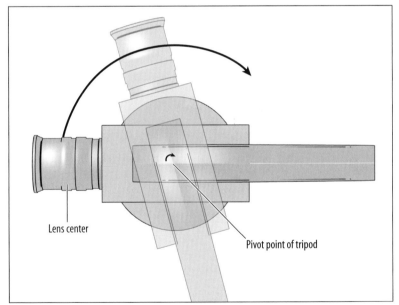

Lens center

Pivot point of tripod

Figure 6.6 The optical center of the lens does not usually correspond to the rotational center of the camera itself. That pivot point is further down on the tripod.

Film Backs and CCDs

To use a baseball metaphor, if the lens is the pitcher, then the film is the catcher. The light gathered by the lens is aimed at the film, which is sitting in the film gate. Match-movers need to be concerned with two aspects of the film gate: the aperture size and the aperture shape. In a film camera, the film sits in the film gate ready to be exposed (Figure 6.7). The front part of the gate has an opening known as the film aperture, which essentially acts as a matte for the image being projected onto the film. Since the film aperture is directly in front of the film, the size and shape of this opening dictates the size and shape, or format, of the image (discussed in more detail later in this chapter).

The size of the film back is important to a matchmover because the film back and focal length together help define the field of view (FOV). The FOV represents what section of the scene will be visible with a particular lens and film aperture configuration.

Film Back and Focal Length

Understanding exactly how the film back and focal length of the lens are related requires a little bit of mental exercise, so here we go (I promise this won't hurt a bit). If you extended an imaginary line out from each of the four corners of the film to the outermost edges of the lens, you would form an ever-widening pyramid shape (technically known as a *frustum*) that represents the FOV for that particular lens/film back combination (Figure 6.8).

Figure 6.7 Film gate

The FOV is a linear measurement of what you can actually see in the scene. If you were to change either side of this relationship, you would affect the angle of view (AOV).

I should also point out that FOV and AOV are often used interchangeably, but they aren't the same thing (Figure 6.9). AOV measures the angle of a 360-degree circle that is visible and is expressed in degrees. The FOV is how much of the scene is visible and is measured in linear units (such as feet or meters).

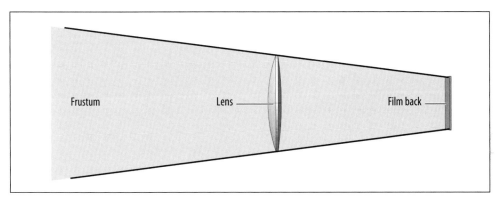

Figure 6.8 The frustum can be found by extending imaginary lines from the edges of the film back to the edge of the lens.

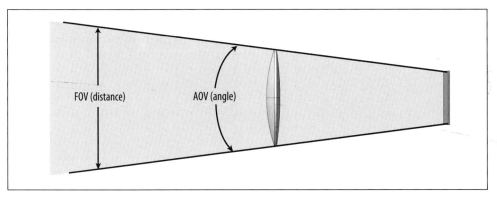

Figure 6.9 FOV vs. AOV

The AOV is usually expressed in degrees, as in the number of degrees in a circle. For example, if a lens has a horizontal AOV of 90 degrees, it can see approximately one-fourth of the scene from left to right. There is an inverse relationship between the focal length of a lens and its AOV—that is, the longer the focal length, the smaller the AOV, and the shorter the focal length, the larger the AOV. This is why short lenses are generally referred to as wide-angle lenses, due to their larger AOVs. For example, using a longer lens causes the lens center to be farther away from the film back, and therefore the frustum is narrower and the AOV is smaller. Making the film back larger while leaving the focal length as is has the same effect (Figure 6.10).

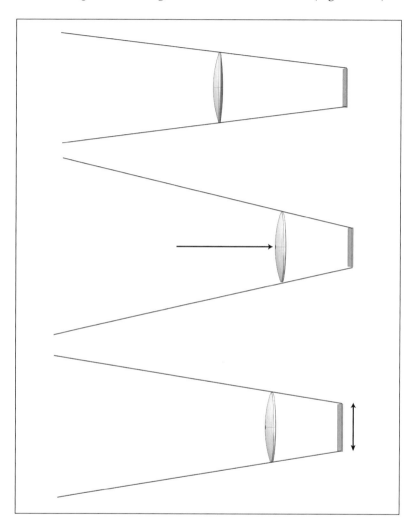

Figure 6.10 The AOV changes if the elements change. If the focal length decreases (second image), then the AOV increases. If the film back increases (third image), it has the same effect as a greater focal length.

Digital Cameras

Digital cameras do not use film and therefore do not have a film gate per se. As I've mentioned before, they use a small chip called a charge-coupled device (CCD) to record the light coming through the lens. In many respects, a CCD is identical in concept to film except that it records the incoming light as an electric signal. The CCD still sits inside the camera behind the lens, and the light from the lens is focused onto it. In a film camera, the film aperture defines the shape of the image, while on a CCD, the shape of the CCD itself (or a pre-defined capture region) defines the shape of the image.

Another important aspect of a CCD that is different from its film counterpart is its size. Advances in technology have improved so much that CCDs have shrunk to sizes much smaller than a 35mm film frame. This can have an effect on how focal length measurements are annotated. When you examine the technical specifications of a digital camera, you'll often find the lenses expressed as "35mm equivalents" and references to "lens multipliers." This is due to the smaller CCD (film back) size. Because the film back is smaller than normal, a wider lens is required to create the same image on the film back (Figure 6.11). So when you see something like "70mm lens as 35mm equivalent," it means that the actual lens is wider than 70mm but produces the same image as a 70mm lens would in a traditional 35mm camera.

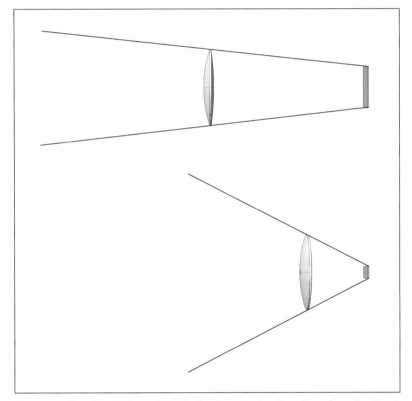

Figure 6.11 Film vs. CCD AOV. Since a CCD is significantly smaller than 35mm film, a shorter focal length must be used to project the image onto the film plane the same way. This means a larger AOV.

The lens multiplier is simply a conversion factor that allows you to convert any lens to its 35mm equivalent. For example, if a digital camera lens that is 10mm has a multiplier of x2.4, the lens is the equivalent of a 24mm lens in a traditional camera.

Using Camera Information

As you might have noticed, the film back and focal length are somewhat malleable when used together. This can be a great benefit or a great big headache when you're matchmoving. Usually when beginning a matchmove, I try to find out the exact film back and focal length used for the shot and use them in my solution. If I haven't been given the film back, I try to find out what camera was used and then look up the technical specifications online or elsewhere. As for the focal length, you are really at the mercy of those taking notes on set. You rely on them to get accurate information as they're shooting and to write up a camera report. Even if you get a camera report with a focal length, it might be wrong.

If you have no information whatsoever about the film back, you could try and take an educated guess using "standard" film backs such as 35mm full app or NTSC DV, but even so, you might not have much luck. If all else fails, you can just let the default settings in the matchmoving software apply and allow the software to calculate the focal length. The only important thing to remember when doing this is that the film aperture measurements must be the same width-to-height ratio (known as the image aspect ratio). By doing this, you allow the software to compensate for any inaccuracies in the aperture. It's important to keep in mind, however, that the focal length settings may not end up solving the same as the actual focal length used on the real camera.

Format

Whenever you are given a shot to matchmove, it is very helpful to determine what format was used to film it. The film format is based on several different factors, including the size and shape of the film aperture. Unfortunately, figuring out what format is being used is not always that easy. It is complicated by the fact that there are many possible formats, and digitization introduces even more possibilities for confusion—even for seasoned pros. In this section, we'll sort through these various formats.

The current size of 35mm film has been the standard pretty much since moving images were invented. This size corresponds to the size Thomas Edison used for his movie cameras in the early days of film. The film passes through the camera vertically via four sprocket holes (perforations) per frame. When the aperture fills the full area between perforations (0.980″ × 0.735″) , the format is known as *35mm full aperture* (or *full app*). If you divide the horizontal aperture measurement by the vertical measurement, the result is the *image aspect ratio,* in this case 1.333:1, usually abbreviated to 1.333. The image aspect ratio is nothing more than the ratio of the width of the image to its height. If you ever want to calculate the image aspect ratio of an image, just divide the width by the height.

Although the size of 35mm film has remained the same, a multitude of formats have come and gone since then. For example, when sound was first introduced to movies, it was recorded optically on the left side of the image. In order to make more room for the sound, the size of the aperture was shrunk to 0.864″ × 0.630″. This format is known as the *Academy format* and is still used today.

The full app and Academy formats have image aspect ratios that are fairly square, more like those seen on a TV. In fact, at the time TV emerged, its picture dimensions were based on the then-popular film formats. In order to distinguish themselves from the fledgling TV images, studios sought ways to maximize viewing pleasure while audiences were in the theater. The result was a multitude of widescreen formats that could be projected on ever-larger scales.

One development in the widescreen wars was the use of anamorphic lenses. These lenses optically "squeeze" the image horizontally so that a greater field of view can be crammed on the film. If you were to look at an image on a piece of 35mm film that was shot with an anamorphic lens, it would appear squished horizontally. Anamorphic widescreen formats get projected in the theater by special anamorphic projection lenses that undo the squeezing effect and restore the image to its proper proportions.

A newer development is that of high definition (HD) digital cameras that create high-quality images without the need for film at all. The image aspect ratio for HD is 1.778, although it is more commonly known as 16:9 (pronounced "16 by 9"). This ratio was chosen as a good compromise between most popular formats.

Of course, this just scratches the surface of the various formats available, and I can't possibly cover them all here. There are a wide range of other formats such as 16mm, 70mm, and IMAX formats for film and NTSC and PAL for video. Refer to Appendix B for more information on these various formats.

Lens Distortion

Lens distortion is a type of aberration that causes images to become stretched or compressed as they approach the edges of the frame. When the edges tend to bend inward, it is referred to as *barrel distortion;* when the edges flare outward, it is called *pincushion distortion.* Because of the nature of distortion, it is more severe around the edges of the image and less severe near the center (Figure 6.12).

Figure 6.12 An example of lens distortion. Notice how the straight edges of the building on the left are extremely bent, while the same effect is less pronounced near the center of the image.

The most common cause of lens distortion has to do with the proximity of stops within the lens. A *stop* (such as the iris in the lens) stops a portion of the light from getting through. If this stop is very close to the main lens, then the image as seen at the lens gets through relatively intact and undistorted. However, if the stop is a significant distance in front of or behind the lens, things are different.

Consider the light that is reaching the lens. A ray that passes through the center of the stop should always reach the image plane at the center of the film plane by definition, as shown in Figure 6.13. But what of light that is entering at the edges of the stop? If the stop is in front of the lens, these rays of light can hit the lens at an oblique angle, causing them to bend more toward the center of the image than they should and resulting in barrel distortion. The opposite is true if the stop is in back of the lens. In that case, the only light that is allowed to pass through the stop around the edges are those rays that tend to bend outwardly and are distorted in a pincushion manner.

Distortion shows up more often with wide-angle lenses and zoom lenses. This is because the circumstances that lead to distortion are more often present in those types of lenses. Zoom lenses tend to exhibit distortion because the elements inside the lens are moving relative to one another and the stop, and therefore it is difficult to create a system that can accommodate this. Such lenses can exhibit barrel distortion at the wide end and pincushion distortion at the telephoto end. To make matters worse, distortion can also be pincushioned near the middle and barreled at the outer edges.

Lens distortion can be tricky to deal with in a large production pipeline (Figure 6.14). This is because the cameras in 3D animation programs do not exhibit lens distortion and therefore all images rendered from them are inherently undistorted. Undistorted CG elements that are composited over a distorted plate might not fit correctly over the plate, especially at the edges of the image. Heavily distorted images usually must be undistorted before matchmoving them, and in turn all artists working on the shot must work with an undistorted plate until the final compositing.

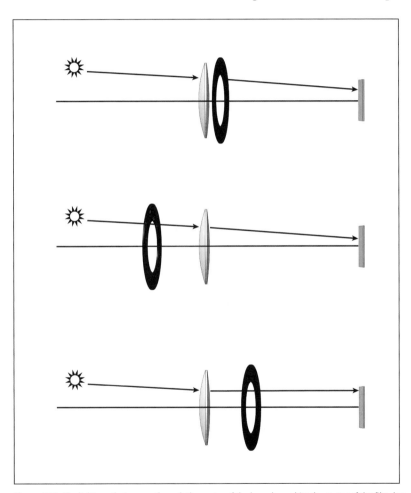

Figure 6.13 The light ray that passes through the center of the lens always hits the center of the film, but light rays from other angles can bend toward the center (second image), causing barrel distortion, or else bend outward (third image), causing pincushion distortion. Which direction the light bends depends on where the stop is located relative to the lens.

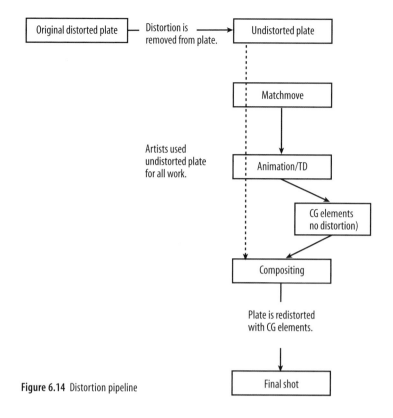

Figure 6.14 Distortion pipeline

Many times the responsibility for noticing and correcting lens distortion falls on the matchmover's shoulders. Lens distortion can be removed by most compositing software, and many matchmoving applications have utilities that can undistort a plate before matchmoving. The thing to keep in mind, though, is that distortion must be reintroduced to the CG elements in the final composite. The amount of distortion that is removed should be noted and passed on to the compositors, so that they can introduce the distortion into the CG elements and then marry it back up with the original distorted plates. This requires a major pipeline shift, and it must be communicated at all levels; otherwise, the objects you have so painstakingly matchmoved will appear to tear away at the edges of frame.

Perhaps one of the more difficult aspects of lens distortion is identifying exactly where it is happening. First of all, distortion most often happens on wide-angle lenses, which are already heavily distorted in a geometric sense. Geometric distortion means that perspective causes a more severe convergence of straight-edged objects, but the straight edges remain straight. Lens distortion actually causes the straight edges to bend as they approach the edge of the frame. Distortion can be difficult to deal with since it is a relatively subtle effect, and sometimes it requires zeroing in on the actual amount (Figure 6.15).

Figure 6.15 Geometric vs. lens distortion. The image on the top is an example of geometric distortion caused by having a wide focal length. The image on the bottom is an example of lens distortion. Notice how geometric distortion leaves the edge of the building straight, but lens distortion causes the edge of the building to pull away from the straight line and leave a larger gap on one side compared to the other.

Digitization

At some point in the process, the images that have been captured by the camera need to be made into digital images that can be used on the computer. Of course, this would exclude digital cameras, such as HD cameras, which generate digital images by default. Exactly how this is done will vary depending on the type of source footage and the desired type of digital image.

Video

Video cameras typically save footage on some sort of magnetic tape. The signal that they record can be either analog or digital. Analog footage that has been recorded on video needs to be converted to digital images that can be used on the computer in a process known as *digitization.*

Digitization usually happens through special hardware designed to convert the signal from the video to digital images that can be used on the computer. For digital video cameras, images are brought over directly to the computer via cables such as FireWire that make getting images onto your computer relatively easy.

The resolution of the digital image depends on the camera and the aspect ratio you are working with. One other parameter that may become a factor is the *pixel aspect ratio.* This is different than the image aspect ratio we discussed earlier. The pixel aspect ratio defines the shape of the individual pixels. If the pixels are square, the pixel aspect ratio is said to be 1.0. Some formats use nonsquare pixels, in which the aspect ratio is usually 0.9, indicating that the individual pixels are slightly thinner than they are tall. When you work in a matchmoving program with nonsquare pixels, you should make sure your project is set up accordingly.

Video cameras can often record footage as interlaced images. When an image is *interlaced,* it is split into two separate fields, each one representing every other horizontal row of pixels. This effectively doubles the number of frames but halves the vertical size of the image.

Film

If the footage was originally shot on film, it will need to be converted to a digital form by a process such as telecine. A *telecine* device steps through the individual frames of film one-by-one, scans them, and converts them to digital images.

Although the basic procedure is relatively straightforward, you may encounter some new variables that need to be taken into account. The first factor is resolution, and this can vary depending on the needs of postproduction. Often film is scanned at 2K resolution, which means that it is 2048 pixels on the longest edge.

Although 2K resolution is the most common size to work with, it is not the only one. Some studios find it easier to work at 1K (1024 pixels), while others prefer higher resolutions like 4K (4096 pixels).

Another aspect of digitizing film that can be problematic is determining what part of the film is to be scanned. Sometimes, the film is scanned from edge to edge (known as full frame), and other times only a portion of the image is scanned. For matchmovers, it is generally better to have the frame scanned full frame. Cropping the image during the telecine can offset the *principal point*—that is, where the optical center of the image is—and therefore make it more difficult to achieve a calibration.

Most of the time, film's frame rate is 24fps, but this can potentially change during the telecine process. If the final destination of the images is video or television, the images may be converted to 30fps. This can be done during the telecine, and it is a process known as *3:2 pull-down*. During pull-down, the 24 frames per second are spread out over 30 frames by splitting some of the original frames over several frames. If the footage you are working with originally came from film, make sure you verify what the final frame rate is supposed to be.

HD

HD footage has the benefit of already being digital, and in that sense, it's similar to digital video as far as digitization goes. It does have a couple of features you should keep your eye on, though.

HD footage can be either interlaced or progressive. Two common flavors are 1080i (interlaced) and 24p (progressive). In most cases, HD footage is captured at 24 frames per second and uses square pixels. The most obvious difference between HD and video is HD's resolution, which can be as high as 1920 × 1080 pixels. This resolution approaches the resolution of 2K images, and as a result has a very high quality.

Keeping It All Straight

As you can see, there are a lot of things to consider when you're trying to figure out a camera. To matchmovers, these items can have a wide range of effects on the way you calibrate the cameras and/or how you need to deliver the scene to other artists. For each of these items, it's important to verify what is required of you and the scenes you need to deliver. Below I've listed the items that matchmovers should be most concerned with and how they can affect a matchmove.

Image resolution You should always try to work at full resolution where possible. Using lower resolutions can potentially introduce jitter or noise in the camera.

Film back/focal length Generally, you know the focal length more often than you know the film back size. Remember that these two items are related, and therefore you should try to find out what the film size is if you intend to solve for a specific focal length. If you don't know the film back size, you may have to let the matchmoving programs solve the focal length for you and make adjustments as necessary.

Image aspect ratio The image aspect ratio is a fixed value based on the dimensions of the images you are working with. It's always worthwhile, though, to check that this ratio corresponds with what you are expected to use.

Pixel aspect ratio This one can be sneaky, since most matchmoving programs can still get a good solution even if this value is set wrong. If you are working with scanned film, it is usually set to 1.0 (square pixels), but if you are working with video, the ratio could be different.

Frame rate This is another one that can get by you if you're not careful. The match-moving programs will solve perfectly fine, and you may even do all of your final matchmove only to discover a frame rate problem when someone else brings it to your attention. The most effective way to deal with this is to double-check your frame rate settings in the matchmove programs before you start working.

Lens distortion Lens distortion will necessitate a radical change in how you work with a shot as well as others in the pipeline. Therefore, it's important to evaluate lens distortion if you suspect it may be a problem. Pay particular attention to wide-angle and zoom lenses, as they are the ones that exhibit lens distortion most often.

Principal point Normally, you don't have to think about this setting, but if you suspect that your image sequence has been cropped, you might want to experiment with this setting if your calibrations are failing.

Fitting In

In the previous chapters, you tracked an image and solved for the camera. Now you're ready to place that camera into a 3D environment and create a scene that is ready for delivery. In the next chapter, I'll show you how to fit the camera correctly into the set so that all of your hard work finally pays off.

Set Fitting

The last step in the matchmoving process is to place the camera into a CG environment or set. This is done in the 3D-animation program, and the end result is a scene that the animators or TDs will use for their work. I refer to this as "set fitting" because the goal is to have a set that fits the plate, but most of the work is actually making the camera fit the set. This is because in most productions the CG set is being used by multiple artists, and any significant changes to the set could have repercussions down the pipeline. In this chapter, we'll look at various ways to accurately fit a matchmoved camera into a CG environment as well as how to use this process to check the final matchmove.

7

Chapter Contents

Fitting the Camera

Fitting the camera into the set serves a dual purpose: it is a means of checking the final quality of the matchmove and also provides some sort of reference for other artists who need to work on the shot. The matchmover uses the set to determine whether the various areas of the CG scene match up with appropriate features in the set. In doing this, the matchmover also provides other artists with a way to find their way around the scene. For example, if a CG character is supposed to run across the floor and jump on a table, the matchmover could provide a plane to represent the floor and a simple box to represent the table the character will jump on. It doesn't have to be fancy; it just has to show the spatial relationships of key objects in the scene.

Re-creating the environment (at least in part) is an important part of the matchmover's job. If you aren't given an environment in which to place your matchmoved camera, then you may need to create the necessary geometry and place it in the right position within the scene. If you are given a CG set, then your job will be to place your camera so that the various set pieces line up with the features seen in the plate. If there is nothing to show other artists where to place their objects, the artists could place objects incorrectly, and the matchmove would appear to be "broken" or not working.

Using our previous example, let's say that you placed a plane representing the floor but didn't place anything in the scene to represent the table. The animator would have no problem having the character run across the floor, but when the character needed to jump on the table, the animator would have to guess the correct height of the table. If he guessed the table was a foot higher than it actually was, the character's feet would appear to slide once she hit the table. The animator might complain to his supervisor that the matchmove was broken, who would complain to your supervisor, who would ask you why it was broken. In this case, the matchmoved camera was correct, but other factors made it appear to be incorrect. You will save yourself a lot of hassle (and a lot of face) by laying out your scenes as clearly as possible and as much as necessary.

Checking the Matchmove

Virtually every scene that is matchmoved will have some sort of set or geometry placed in it. As mentioned in Chapter 1, "The Basics of Matchmoving," this is required for a final high-resolution check to make sure that the 3D objects are moving in the same manner as the objects seen in the plate.

Proxy Geometry

Most of the time, the matchmovers place a simplified version of the full scene called a *proxy sets,* or *objects.* Proxy objects are, as the name suggests, placeholders for the final geometry that will be used in the final scene (Figure 7.1).

For matchmovers, proxy objects don't have to be highly detailed, but they do need to be accurate enough to tell whether the set is "locked down." Again, this will vary depending on what's going to be placed in the environment. A polygon plane may suffice for a ground plane in an interior scene, but a simple plane might not work at all if the shot is of rolling hills where nothing is flat.

The proxy set should cover all of the areas where 3D objects are going to interact with items in the plate. If something is going to bounce off the wall, then you need to have geometry for the wall. If the object needs to fly out the window, you need to indicate where the window is in your 3D scene. If the object is going to sail through the air, you may need to place an object that represents its approximate flight path. By placing the appropriate geometry in the appropriate place, you will be able to compare a render of the proxy object to the original plate and check to see whether it's slipping at any given moment.

One problem you might encounter when trying to build up a proxy set is not having any information on the objects in the scene (for example, you might not know exactly how high the table in your scene is). If you have been given no information, then you may have to resort to educated guesses. A good place to start is to study the scene and the objects in it. Are there any objects of known dimensions in the scene?

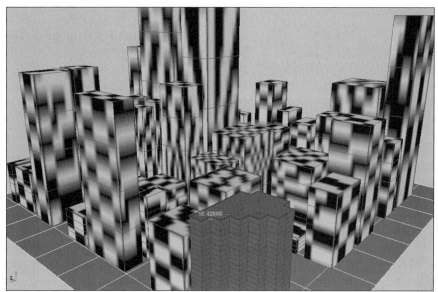

Figure 7.1 Low-resolution proxy objects

Look around; most doorways are of a standard height. Are there tiles on the ground? Cars on the street? Sometimes you might be given an actor's height, and that may provide some scale reference. You'd be surprised how much scale reference you can garner from most footage just through the power of observation. If you are guessing at the height or distance of certain objects, you should check the measurement by creating the object at that scale and seeing if it works with the plate. If not, you'll have to try adjusting the object until you find a measurement that works. Once you have it matching with the plate, you'll want to make sure that the measurement is plausible. For example, if my average-sized table works out to be 2 meters tall, I know something is wrong.

Although the proxy set is low resolution, it can still have a high degree of accuracy for key surfaces. For *Hellboy*, I built a proxy set of church ruins. This set was based on a relatively sparse set of survey points. The survey data was captured by a professional surveyor who used sophisticated survey equipment to accurately plot various points on the set in 3D space. These survey points measured the heights of the gothic arches, the height of the steps, and the position of key lights—about 100 survey points in all. From that data and photos of the set, I was able to produce a model that was very accurate at the survey points and reasonably accurate everywhere else. The final proxy set contained about 1400 polygons, which made it light enough to work with but accurate enough for matchmove purposes.

For shots in which a character is being matched into the plate, you might want to place something in the scene that represents the character. Most often, the model is still being built while matchmovers are working. But if there is a low-resolution version that is the correct scale, you could use that. If not, you could always use a generic character or even a simple box scaled to the appropriate height. This will not only give you some idea of how the character matches into the plate, but will also clearly show the animator where the character needs to be.

Checkerboards

Of course, there are obvious shortcomings to proxy geometry in that it is low resolution. Matchmovers need a way to show that the entire scene is matched properly without actually modeling the entire environment. That's where checkerboards come in.

If you were to examine most matchmove department's *dailies* footage, you would find strange renders of 3D objects with checkerboard textures laid over the original images. These checkerboard textures help matchmovers see how well the 3D object is sticking to the plate in the areas where there is a lack of geometric detail (Figure 7.2). For example, you might have a single plane representing the floor, but with a checkerboard texture, you can compare various parts of the CG floor with the features of the real floor and see if they are slipping. Other textures would work as well, but the checkerboard is sufficiently CG-looking to be easily distinguishable from the background (unless you're matchmoving a checkerboard!).

The proxy object with its checkerboard texture is rendered as semitransparent in order to see the CG element as well as the plate underneath. Rendering objects as semitransparent can slow down renders, so you could also render the objects at full opacity and then do a quick composite in a compositing program to make them partially transparent.

Exactly how this is done is up to you, but in the end, you will want to compare a semitransparent version of the object over the plate at full resolution and at real speed. This will be the ultimate test of the matchmove, because you will be able to analyze the object/feature relationship throughout the shot, not just at the boundaries of the geometry.

Figure 7.2 Checkerboards

Fitting the Set

Sometimes you will be asked to fit a set that has already been built. How much of the set is constructed for you will depend on what is required of the scene; it could be very rudimentary, or it could be a complete, high-resolution set.

Moving the Camera

In general, the more areas of the shot you must match, the more difficult it becomes to align all parts of the set with the plate. It also becomes more difficult if you are trying to match up a CG set with existing sets in the plate. If you are putting a completely CG environment around an actor on a green screen, the matchmove should be fairly tight, in particular near the areas where the actors interact with the set, such as where their feet meet the floor. Perhaps the most stringent requirements are placed on matchmoves for digital set extensions. These are pretty tough because the areas that are being matched must do so extremely accurately. The fact that the objects being matched are not moving makes it readily apparent when the matchmove slips—even a small amount.

If you are matching into a complete set, the first order of business is to put the camera in the right position within the set. Moving the camera presents a tricky situation: The camera that you receive from matchmoving software is generally keyframed on every frame. If you want to move the camera, you must find a way to do so without changing its overall animation (Figure 7.3). For example, if you simply moved the camera into the correct position on frame 1, it would no longer relate properly to the keyframe on frame 2. The easiest way to deal with this is to create a simple camera rig, similar to the one we used in Chapter 1 to move the camera into its starting position. This can be done by simply parenting the camera under another object (usually a null) and then moving that null. The matchmove camera can then be repositioned in the set, but will retain its original motion.

The way you approach the set fitting will depend on how the camera is moving. Pan shots are considerably easier to fit than translation shots. When matchmoving software spits out the results, it only contains the rotational information of the camera, so all you need to do is find out the location of the camera for one frame, and the rest of the shot should follow along.

When fitting a pan shot, I generally parent my camera under a null and find a frame where I can see a large portion of the scene. Then I try to find the position within the set where the camera was located. From there, I adjust the rotation of the camera around (using the parent null) until I can find a match. In this respect, it is identical to a perspective match (similar to the tutorial we did in Chapter 1). The only difference here is that after the camera is working for one frame, scrubbing through the footage (that is, dragging back and forth in time) will show whether it holds up once the camera rotates.

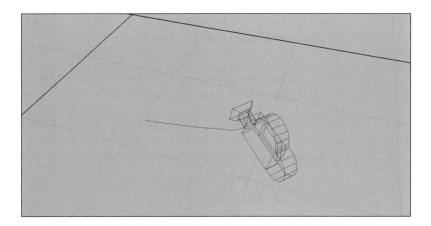

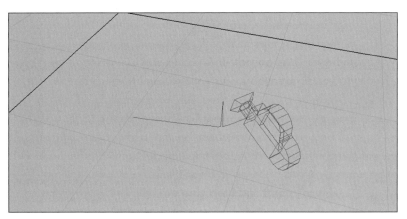

Figure 7.3 The matchmove camera contains keyframes on every frame (top). If you move the camera independently, it will only change the position for the current frame and cause spikes in the camera motion.

Scaling the Camera

Translation shots are trickier to deal with because you must figure out the "scale" of the camera move. That is, you need to know not only where the camera started, but also how far it went during the course of the shot. To be more specific, when you define the scale of a camera move, you are defining the camera's starting and ending positions. This is particularly true when you are fitting a camera into a prebuilt set, since it will more readily show any problems with the length of the camera move. Most often these sets are built to scale, and this scale is agreed upon so that all artists working on the shot don't accidentally deliver a model that is much larger or smaller than other objects in the shot. If your camera is perfectly accurate but not scaled correctly, the matchmove won't work. Why? Because a translating camera needs to reflect the exact amount of distance traveled.

The first place you should start when trying to scale a translating camera move is in the matchmoving software. In these packages, you can set up a coordinate system that usually includes a field for the scale of the scene. The scale is set by defining a distance between one or more features in the scene. For example, you might know that the length of a table is 2 meters. Knowing this, you could track the corners of the table and then define that in the coordinate system as having a scale of 2m. When you bring that camera into your 3D software, the two nulls that represent the corners of the table will be 2m apart, and your camera will move relative to that scale. This usually gets you close to the proper scale of the scene if you have a reasonably good solution. Even if the scale is only in the ballpark, it's better than nothing at all.

Although you can set the scale accurately in the matchmoving software, you may still need to adjust it in the 3D package. This is usually noticeable when your set fits properly on one frame but, as the shot progresses, gradually begins to slip off. A camera rig will again come to the rescue on these occasions. First, you should fit the set on one frame, preferably at the beginning or end of the camera move using the single null rig that I described earlier for panning cameras. Next you should go to the opposite end of the clip—that is, if you initially matched the first frame—then go to the last frame of the camera move, or vice versa. You will see that the camera either moves too little or too far because the objects in the CG scene wouldn't line up properly with the plate. You can then scale the null to which the camera is parented in order to adjust it (Figure 7.4).

If you use this method, you should take care about the point from which you are scaling the camera's group. Make sure that you scale from the camera's position on the frame at which you did your initial set fitting. If you don't do this, then scaling the null might correctly help find the end position of the camera, but during the process it will break the matchmove for the initial frame.

This method works because when you scale the null above the camera, the camera inherits the scale as well. Although scaling a camera doesn't have much of an effect on the camera itself, it does scale the camera's motion—that is, the motion path gets larger or smaller, which is what we want. When you scale the null up, the camera moves farther from beginning to end, and when you scale it down, the camera's move gets shorter. It works because it doesn't affect the initial frame on which you lined up your camera. So if you can line up your camera on the first and last frames of the move, then chances are everything else in between will match up perfectly as well. This is the case even if the speed and direction of the camera are not a constant value, because all we are doing is adjusting the relative positions of the keyframes to one another.

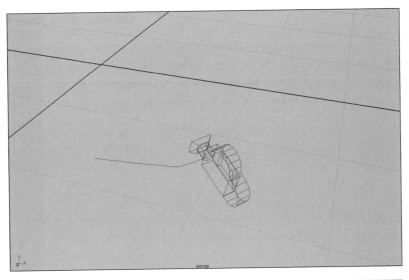

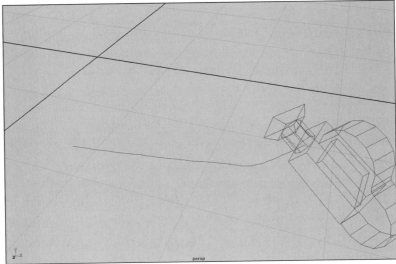

Figure 7.4 Scaling a camera move

Camera Rigs

Some matchmovers (and animators for that matter) use a slightly more complicated rig that allows more control over how the camera moves. This involves parenting three nulls above one another and the camera and limiting how they can be used (Figure 7.5).

Figure 7.5 A three-tier camera rig

One common version of this is to parent the camera under a null. That null is only used for scaling. Then the scaling null is parented under another null used only for rotation, which is parented under yet another null that is used for translation. When working with this rig, you limit the type of adjustment to each respective null—translate for translation, rotate for rotation, etc. The benefit of this method is that you can really isolate each set of *channels*, and it is clear to other artists what is happening to the overall camera move. The downside is that it can be cumbersome to work with. And given that you could potentially have offset pivot points on each of the nulls in the rig, it could be confusing to yourself and others, especially for complicated camera moves.

Set-Fitting Tutorial

To see how this all works, let's finish up the matchmove that we began in Chapters 3 and 4. In this example, I've provided a set in which to fit the actor and a proxy set from which we can test the matchmove to see if it's working.

For this tutorial, I'll be showing the steps using Maya, but as in previous chapters, you can apply these techniques to virtually any 3D-animation program.

1. To begin with, let's check out the results of our export from Chapter 4: open the final file from your work there, or open `bluescreen_finalExport.ma` in the Chapter 7 folder on the companion CD if you're jumping in at this point. You should have ended up with something similar to the project seen in Figure 7.6. The nulls in the scene represent the features you tracked on the plate, and the camera should be slowly translating to the right.

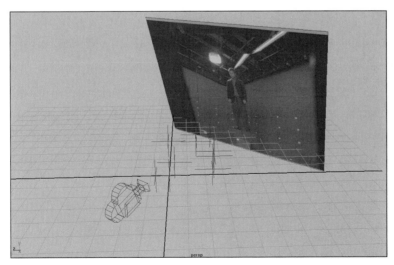

Figure 7.6 The matchmoved scene

2. Look through the camera; the nulls should match up to the features you tracked, including the markers on the wall and near the actor's feet (Figure 7.7).

3. If you look at a list of the objects in the scene, you'll see that there is a camera imported from MatchMover and all of the trackers (here as locators) that have been grouped together. In order to make the camera fit properly into the set, you need to be able to move it around without messing up its animation. You can do this by grouping it together with the trackers in this scene (Figure 7.8). You can also achieve this by having the camera and the trackers parented under another null. The easiest way to do this with our scene is to drag the camera into the group that contains the trackers: in the Outliner, middle-mouse-drag the camera into the tracker group. The main thing is that the camera and trackers can be moved together.

Figure 7.7 Looking through the matchmove camera

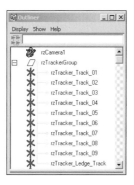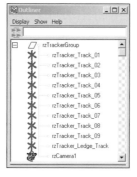

Figure 7.8 Grouping the camera

Adding Test Geometry

In this scene, you'll start by adding some simple geometry that will help you check the matchmove before you start fitting the camera into the full environment.

The most important thing to consider in this matchmove is that the actor's feet need to contact a CG object. Since that is the main focus of your attentions, you need to have some geometry in the scene that will let you know the location of the box that the actor is standing on.

1. Make sure you're on frame 1, then create a polygon cube (Create > Polygon Primitives > Cube). Once the cube is created, move the pivot point of the cube to its front corner, the corner closest to the camera. To do this, select the cube, then hit the Insert key. Hold down the V key while you drag the pivot point to the corner of the cube (Figure 7.9).

   In order to get a correct placement of the cube, you need to match it up with the same position as a locator from the matchmove. Align one corner of the cube to the locator named rzTracker_Ledge_Track. This represents the position of the back corner of the box the actor is standing on. You'll use this as a way to get the cube into position.

2. Once the corner of the cube matches up with the corner Ledge_Track null, slide it forward on the X-axis until its front corner is on the corner of the box seen in the live-action plate. From there, it's a simple matter to scale the X and Z sides of the cube until it's the right size (Figure 7.10).

Figure 7.9 The proxy cube aligned with the corner of the cube in the plate

3. Now that the cube is in place, you need to make sure that it stays in the right place during the camera move. Go to the last frame of the shot and examine the cube's position. It should maintain a good alignment with the box the actor is standing on (Figure 7.11). If your cube is not lining up, try realigning the cube with the locator again and retracing your steps.

 Note: This cube comes in reasonably well-oriented because of the extra care we took to establish a coordinate system in MatchMover Pro. We could have done the same thing without setting it up in MatchMover, but the process of fitting the camera in Maya would have taken longer and been more difficult.

Figure 7.10 Cube in position

Figure 7.11 Cube on last frame

4. The next thing to do is to define where the walls are. This essentially ends up being the same as when you placed the cube. Make a polygon plane that is 1 in scale on all axes, snap its pivot to its corner, and then snap the plane to a locator on the right wall. From there, scale the plane until it is a better size.

5. An important aspect of setting up this wall is that it be flush with the locators on the wall that you've tracked in MatchMover Pro. When you have the wall in place, do the same process but to the left wall (Figure 7.12). The purpose of placing the cube and these two walls is to verify whether your camera is matching properly; therefore, the walls should be close to what you've tracked.

In the end, your scene should look something like Figure 7.13.

Figure 7.12 Right wall in position

Figure 7.13 Proxy geometry done

Texturing the Objects

If you were to render these objects now, you wouldn't see how well the geometry is registering with the plate because the objects don't have any surface detail. You need to place some checkerboard textures on the objects so that there is something to compare. This doesn't have to be anything too fancy, just a simple checkerboard texture. Most animation programs have a material preset or procedural texture to do this, but you could also use a checkerboard texture map if you wanted to. The texture should be small enough so you can see where it intersects with various features, but not so small that it becomes visually confusing.

To do this in Maya, open the Hypershade and create a new Lambert Shader (Create > Materials > Lambert). Double-click the Lambert icon to open its attributes and click on the small checkerboard icon to place a texture on the color channel. Choose 2D Textures > Checker to create the shader and close the Attribute Editor. Now middle-mouse-drag the shader onto each of the objects (Figure 7.14). You should be ready to render.

Figure 7.14 The checkerboard render

The First Tests

If everything seems to line up in the camera view, then the next step is to see how everything looks in motion. I usually like to make a wireframe preview at this stage, since it doesn't take as long as a render and it will help show any serious problems.

> **Note:** Wireframes are a good initial check that can show most problems, but they also are not anti-aliased, which could hide subtle camera jitter problems or make it seem like there is more jitter than there really is.

1. In Maya, right-click the Timeline and choose Playblast. When checking the playblast, you're looking for any slipping or perspective problems that don't look right. For example, if the actor seems to drift off the cube, then you need to recheck your set to make sure it is in the right place.

2. If the playblast looks good, then you're ready to render out a test plate. This test render should be full resolution with a decent amount of anti-aliasing on it. In this clip, I would render without motion blur turned on, since the camera isn't moving that fast (Figure 7.15).

Figure 7.15 The checkerboard objects over the plate

3. Once your render is finished, look at the way the checkerboard objects line up with the footage. You're checking to see whether the objects line up correctly: Do they stay in the correct position? Do they follow the bumps and jolts of the camera correctly?

This shot is pretty straightforward, but if you do run into problems, here are a few things to check:

Frame rate Verify that your scene is set up to the correct frame rate. If the frame rate is wrong in this scene, then it could be that your settings were wrong in the matchmove program. Change the frame rate in your MatchMover Pro project, then reexport (you shouldn't need to re-solve) and open the Maya scene again.

First key Sometimes, the matchmove programs will export the keyframes starting on a different frame than you intended. For example, your footage may start on frame 1, but the matchmove program exported a scene that starts on frame 0. This usually presents itself as a set that looks like it fits reasonably well but is very jittery and erratic.

Misaligned objects This is perhaps the most likely culprit in this tutorial if your objects seem to be slipping, especially if the slip is very slow and subtle. Go through the previous set-fitting steps again and make sure that your proxy objects are correctly positioned relative to the locators you got from the matchmove program.

4. If everything looks good, save out your scene including the proxy geometry.

Placing the Matchmove in the Set

Now that you've verified that the matchmove works, you're ready to drop the camera into your set. The fact that you've taken care to use some proxy objects will greatly facilitate this process.

1. You could have loaded the final geometry into your matchmove scene, but let's do things the way the matchmove camera is typically used. In most cases, the animator or TD will load the matchmove camera into their scene, since the matchmove scene is often very small and doesn't contain too many objects. If you have the scene we've previously set up open, close it (of course after you've saved it!).

2. Open up the scene with the final set in it, named DowntownMM.ma (included in Maya format in the Chapter 7 folder on the companion CD). This set contains both a full-resolution version of a downtown area plus a low-resolution proxy version. The proxy version has been placed on a separate layer so that its visibility can be turned on or off, as has the high-resolution geometry. In addition, there is a "hero" building that represents the building our actor needs to be standing on (Figure 7.16).

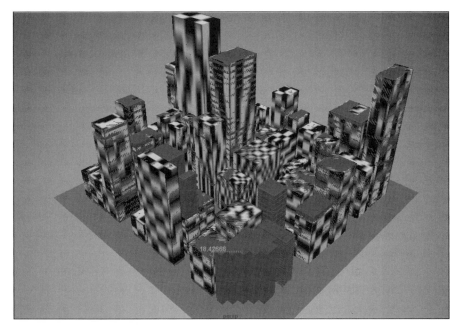

Figure 7.16 The set we will be using

3.   Import the scene you just created for the matchmove camera. In Maya, this is done by choosing File > Import.

Initially, the camera may not be easily visible, since it sits somewhere near the origin of the scene which right now is buried under one of the buildings. Our goal is to move the camera into position on the top of the hero building at the front of the scene. (The hero building has a zigzag edge and is at one of the outer corners of the model.) To make this set a little easier to navigate within, you may want to hide all the high-resolution objects except the hero building and leave on just the proxy buildings for now. The easiest way to do this is to turn off the layers that correspond with the high-resolution buildings.

4.   Before you can move the camera, you need to make an adjustment to the way it's set up. You'll remember that you placed the camera under a tracker group in a previous step so that you could move them together, but you'll also need to do the same thing for the proxy geometry you added earlier. This way, the proxy geometry maintains its relationship to the camera as well. In Maya, open up the Outliner and middle-mouse-drag the three proxy objects (the cube and the two walls) under the camera's group (Figure 7.17).

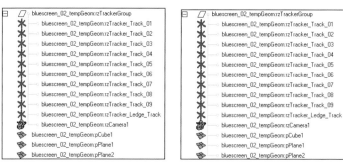

Figure 7.17 Regrouping the camera

5. If you look through the matchmove camera, you'll see that the camera is doing the right thing; it's just at the wrong place. Now we'll start getting the camera into the right spot in the set. Select the camera group and move it up to the rooftop of the hero building (Figure 7.18). For now, don't worry too much about the precise placement; rather, get it into the right area of the scene.

Once the camera group is close to the edge of a top corner of the hero building, you can see some problems right off the bat (Figure 7.19). First and foremost, the scale of the camera scene is significantly smaller than the scale of the scene used for the buildings. Second, the camera is facing the wrong direction relative to the building. We'll use our camera group to fix both problems.

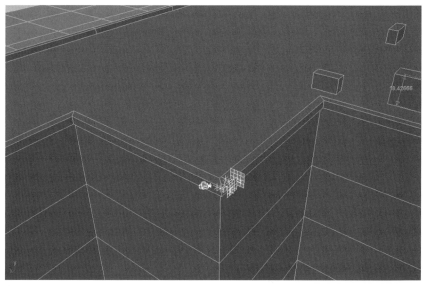

Figure 7.18 Getting the matchmove camera into its initial position

6. The scaling seems to be off by at least a factor of 10 here, so scale up your camera group by 10. Make sure to scale it up on all three axes equally. This seems to make the camera and cube look much more like the scale of the scene. You can adjust it again later if you need to, but for now, this will work for our purposes (Figure 7.20).

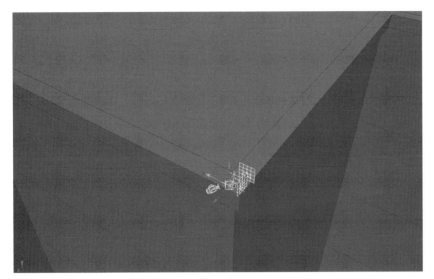

Figure 7.19 The camera is in the correct position, but the scale is too small.

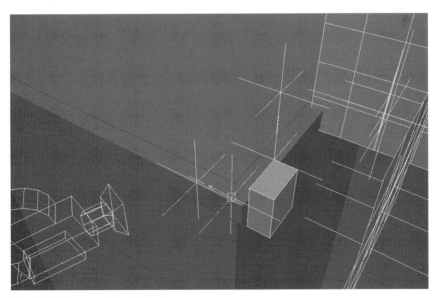

Figure 7.20 The camera at the right scale

7. To rotate the camera into the right position, you follow a similar step, except rather than scale the group, you rotate it. But before doing so, let's save ourselves a little bit of work. Ultimately, we'd like to have the front corner of the proxy cube line up with the corner of the ledge on the building, so it would be helpful to be able to rotate around that front corner of the cube. This can be done by moving the pivot point of the camera group to the corner of the proxy cube. In Maya, just hit the Insert key and then hold the V key to snap the pivot point to the front of the cube (Figure 7.21).

Note: In some programs, moving the pivot point can have unpredictable results on the animation on the camera. A way around this is to create a null object and snap it to the proxy cube, then parent the camera group under it.

8. Now that the camera group pivots around the corner of the proxy cube, snap the camera group to the front corner of the ledge (Figure 7.22). Then just rotate it around the Y-axis until the edges of the ledge seem to be where the edges of the proxy cube are (Figure 7.23). In this case, our coordinate system works out pretty well and is an even 90° off. Simply rotate the camera group 90° on the Y-axis and *voila*, a nice fit.

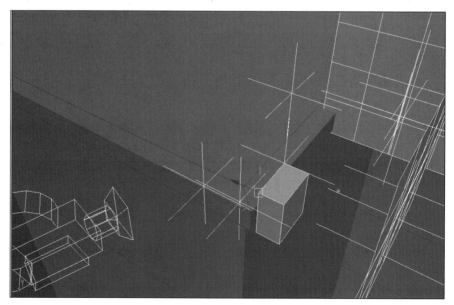

Figure 7.21 Moving the camera group's pivot point

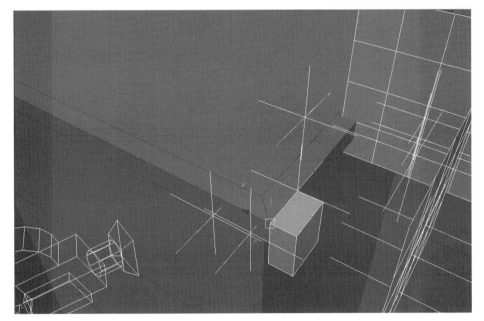

Figure 7.22 Snapping the camera group into position

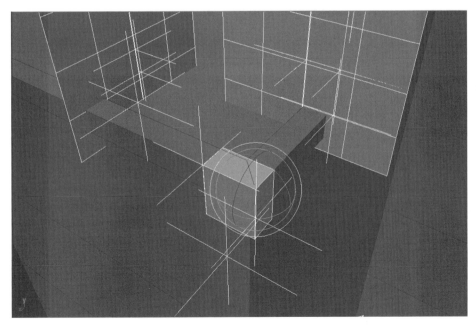

Figure 7.23 Rotating the camera group

9. Since the proxy cube matched up with the plate, and you've matched the proxy cube to the ledge, it follows that the ledge should look as though it's in the right plate now. Look through the camera to verify this (Figure 7.24).

Of course, you'll want to check that the matchmove still works at the last frame as well. When you're all done, it should like what you see in Figure 7.25. Make a playblast to make sure that nothing "broke" during the process of getting the camera into position.

10. Once you're satisfied that the matchmove is working, save this scene as a new version and call it `Downtown_MM_setFit.ma`. We'll use it again shortly as we get the scene ready for final delivery.

Figure 7.24 Camera group in place (first frame)

Figure 7.25 Camera group in place (last frame)

Matchmove vs. Layout

Much of what we've just done in fitting the set is similar to another type of visual effects job: *layout*. This is a discipline that in many ways overlaps with the duties of the matchmover. Many larger studios have a layout department or team of artists whose job is to make sure that everything looks right when looking through the camera.

The key difference between a matchmove artist and a layout artist is that matchmovers are concerned with cameras, in the sense that they accurately match the camera that was used to film the scene. Layout artists are concerned with what is being seen through the camera in a more artistic sense. They set up cameras that show what CG objects are visible in a shot and the general motion of those objects in the scene. So at its most fundamental level, you could say that matchmovers are concerned more about the technical aspects of the camera, whereas layout artists are concerned with creative problems. Of course, that's not to say that a certain amount of creativity isn't involved in matchmoving and that layout can't be extremely technical; it's just a matter of focus.

There is often quite a bit of overlap between the two disciplines. Layout artists often create cameras from scratch and animate rough matchmoves. These cameras can later be swapped out with the fully matchmoved cameras from matchmovers. Sometimes, matchmovers are the layout people as well (much like what we've just done in the tutorial), and they must place the camera in the set in such a way that it looks aesthetically pleasing.

Since there are a lot of similarities between the two disciplines, it is generally useful for layout artists to know something about matchmoving and vice versa. Either way, you're working with cameras and trying make everything look good, so a little bit of cross-training in this area can only be a good thing.

Altering the Coordinate System

When I discussed matchmoving programs in earlier chapters, I talked about how to set up a coordinate system. When possible, I like to set up the coordinate system in the matchmove program, but there may be times when you will be unable to set it up (such as with pan shots) or can't set it up correctly (as with weak solutions). In these situations, I've found it's easier to orient and scale the scene inside the 3D animation program.

In matchmoving (and in matchmoving programs), the solution represents a relationship between the 3D camera and the 3D markers. The solution remains valid as long as any action performed to the camera is also performed on the 3D markers and vice versa. For example, if you wanted to rotate the camera 180° on the Y-axis, you would also need to rotate the markers (from the same pivot point, no less) the same amount. This would also apply to translating or scaling.

It is always helpful to do as much as you can in the matchmoving software, but if it gives you too much of a problem, you can take heart knowing it can probably be tweaked in the end 3D scene.

There are three aspects to the coordinate system setup to consider: translation, rotation, and scale. *Translating* the matchmove has the effect of repositioning the camera within the scene and includes defining where the origin of the scene is relative to the camera. *Rotation* defines the overall orientation of the scene and helps define the alignment of the three axes, most important among these would be the up-axis (usually Y). The *scale* of the coordinate system defines how far it is from one marker to the next and how far the camera moves through the scene.

The key to altering the matchmove's coordinate system is that whatever you do to the camera, you must also do to the nulls from the matchmove. They all must move, rotate, and scale in unison. If not, you'll break the matchmove. The easiest way to do this is to group them together or parent them under another object and then perform your translation, rotation, or scaling to that object.

Delivering the Scene

The matchmove is, of course, only one part of the large amount of work that goes into an effect shot. Studios have their own unique requirements for how a matchmove scene is delivered to artists further down the pipeline based on their workflow, software they use, etc. But there are some general practices that make good sense for any matchmover. Ideally, your scene should leave no room for confusion to artists downstream. A well-organized scene can mean that you never have to revisit it again.

The matchmove scene should conform to the standards of the project you are working on. The scale should be the same scale everyone else is using, and the up-axis for the scene (usually the Y-axis) should, in fact, be up. Nothing will get a matchmove kicked back faster than a scene that is lying on its side or is 10 times too big.

You should also clearly label everything in your scene. Often there are multiple cameras in a scene for various reasons, including cameras from other artists. You will want to identify which one is the final matchmove camera. It might also be helpful to identify important nulls in the scene (although it may not be necessary to label them all, especially if you are dealing with a thousand or more automatic tracks). In fact, some matchmovers prefer to delete most of the nulls that result from the matchmove process.

Another good practice is to lock down the scene so that it can't be modified. Cameras can accidentally get moved or deleted by other artists or sometimes even the matchmovers themselves. This little bit of effort before final delivery can save you a lot of work if you don't have any backups, and if there's anything worse than matchmoving a tough shot, it's matchmoving it twice.

> **Note:** In Appendix A, I've included a delivery checklist that will help you quickly button up a scene so that it will not be confusing to other artists or potentially even yourself.

Tutorial Continued

Let's finish up our matchmove by getting this scene ready for final delivery and going through this checklist.

1. Open up the scene Downtown_MM_setFit.ma you saved earlier in this chapter or you can load the file from the Chapter 7 folder on the companion CD.

2. Select your camera and rename it mm_cam. It also makes sense to name the group the camera is under mm_cam_group so that everyone will know where to find it.

   The most important feature to identify in this scene is probably the ledge the actor is standing on. Since this is already identified, and your tracker on the ledge is already named appropriately, you don't need to do anything there.

3. If possible, lock all of the channels on the camera, including the focal length: in Maya, drag-select the channel names in the Channel Box and then right-click and choose Lock Selected. This will prevent someone (including yourself) from accidentally moving or changing the camera.

4. You have three proxy objects in the scene that you used to help check the match-move, but they're probably not going to be used by anyone else. Just in case, though, simply hide them (Ctrl+H) rather than delete them.

> **Note:** In most larger production studios, it's nice to only have the matchmove cameras in the final match-move camera scene. This way, the animators or TDs can simply load the final camera into their current set. In this case, we're leaving in the main geometry.

5. Save your final scene. That's it! With an appropriately named scene, this project is ready to deliver. This scene can now be given to other artists (or used by yourself) to render your CG objects with.

And Now on to the Real World ... Sort Of

We've spent much of the first half of this book either working in software programs or else dealing with the concepts behind matchmoving. In the next chapter, we move on to what matchmovers do on a live-action shoot and how they can make their lives easier.

Being on Set

One of my favorite parts of my job as a match-move supervisor is being on set during a live-action shoot. Of course, there isn't always a matchmover on set during the shoot, but when the opportunity presents itself, it's good to be prepared.

In this chapter, I discuss the roles of a match-mover while on set and the types of information they need to gather. The techniques I describe here are framed within the context of film work, but could easily be applied to smaller-scale productions. I'll show you how to gather the information you need and give you a few pointers for on-set etiquette.

Chapter Contents

Getting the Right Information

A matchmover's responsibility on set can be summed up in one word: information. Since your postproduction job is to reproduce the camera, and to a lesser extent the environment, your live-action production job is to gather as much information about the camera and environment as possible. Your secondary mission is to make sure that shots are filmed as matchmove friendly as possible—which is sometimes easier said than done.

The best advice I can give you when it comes to the set is to measure everything. The more measurements you have, the better. You should measure all relevant objects that might interact with the CG elements and even those that don't. You never know when a director will suddenly change his mind.

The measurements to take will vary depending on the location, production needs, and your own needs as a matchmover. Interior shots are usually a little bit easier to measure because they tend to be geometric and regularly shaped. In particular, it is good to measure the dimensions of furniture items and their relative position to one another. That's not to say you will measure every beveled edge of a table leg—the height of the table and the width and depth of the tabletop are usually sufficient. Measure the height of the walls and the distance between them, the size of the windows, doors, and the height of any steps or stairs. In other words, try to rough out the entire set with measurements.

It's helpful to make drawings of the set as though you were looking down from above (Figure 8.1). This allows you to create a map with key measurements. Where necessary, you can make additional drawings of chairs or the profile of a cabinet or complicated objects and side views of the set. You can never have too much reference, so diagram anything you think might be important.

Finding the right time to take your measurements can be surprisingly difficult. In most cases, I recommend waiting until as close as possible to the actual shooting. This is because the sets will be in a constant state of flux right up until the director says, "Action." It is somewhat less desirable to measure the set the day before (except on large, immovable objects) since it will probably be quite different the next day. Sometimes it's more practical to take your measurements between takes or even after the shooting, although you have to be careful not to wait too long, because sets are often struck (torn down) as quickly as they are assembled.

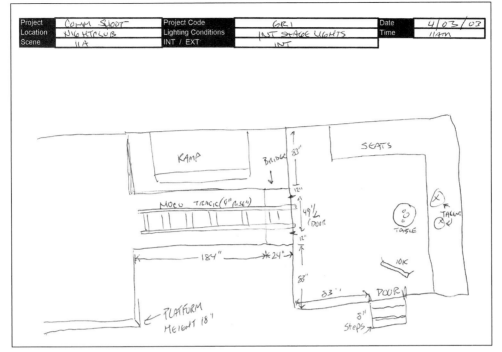

Project	COMM SHOOT	Project Code	GR1	Date	4/03/03
Location	NIGHTCLUB	Lighting Conditions	INT STAGE LIGHTS	Time	11AM
Scene	11A	INT / EXT	INT		

Figure 8.1 Set diagram from a live-action shoot

If you do take measurements between takes, be extra careful to (a) not be in the way of other crew, such as make-up/costume folks and grips/gaffers who are also making adjustments at that time, and (b) not disturb anything on the set. When the set is exactly the way a director wants it, or it has been filmed and needs to be refilmed, it is referred to as a "hot" set. If a set is designated as a hot set, nothing should be moved or disrupted. This second point would hold doubly true for shots that contain effects, since multiple takes may need to be composited together later, and any misregistration of set elements would be immediately noticeable. If you need to measure the size of props, you could wait until after they're shot and removed from the set to measure them, although again, you should act quickly because they may be whisked off without you noticing.

I also like to note the relative position of the actor's mark as well. Often this is marked with a T-shaped tape mark on the floor. This can be useful in determining the distance to the camera later on. But be aware that these marks are often pulled up and moved quickly.

Getting Camera Information

Since half of your work in postproduction involves the camera, it is natural that you will also take down a lot of information about the camera. Much of this information will be taken before, during, and after the shoot.

Before the Shoot

Here is a short list of things that I like to record about the camera before the shoot:

Camera make and model This is one fact I always try to get on set, because this will help you to determine that all-important measurement, the film aperture. Often the film back measurement isn't known by anyone on set, so if you can get the make and model of the camera, then you can generally look up the technical specs for that camera online or elsewhere later.

Camera mount This is what the camera is attached to, such as a tripod, dolly, or crane gimbal. Where possible, write down the make and model. At the very least, it can be helpful to make a quick sketch of it. This can be helpful in troubleshooting and visualizing camera moves during the matchmove.

Film stock This one isn't really necessary for matchmoving (although I suppose it could be used to help determine grain characteristics), but I grab it as a courtesy to compositors and others. I figure no one else is going to be scrutinizing the camera as thoroughly as I am, so why not? You can usually find out this information from a camera operator, or else it is sometimes written on the side of the film cartridges that are mounted on the camera.

During the Shoot

During the shoot, I begin to focus on other aspects of the camera. These are aspects that can change from take to take, so it's conceivable that you may end up writing down the information multiple times. I like to use a camera information sheet (Figure 8.2), which has columns for all the data I'd like to get. The sheet contains a field where I can mark which shot and which take is currently being filmed. This serves as a means of indexing the shot against the information I've gathered.

Once the shooting begins, the takes can fly by, so it's important to note important changes as they happen. Personally, I like to stay close to the camera without being in the way. That way I can keep track of any camera changes and note them as they happen. Short of that, I will monitor the shoot from the video feed and only approach the camera operator when I need additional information. The information I like to get includes:

Lens information This is perhaps one of the most important pieces of camera information to get, and sometimes the trickiest. It's best to wait until right before shooting or in between takes to find out the focal length used for the shot. You have to take care here, because the director or DP (director of photography) may swap lenses out quite rapidly and randomly depending on their vision for the shot. These could even change in between takes, so you'll need to keep a close eye on this.

If you see the director or DP walking around with a *stick* (a small stick with a lens mounted to it, used to previsualize what a certain focal length will look like without actually moving the entire camera), a lens change may be imminent.

It's worthwhile to note other lens attributes, such as whether the lens is fixed or variable. If the lens is variable, did they zoom it during the shot? It's also helpful to note whether or not it is an *anamorphic lens* (although this last fact would probably be given to you well in advance and would not be likely to change during the shooting). You should also check whether the camera operator is using any *diopters* (magnifying lenses) and note their power (x2, x10, etc).

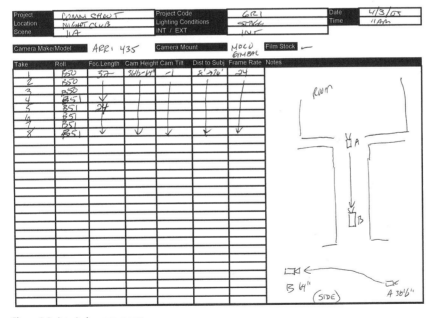

Figure 8.2 A typical camera report

Camera height This information can be of great help during CG set fitting by the matchmover. You'll want to measure the distance from the ground to the center of the lens for the best accuracy. If the camera is moving, you should try and take the height at the beginning and end of the move. I usually mark on my camera report the beginning and end of the camera moves with an *A* and a *B*, showing the approximate path the camera took to get from one to the other. The camera height can be the biggest help with pan shots. You can really crank through a pan-shot matchmove if you know how high the camera is, since that is essentially the only translation you need to know. You simply place the matchmove camera at the correct height and aim it in the right direction, and you're nearly finished (Figure 8.3).

Distance to subject This measurement can be very helpful because it represents a known distance between the camera shooting the scene and an object that is going to appear on film. This measurement often is the distance to the actor and is again measured from the film back or lens center. If CG objects are to be placed a certain distance behind the actor, it might also be worthwhile to measure from the camera to a wall (or other objects) behind the actor. Rather than measuring these yourself, you might check with the camera operator, since they often measure the distance to the subject and other objects for their focal distances.

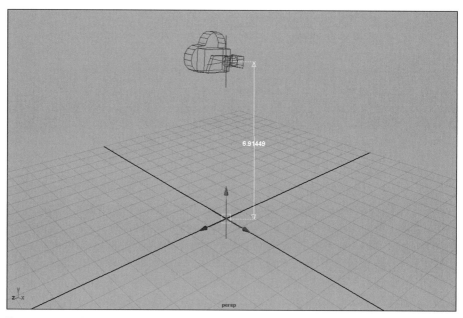

Figure 8.3 For pan shots, getting the right camera height and tilt are half of the battle.

Camera tilt Most camera mounts provide a fairly precise way to tilt the camera along all three axes. This information can usually be obtained from the camera operator or grips operating the dolly or crane.

Frame rate Although it has little effect on the matchmove process, the frame rate can affect how you need to deliver your scene to other artists down the pipeline. You should note if they switch to overcranking (faster frame rate) or undercranking (slower frame rate). This is often for slow motion/fast motion effects or to accommodate low lighting situations.

After the Shoot

Once the shooting is complete, there may be a few additional things you should take note of. It's the perfect time to get any information you missed. The key here, though, is speed. A set and camera can be broken down quite quickly, so if you need to take some measurements, make it clear to the crew that you need to do so.

After the shoot, I often photograph any key props that I couldn't move during the shoot. This also is a good time to have the camera crew film your distortion grids (which I'll talk about later in this chapter).

Marking Up the Set

While gathering good information is the best thing you can do for the matchmove process, you might also have some degree of control over what is actually seen in the shot. Most film production crews are familiar with the need for marks of some sort on a green screen, but they may not necessarily know exactly what they're for, where to put them, or how many you'll need. That's where the on-set matchmover comes in. Your job is to make your job as easy as possible.

Adding additional markers to the set is a delicate affair. You need to add enough markers to help you during 2D tracking, but not so many that they are difficult for compositors or roto/paint people to remove later. Decisions of this nature should be made with the visual effects supervisor, since they can potentially create problems that you did not anticipate.

In general, a blue screen or green screen should always have some sort of marks on it to allow for tracking either by matchmovers or compositors. These marks come in all shapes and flavors, from green dots to white Xs of gaffer's tape. It's best to place them in regular rows of a known distance. This can be helpful in determining the scale of the scene when no other objects can be used to establish scale. Avoid making them too big, because that would make it hard for the artists who will need to extract the foreground objects from the background when the markers pass directly behind them.

Where possible, I recommend using existing pieces of the set or props for tracking purposes rather than placing "artificial" markers in the scene. This is more desirable because these objects won't have to be removed later.

Even when you are shooting on a complete set, it may be necessary to place markers in areas where there is a low amount of visual detail or other factors that would make it hard to track. If you place matchmove markers in the scene, however, they will need to be painted out later, so you are fairly limited in what you can use. Often the color of the marker is carefully chosen to make the matte extraction process easier. For example, light green markers can be used on a green screen shot. The scale of the markers should fit the scale of the shot, be easy to track, and be easy to remove from the original plate. For wide shots of large landscapes, you might be able to use tennis balls or golf balls. Avery makes $1/4''$ removable garage sale stickers (Avery 06166) which are great for medium to long shots. They come in a variety of colors and are easy to remove. In tighter shots, you might only need pea-sized stickers made with a hole punch.

Note: You can use virtually anything for a tracking marker, and it doesn't have to be a specialized gadget. I've heard of matchmovers using everything from LED keychains to ping-pong balls with small lights in them. For larger matchmove markers that need to rest on the ground, I prefer racquetballs cut in half and marked with an *X* in brightly colored tape. Basically, it comes down to whatever gets the job done.

Working with Others On Set

Even on small-scale shoots for commercials, there can be dozens of people involved in filming a scene. When you get into features, the number can be even higher. With so much going on, it can often be confusing and move way too fast. Everyone is very focused on their particular task, and things need to move fast; after all, shoots can cost tens of thousands of dollars an hour, and there's no time to waste. Before going on a shoot, you should make sure you are prepared, have all of your equipment ready, and know whom to ask for help when you need it. I'll cover the necessary equipment later in this chapter, but first, here's a list of people who are good to know on set:

Assistant director The assistant director (AD) is the director's go-to person. They often deal with the "nuts and bolts" operation of the set and make sure that everything gets done. ADs have a lot of responsibilities during a shoot and are usually very busy people, but they can also be of great help if you have needs from the production in general. You should make sure that the AD knows who you are, and you should let them know if your work will affect anything involved with the shoot. If you need a couple of minutes in between takes to get a measurement, you should make sure they're aware of it.

Visual effects supervisor The VFX supervisor's role on set is to make sure that everything that needs to happen in regard to effects actually happens. How they do this varies from one person to the next. I've worked with some who prefer to work with me closely and others who prefer that I go off and get the information on my own. VFX supervisors are also very busy people. They have a lot of things on their plate besides matchmoving. They are depending on you to get your information on your own, but in the same regard, they can let you know what effect is happening during any given shot and what information you will need to obtain. They also will have more direct access to the director should that become necessary.

Camera operators/assistant camera operators One of my most important contacts during the shoot often ends up being the camera operator or one of the assistant operators. Their job is to handle the camera, change lenses, measure focal distances, and change film. They know better than anyone else what is actually going on with the camera. I like to shadow them and get the data I need during the takes. They're a great source for lens information, distances, and camera height. Often they are measuring these anyway, in which case it is little bother to them to pass that information on to you. I try to stay out of their way as much as possible and only interject myself at opportune times, such as when they're waiting on the director or DP between takes. Many times, I've found that they get used to my information-gathering routine and start to yell out lens information before I even ask.

Script supervisor A script supervisor can be a great help to a matchmover. A script supervisor's job is to monitor the shoot and make sure to annotate any number of things that are going on. They generally keep track of things like the film roll, takes, slate numbers, focal length, and t-stop. If I must make set measurements or perform other tasks in between takes, I might not have enough time to record focal length or lens changes. This is where it's handy to coordinate with script supervisors. You can apprise them of the information you need (within reason), and they can usually include that in their notes. Of course, if you do this, you should make sure to get a copy of those notes at the end of the day.

Because a script supervisor has to gather information from various people on the set, this is also a great person to ask when you need to find out who is who on the set. However, since they're recording so many other things, the data you get from them might not always be clear. It's a good idea to quickly double-check the notes before you leave the set so you can clarify anything that you don't understand.

Producers Generally, if you have been invited to the set, it will have been at the request of a producer. Producers manage the time and budget of the production, and in that capacity they are highly motivated to help you succeed at your job. Sometimes, a producer is the only face you know when you first arrive on the set, so they can help introduce you to key people and get you briefed on the day's events. If you have any difficulties getting information, or you're not sure whom you need to talk to, a producer can make it happen. There are usually producers specifically for the visual effects team, so your best bet is to work with them first rather than bother the film production unit's producers.

Grips Grips are the muscle of a movie set. They build stuff, move stuff, and make stuff on demand. They are the MacGyvers of the movie business. As such, these are the guys you can ask for things like C-stands, tape, measuring tapes, apple crates, etc. They can sometimes even lend you a hand moving items or serving as an extra pair of hands, although you should check with their supervisor (the key grip) or the assistant director before getting them too involved in a task, because they might be needed elsewhere.

During shooting, sets are extremely busy and fast-paced. Everyone is doing their jobs as quickly and as flawlessly as possible. Most of them have been through it too many times to count, and they know how to work within the framework of the production.

As an on-set visual effects artist, you have to be persistent to get the information you need. You have to remember that everybody has their own thing to do, and getting the right information is your job. There are times when you will need to ask for help, and crews are usually very accommodating, but you should always be aware of how your actions will affect the live-action shoot. The one thing you probably don't want to do is bring the shoot to a halt while you bust out your tape measure, especially if you could do it at another time. On the other hand, once shooting starts, it tends to roll like a freight train, and if something is important, speak up!

Before any shooting starts, I usually tour the set to get an idea of what has been built so far and how close it is to completion. I try to find and introduce myself to the VFX supervisor, the script supervisor, the camera operators (including the assistant operators), and the key grip.

When I talk to the VFX supervisor or producer, I try to get an idea of what is on the schedule for the day and perhaps find out what information I'll need and when I'll be able to get it. I check in with the script supervisor in order to find out what information they're keeping track of. I talk to the camera operator and assistants to see which one of them I can count on for the information I'll need during and after takes (often the main operator is too busy working with the DP or director to work with me directly). And I let the key grip know what types of things I'll be doing and when. Sometimes when you need someone to hold the other end of a tape measure and no one else is available, the key grip might be able to get a grip to give you a hand. By visiting these people and letting them know what I'm going to do, things go more smoothly because we're all on the same page.

Building a Matchmove Kit

Whenever I go on set, I bring along a "matchmove kit" that has all the things I need to obtain and record my information:

Digital camera One of the best things you can do is document the set with pictures. It helps to remind you of how things were arranged, and it can also help with measurements if necessary. I always take hundreds of pictures during a typical shoot. If it goes over multiple days, I upload the day's pictures to a laptop and then shoot new pictures the next day.

Camera reports These are sheets for writing down lens information and other camera information from take to take. (See Appendix A for a sample.)

Set reports For making drawings and measurements of the set (see Appendix A).

25′ metal measuring tape For shorter distances and vertical measurements. I carry this around with me the whole time. It has a clip so I can wear it on my belt.

100′ cloth tape For measuring longer distances.

Electronic laser measuring tool This is a little bit expensive, but it measures with a laser beam instead of tape. It's great for getting really long measurements (mine can reach almost 50m!), and it also can get measurements that are hard to do with a tape, such as floor to ceiling measurements. The only drawback is that it doesn't work well on glass and mirrored surfaces and can have problems measuring in intense sunlight.

Electronic angle measuring tool This is a small gadget that looks like a miniature level. If you lay it on a surface, it will tell at what angle the surface is sloping. There are also non-electronic versions that are a little larger but work just as well.

Level A standard level from a hardware store. There may be times when you want to check whether or not a surface is level.

Matchmove markers I have several cans of racquetballs that I've cut in half and marked with an *X* with tape. I also have multicolored removable garage sale stickers and small LEDs (for nighttime shoots).

Roll of ¼″ gaffer's tape This serves a lot of purposes, from marking Xs on blue screens to taping a tripod head back together. Most grips carry 20 of these on their toolbelts, but it's good to have your own.

Distortion chart Used to measure lens distortion; I'll talk about this in just a second. (There's a PDF of a distortion grid in on the companion CD).

Grease markers, pens, and pencils You'll always need something to write with.

Of course, these aren't the only things you can have in your kit, but it should cover most of the things you'll need. It also reduces your reliance on others, so that you don't waste time tracking down tools.

Distortion Grids

There's one final piece of information that I try to get: a distortion reference. Distortion is sometimes difficult to quantify in the final sequence you are matchmoving, especially if there are no straight lines in the shot. It's easier if you can get a distortion reference in addition to the live-action plates. A distortion grid is nothing more than a grid of lines. This grid can be filmed by the camera operator at any time and should be shot once for each lens that was used (Figure 8.4).

Usually, I ask the operator if they can shoot the distortion grid after all of the shooting is over, or when they get ready to move between different sets. The grid should be set up facing the camera as squarely as possible and close enough so that it fills the entire frame of film. They don't need to shoot very much film, usually about a second or so (technically, you only need one frame for this).

You will need to get distortion grid shot using each of the lenses that were used during the shoot, since the various lenses might have different levels of distortion. Furthermore, if a variable lens is used, you should have them shoot the grid full wide and fully zoomed.

If they're using multiple cameras and the cameras are of the same type, it may be possible to shoot the distortion grid using the camera that isn't currently filming. You can use these grids once you get back to the postproduction in order to get more precise calculations on the amount of lens distortion. They're not critical, but they can really help with that thorny problem.

The grid itself should be printed fairly large—at least 18″ × 24″. This will help the camera operators during their framing of the grid and keep them from having to get too close to the grid while shooting wide lenses. You should also make a little space for a label in the center of the grid. You can use this space to note which lens you are shooting. As you change lenses, write the new information on a piece of tape to cover up the old takes. Placing it at the center of the grid shouldn't be a problem since distortion is less pronounced in the middle of the image.

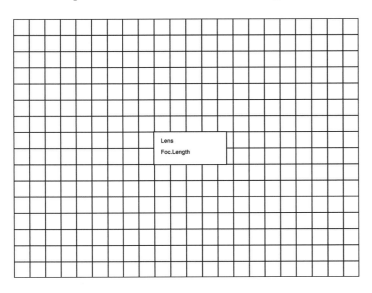

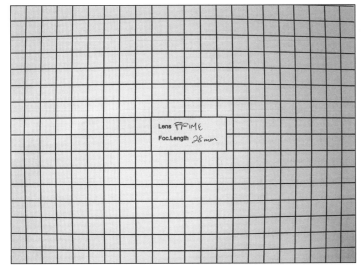

Figure 8.4 A distortion grid before and after shooting

Filling In the Details

As you can see, getting the information you need, keeping track of it, and finding whom to get it from and when you should get it can get a bit complicated. But it's more than worthwhile, in my opinion, to be a part of the filmmaking process. I can wrap up my thoughts on this subject by saying, get in there and get what you need, but stay out of the way and have fun.

Matchamation

The process of matching up a CG character or object to a live-action plate is known as matchamation (also known as rotomation). Matchamation techniques are a blend of matchmoving, animation, and, on some level, rotoscoping techniques—hence the hybrid name.

Matchamation is not an easy thing to do well, and I haven't heard too many people describe it as fun, but it is a unique challenge that requires a unique approach. There are no shortcuts per se, but I've included this chapter because there are ways to make matchamation a faster and less painful process.

9

Chapter Contents

The Basic Technique

Before getting started with matchamation, there are a few things that must be in place. First of all, you need a matchmoved camera for the scene. Any time you place CG elements into a live-action scene, you'll need a camera. The matchmove is done in exactly the same way as we've done in previous chapters.

The second thing you need is a CG model to match to the plate, and it needs to be as accurate as possible. The more inaccurate the model, the more difficult it will be to line it up to the plate. Ideally, the model is based on a scan of the actor or built from blueprints, but unless you're working on big-budget movies, you'll probably have to make do with reference photographs and educated guesses

The exact procedure for matchamation can vary greatly depending on the needs of the scene. But I have found the following steps to be a good way to go about it. These steps assume that the camera has been correctly matchmoved and fit into the set, so make sure you've accomplished those items first.

Establish the Distance to the Camera

When you're ready to start matchamating, the first thing you need to do is establish the distance between the object you are matchamating and the camera. You should take your time during this step and try to accurately work out this distance. If you misjudge this distance, you may not realize it until much later and end up redoing a significant portion (if not all) of your matchamation.

If you're lucky, you've been given the distance to the object. This measurement is sometimes written down on live-action shoots as the focus distance, but matchmovers can use this distance as a guide to how far the camera was from the object. Of course, this assumes that the camera was focusing on the object you are matchamating.

It should be readily apparent whether the distance is working or not if you place your model at the same distance from your CG camera. If you do not have measurements, the best way to find this distance is move the model directly away from the camera. Then, while looking through the camera, move the model until the scale seems correct.

If you are matchamating a character, check that the size of the head is the same, that the spacing of the eyes is the same, that the shoulder width is the same, etc. Characters can present unique challenges for matchamation because they can move in so many different ways, and they often require an exact fit.

Set the Initial Pose

Once the model is the correct distance from the camera, you're ready to start getting the object into the correct starting position. Setting an initial pose serves two purposes. First, it gives you a starting point for your animation, and second, it helps you spot any inaccuracies in the model.

The first thing you need to do is figure out which frame you want to use for your starting position. Sometimes it makes sense to start at the beginning of the clip, but not always. Pose your model on a frame where the object is not in the middle of a movement (if possible) or perhaps transitioning from one movement to the next. It is also helpful to match up the model to the object you're matchamating on a frame where the object is in a relatively neutral pose. For example, if you are matchamating a character, choose a frame where the actor's movements aren't too extreme.

The difficulty in posing the character or object is directly related to the complexity of the rig used for model. For this reason, it is often more difficult to get a character model rigged with full *inverse kinematics (IK)* controls to pose properly than it is for a simple model with no rig at all.

Sometimes, there may not be a rig, but you will need to create one in order to facilitate the movement of the object. At other times, the object will be fully rigged, and you will need to remove some or all of the rigging to more easily animate the object. This is particularly true of character models/rigs. These are usually set up with complex, multilayered controls such as IK that allow the animators to move the model as though it were a puppet. Many times, these types of controls actually make it difficult for matchamators. In these cases, the matchamators often strip out the IK controls and rely on *forward kinematics (FK)* techniques during their animation. If you are working in a larger production environment, make sure that you can alter the rig before doing so. Sometimes, additional work may be done to the character after you matchamate it, and removing or disabling the rig may present problems for other artists down the line.

During this initial pose, you may notice some problems getting things to align. If this happens, you may need to make adjustments to the overall distance to the camera. Or perhaps it points to accuracy problems with the model. A distance problem usually presents itself as an overall scaling problem—that is, the head is too big, but so is the body and the rest of the model. If you notice that different parts of the model seem to fit in different ways, the model may need to be modified.

This first pose can be refined later if necessary, but at this point it can serve as a test for global problems. This is the time when you should be determining if the overall positioning and model accuracy are correct.

Using Nonlinear Animation Techniques

I've often found that animators take to matchamation much more readily than people with no animation experience. Although matchamators are simply matching the movement of a character to the plate, the basic principles of animation still apply—perhaps more so than normal. One method used by animators is nonlinear animation. In the jargon of animators, this is often referred to as *pose-to-pose* animation. This is the opposite of another style known as *straight ahead* animation.

In pose-to-pose animation, the animator sets key poses on certain frames (not necessarily in order) and then fills in the in-between key poses as necessary. With straight ahead animation, the animator starts at the beginning and works straight through, creating poses in a linear fashion from the beginning of the shot to the end. Nonlinear animation has the advantage of being more natural looking because you get some of the in-between animation "for free."

Nonlinear animation techniques also work well with matchamation because they allow you to start with basic roughed-in poses from which you can refine more subtle movement. This makes it easier to "zero in" on a correct animation without creating a lot of extra keyframes.

Another principle of animation that is useful in matchamation is that of animating objects and particularly characters from the center out. For example, when animating a character, you would begin by animating the body elements first, then the head, arms, and legs, and finally hands, feet, fingers, and other secondary animation. In this way, you greatly economize the amount of revisions you need to do as you search for the correct poses for the model. If you animate the head first and then realize that the body is in the wrong position, you will have to reanimate the head once you repose the body. I usually try and make sure that the body is as accurately placed as I can make it before getting into any significant animation of the arms, legs, etc. It is a relatively small time savings, but matchamation is already a time-consuming process, so there's no sense in making it take any longer.

Analyze the Movement

Before you start animating, it's helpful to take a moment to analyze the movements of the object you will be matchamating. By watching the movements, you can find out about the general movement of the object, the overall timing, and the problem areas.

I like to create an exposure sheet (also called an *x-sheet*) of the movements I will be creating. This is simply a list, frame by frame, of the key movements of the objects. X-sheets are used by traditional animators to help them plan timings of animation and lip sync, and I've found it quite useful for creating a plan of attack during matchamation.

When writing on my x-sheet, I use a series of arrows to indicate the general direction of movement. To an animator, these types of notes should seem very familiar, since these same techniques are used to animate a character by hand.

Using an x-sheet helps you to identify the main movements by the character or object in the plate. When making notes about the movement, try to identify the "extreme poses": the points at which the object is at the beginning or end of a motion. For example, when matching an actor's arm swing during a walk, you would note at what frame the actor's arm is fully forward and at what frame it's fully back.

By noting the main positions of the object, you avoid creating unnecessary keyframes or having keyframes that aren't in sync with the motion. What you don't want to do is set keys every 10 frames and then go from there. This might leave you with a first pass that is slightly out of sync and difficult to edit. By noting the main movements ahead of time, you can make sure that you are only setting keys where they are absolutely necessary and that they are in sync with the movements seen in the plate. Analyzing the footage may take extra time on the front end, but it can save hours or days on the back end, and it might save you from matchamating the object again.

Note: I've provided a blank x-sheet (`x-sheet.xls` or `x-sheet.pdf`) in the Extras folder on the companion CD. You can print this out to use as a starting place for your own matchamations.

First Pass

Now you're ready to start getting into the "meat and potatoes" of the matchamation. Using an x-sheet, you simply go through the sequence and start posing the character. Since you've planned out where the main movements are located, you can quickly go to those frames to make the keys, adjust the pose, and then move on to the next pose.

On the first pass, you'll mostly be concerned with accurately posing the model on the main keyframes as listed on the x-sheet. You might notice that the model strays a bit between keyframes, but you probably don't need to fix those areas just yet. This first pass is really to help define the poses for the entire shot in a global sense. It helps show whether the initial distance and pose were correct, and it also helps to show any major problems with alignment elsewhere in the sequence.

During this stage, you might see previously unnoticed problems with the model or the initial pose. Having only set the barest of keyframes, you can still go back and make modifications without too much difficulty. This gradual, iterative approach helps you identify and correct big problems early, and in the long run, it saves you a lot of time and hassle.

The last thing to remember during this stage is to periodically check your object's animation in a perspective view. If you're only looking through the camera, it's easy to pose the object in a position that is inconsistent with the rest of the animation. When you look at the object in a perspective view, you'll catch problems like an object that suddenly jumps forward or rotates in a strange manner during a few frames.

Assuming your model is fairly accurate and rigged in a manner consistent with the real object, you should always strive to keep the movements of your character or object within the bounds of what it could physically do in real life. This is particularly true for characters. You don't want your character's arm to bend backward at the elbow or move in some other unrealistic motion. Check your first pass in a perspective view occasionally to ensure that you're not posing the character in a strange way. This prevents animating too many false-start poses and ensures the most accuracy.

Additional Passes/Tweaks

Once you're satisfied with the first-pass keyframes, you can turn your attention to the rest of the frames. During the first pass, your model is locked only to the keyframes you have set. Chances are that in between those keyframes, the model drifts away. In order to nail these frames down, you'll need to set more keyframes.

Try to lock down the in-between frames with as few keys as possible. The thing to avoid at this point is adding too many keys. If you have multiple, hand-placed keys packed tightly into a narrow frame range, you run the risk of having jittery or erratic movements.

The best way to avoid adding too many keys is to borrow a technique from rotoscoping. Let's say that you have some keyframes from your first pass at frames 1 and 10. The animation program interpolates the motion between these keyframes, so chances are that the object is close to where it needs to be, but not exactly right. The best place to put your next keyframe would be halfway between existing keyframes—around frame 5 or 6. In many cases, the halfway point between keys represents the largest possible deviation. Therefore, if you fix it at frame 5, it is likely that you'll also fix it (or at least get it closer) during frames 2 through 4 and frames 6 through 9. On subsequent passes, you may find that you need to further subdivide and add keyframes between the existing keyframes until the motion works.

During this process, it's a good idea to constantly create real-time previews to check for excessive jitter. Depending on the number of overall keys, during the second pass you may decide to add only one keyframe in between the first-pass keys and then deal with the other keys on subsequent passes. Eventually you might find yourself down to cycling between two closely spaced keys. It's good to bounce back and forth between two frames and watch all aspects of the model to see how they're lining up. By staring at the frames, you can get a more intuitive sense of how the matchamation is working. It's hard on the eyes, but nonetheless an effective technique.

Making Model Changes

No matter how accurate your model is, there will be parts that simply won't align (even if the actor was scanned). These misalignments usually present themselves as a consistently ill-fitting portion of the model. In these cases, I usually suspend judgement on those areas as long as the majority of the model is lining up properly. Rather than fight the problem areas for days and possibly reanimating the entire character, it is sometimes easiest to solve the final stages of matchamation with some modeling tweaks.

Perhaps the best tweak is to modify the geometry to "accommodate" the imperfections. I like to refer to these post-matchamation modeling tweaks as "shapefixes." Shapefixes are often created by modelers or matchamators by making an extra deformation to the model and adding it as a *morph target* to the model. These morphs can last as little as one frame, and they simply warp the mesh ever so slightly to match up perfectly. If the matchamator has done the job correctly, the model should only require relatively minor changes.

In most matchamation, only the basic model is required to be aligned. However, there are times when facial expressions are so extreme that you may have to matchamate those as well. I've found in these cases that a process similar to shapefixing is helpful. First, the model is matchamated, including the head. Since the facial expression is changing, you will probably need to match the eyes, nose, and maybe the upper teeth to the plate, since these features are relatively immobile. Then the modeler creates the facial expressions based on the plate with the matchamated model viewed over it. Those facial expressions are then animated by either a matchamator or an animator.

Shapefixing should be done with care, since it could affect the final outcome of the shot. After you have corrected the shape, you should check the object in a perspective view to see how much it has deformed. The acceptable level of deformation will vary depending on why the object needs to be matchamated in the first place. If the model is being used for things like particle emission or dynamics, it may be a little more forgiving. But if the model must be seen directly integrated with something on the plate, you may not be able to deform the model very much, if at all.

Working with Imperfect Data

No matter how good your model is or how well it's rigged, there will always be small problems. If the model is imperfect, you need to find out which areas are not correct and which ones are. Unfortunately, there isn't any easy way to do this except through trial and error. Sometimes it may be a matter of comparing a number of features and choosing which ones you trust the most.

Let's say you are trying to line up a head model with an actor on the plate. While the overall shape of the head is working, the eyes, nose, and mouth are not. You could try aligning the eyes and see if the nose and mouth are the right proportion relative to the face on the plate. If all three of these seem okay but the head seems the incorrect scale, you could make a reasonably safe assumption that the head is wrong. However, if the eyes, mouth, and nose are not correct, the proportions of the model could be off in some other way.

Another common problem is that the rig is not set up in a way that you can pose the character as required. The simplest solution for this is to only use rigs that can accurately mimic the structure and dynamics of the real object. Sometimes matchamators will "break" the rig in order to get the correct pose. That means you may have to partially disable animation controls or controls driven by expressions, scripts, or plug-ins.

Matchamation Tutorial

The best way to learn how to matchamate properly is, of course, to matchamate something. I've put together a tutorial in which we will create a matchamation for a bird's head so that animators can later lip-sync the bird saying a clever line.

Setting Up the Camera

The first thing to do before any matchamation is to matchmove the camera. In this shot, the camera is locked off, so that makes the job quite simple. Really, all we need to do here is create a camera and do a simple perspective match. We already did this part in Chapter 1, so I'll skim through it pretty quickly here.

1. Start a new project in your 3D animation program and create a camera. Add the image sequence `Bird_square.###.jpg` from the Chapter 9 folder on the companion CD as your background or camera image plane.

Tutorial footage courtesy Trevor Tuttle

2. As before, you don't have any information on the camera for this shot, so make an educated guess. Just from looking at it, you can tell that it was shot from a very low angle, probably less than a foot off the ground. I placed my camera 6″ off the ground (15.24cm). The lens seems fairly long, at least 50mm. Try these settings.

3. Add a polygon ground plane just to get some sense of how your perspective is working, and scale it large enough so that the plane is visible through the camera.

4. Rotate the camera until you get an angle that makes the ground plane look about right in regard to perspective. This is a little bit difficult because the beach is obviously slanting a bit to one side and possibly up away from the camera. Since you only really care about the bird's head, the exact perspective isn't important. Once you've got the camera set up similar to Figure 9.1, save your scene.

> **Note:** In this tutorial, we will be modeling the bird's head to match the plate. This gives us a little bit of freedom while setting up the initial matchmove camera. If our camera is slightly off, we can probably compensate by changing the model. This is not always the case, though. If the camera is moving significantly, your matchmove, and subsequent set fitting, will need to be solid. Also, if your model is very accurate, as in a scanned model of an actor, your matchmove will have to be very tightly set up. Since neither is the case here, we can be a little looser than usual.

Figure 9.1 Camera in place

Creating the Proxy Object

Now that we've got a camera, we need something to match to the plate. In this section, we'll create a proxy object of the bird's head to use to match the motion.

1. Make the head. How you do this exactly will vary depending on what software you are using. There are two things to determine here: the size of the bird's head and its distance from the camera. I began with the assumption that the bird's head was about 3″ long, from where the bill begins to the back of its head. So I created a 3″ sphere (7.62cm) and then pushed it out in front of the camera and moved it around until it fit on the left and right sides. The sphere should have a reasonably low number of subdivisions on it—I used 10 × 10 divisions. This gives you a shape that is detailed enough to follow the contours of the bird's head and yet not so dense that you can't see the plate underneath the geometry.

2. Rotate the sphere so it's aligned with the axes of the actual bird's head: one pole is at the bird's bill and the other at the back of its head. This will make it easier to align the head properly as you animate it.

3. Deform the sphere so it's more like the shape of the bird's head. To do this, I pulled the individual vertices around to match the shape (Figure 9.2). I also scaled the sphere slightly on the Y-axis and also the X-axis to make the head narrower. This will be important once the bird starts turning its head. To verify how narrow the sphere needed to be, I went to the last frame where its head is facing the camera and checked to see if mine matched.

4. Next we need a bill. Again this can be a very simple object. I started with a cube that had two subdivisions on all axes. I moved it into position at the end of the sphere and moved its vertices until it was the right shape (Figure 9.3).

Figure 9.2 The proxy bird head

Figure 9.3 The bird's bill in place

> **Note:** When you make the bill, line up the vertices with the various markings and features on the bird's bill in the plate. By doing this, you give yourself anchor points to which you can strive to keep aligned during matchamation. For example, I placed vertices along the edge between the black and yellow parts of the bill.

5. One other thing that might help align the bird's head is to identify where the eyes are, so add a sphere on the side of the head and align it with the eye.

Creating a Matchamation Rig

Now that we have some basic models to move around, we need to make sure that our models move in the appropriate way.

1. Parent the eye and bill to the head object. This allows the bill and eye to move together with the head when the head is moved.

2. If you play through the footage, you will notice that the bird's head is not the only thing that is moving; the bird is also moving its neck and body. You need to put a simple rig in place to mimic these various points of movement. This will make getting the head in the right place somewhat simpler. Start by adding a null object and moving it to right in between the bird's legs and somewhat up a bit. This is the center of gravity of the bird's body (basically its hip joint).

3. Add a null into a position that roughly approximates the base of its neck. Again, this won't be possible to accurately place, but you want to provide a place that pivots around where the neck meets the body.

4. Now you need to link up your model to the rig. First, parent the head object to the neck null (make sure that your parenting options don't allow the head to move during parenting). Then parent the neck null to the hip null. This sets up a very simple rig in which moving the hip null moves everything in the chain, moving the neck null moves everything above it, and so on. This should allow you to mimic the movements of the bird fairly easily (Figure 9.4).

Figure 9.4 The matchamation rig's parenting structure

Analyzing the Motion

Before we get into the actual business of animating the model, let's take a moment to analyze the motion of the bird's head. A little bit of time spent in advance can be a great time-saver down the road.

Figure 9.5 shows an x-sheet (a blank version of this is included on the companion CD) on which I've marked the major movements of the bird's head. I use a sort of shorthand set of marks to indicate the movement of the bird's head and body. Each arrow is drawn on the frame in which the motion ends, and the direction of the arrow indicates the object's motion needed to get to that position. You can use whatever annotation works for you, but I like to draw small arrows to indicate the direction of movement and other important notes. If the head rotates to screen left, I make a small curved arrow to the left; if it moves to the left, I use a straight arrow to the left. Sometimes the object needs to stay in the same place for several frames. I indicate this using the word "hold," which means that the bird holds the position until that frame.

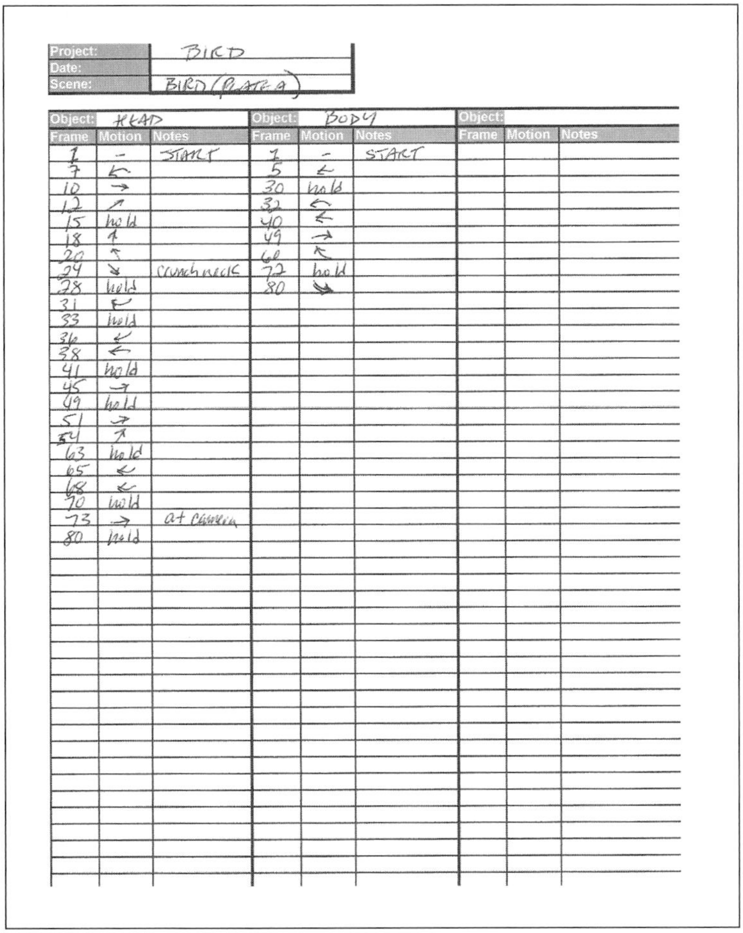

Figure 9.5 My x-sheet for this shot

I also made a separate column that lists the movements of the body. This will come in handy when we get down to animating with the rig.

Go through the clip and try and make your own x-sheet. Note any major changes in motion or holds. Try to only mark the main movements and not get hung up on smaller motions; you'll fill those in later as you matchamate. Once you're done, compare your results to those I've given. They may not match frame for frame, but they'll probably be close.

Optimizing Your Workspace for Matchamation

There are a few ways you can set up your workspace in your 3D animation program that will make matchamating a little bit easier. The exact steps will vary, but most of these items can be done in every program.

Wireframe overlay Viewing the wireframe mesh over the plate is crucial to any matchamation. You may find it helpful to change the color of the wireframe to make it more visible. For example, in this tutorial, I found it was easier to see a dark blue or red wireframe instead of the default white or gray.

Backface culling Most animation programs give you the option to see the wireframe with backface culling turned on: the wireframe then doesn't show any geometry that is facing away from the camera. This helps eliminate confusion because you only see the parts of the mesh you care about. The reduction in clutter on-screen is dramatic, and I highly recommend working in this mode.

Automatic-keying Most animation programs have an automatic key feature that places the keys automatically as you move objects. Whether you use this feature or not is a matter of preference, but I've found that it is quite handy for matchamation. This feature can be used to set keys whenever an object is moved or adjusted. Some programs let you autokey only when an already-keyed object is moved. Again, this is a matter of preference.

Hotkeys During matchamation, you will find yourself bouncing back and forth a lot between frames. It's very helpful to learn or set up the hotkeys for your program so that you can quickly go to the next/previous frame and the next/previous keyframe. This allows you to stare at the model while changing frames without having to take your eyes off the screen. This is particularly beneficial when you're trying to nail down subtle movement.

First Pass

Now that we have a model and it is rigged to animate, we can start getting down to the business of matchamating. The focus of our efforts will be to make the bill and head match properly, but since the head follows the body, it will be helpful to start matching the body's movements first.

1. Select the body null and set a keyframe for it at frame 1.

2. Look at your x-sheet to see where you've guessed at the next keyframe's position. On mine, I saw that the body shifts to the left ending around frame 5. Go to frame 5 and move the locator so that it is more to the left. This movement to the left isn't just relative to the screen. The bird actually shifts its body away from the camera slightly. In my setup, this translates to a Z-axis movement, so I moved the null on the Z-axis.

3. After you set the key, scrub the footage between frames 1 and 5 and check to see how well it works. The in-between keys may not fit exactly, but they should give you the general sense that the null is moving far enough or not too far (Figure 9.6).

4. Now repeat this for all of the body keyframes you've noted on your x-sheet. If you've listed a keyframe as a "hold" keyframe, you can simply copy the keyframe that came before it. (In Maya, you can do this quickly by middle-mouse-dragging the previous keyframe to the frame for the hold frame and then hitting the s key to set the key.) You can also use the automatic keying while making the adjustments, if you prefer.

> **Note:** If you use the autokey feature, make sure that it keys all channels when making the key. You can inadvertently destroy object placement for previous keys if you don't key on every channel. For example, let's say you key all the channels on frame 1, then only key the X translation on frame 5, then only the Z translation on frame 10. The Z translation interpolates between frames 1 and 10 only and changes the Z translation value for frame 5, thereby ruining the placement of the object at frame 5. Keying all of the channels for every keyframe generates extra keyframes, but it guarantees that your object placement remains exactly as you set it.

5. As you set the keyframes for the body null, scrub back and forth on the timeline to check the movement. Make sure you are getting the rotation of the body as well. The head probably won't match up well at this point, but don't worry about it just yet. The goal is to get a little bit of a head start toward the overall motion. By adding some of the body motion, you can get a sense of how the head needs to move.

Figure 9.6 Placing the next key on the body

6. Once the body null is animated, start working on the neck a little. This will help with the neck crunching movement that the bird makes as well as some of the head rotation. The method is the same as the body: set keys on the neck null to keep it centered on the neck region. When setting the keys for this control, it may be helpful to first set the translation, then go back for a second pass to do the rotation of the neck. Remember, the null doesn't have to follow perfectly, just pretty closely. Try comparing how the null was close to a marking or shadow on the bird's neck and then try to keep it close to that feature during the first pass.

7. Now it's time to animate the head. Again, start at frame 1 and set your keyframes throughout the sequence. This is where the x-sheet comes in real handy, because you don't have to think too much about what frame your keyframes are going to be placed. You can focus instead on how the head is moving from keyframe to keyframe. Work your way through the x-sheet, placing the keys and repositioning the head so that it matches the plate.

8. At this stage of the game, you're just trying to make sure that everything is working at the keyframes. You want to make sure that the gross movements are working before you get into the fine-level detail. After all, it will be easier to make smaller adjustments later if you know that the overall movement of the head is working (Figure 9.7). Make a preview of your animation so far and make sure the animation is not doing anything extreme. If it is, correct the parts that seem out of place relative to the rest of the movement.

You may notice that the head comes away from the head in the plate during the in-between frames. Don't worry about that for now (although it's tempting to fix it now). It's really easy to get bogged down in the details and end up wasting a lot of your time.

9. After you've keyed all of the keyframes on your x-sheet, look at your animation at real-speed by doing a wireframe preview. This will look a little bit "floaty"— that is, the object will drift around. What you're looking for are any major separations or pops that you didn't intend. You'll tighten up the animation in the next pass, so don't get too finicky just yet.

10. You should also preview your animation in a perspective view (Figure 9.8). This will show you how the head is moving in 3D space and highlight any unrealistic motion. Sometimes, when you're only working in the camera view, it's easy to push the head much farther than it actually would have moved. If you preview the animation in a perspective view and find that the head is moving a meter back during one of the frames, you know you need to adjust that before continuing. I recommend you make this check frequently throughout the matchamation process to make sure your model is moving in a realistic and consistent manner.

Figure 9.7 The first pass

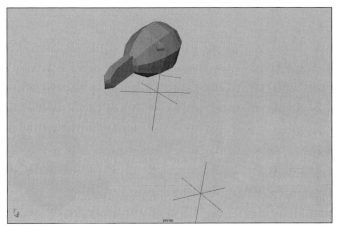

Figure 9.8 The first pass as seen in a perspective view

Second Pass

The first pass serves as a way to get the overall motion worked out. The second and subsequent passes are then used to really dial in the exact movement. I usually focus on getting the in-between movements as tight as possible during this stage. A good example of this is when the bird turns its head. We've set keys when the bird is facing left and when it's facing right, but during the turn the model slides off a bit. The second pass is where we take care of problems like this.

1. Start at the beginning of the scene again. If your x-sheet looks like mine, you'll have keyframes for the head object at frames 1 and 7. A good place to see how well the matchamation is holding up is to go halfway between the existing keys. Scrub between frames 1 and 7 and find the point where the model is most out of alignment. In my animation, the head model slides to the left too far. The frame where it is most out of alignment is at frame 3 (Figure 9.9).

2. Place a key at frame 3 and adjust the model again so that it fits. Remember, you want to be consistent with the motion of the bird's head. If it moves, then your model should move. If it rotates, your model should rotate. After setting the key, check the movement in a perspective view and make sure it's not too far out of place relative to the rest of the movement.

3. Scrub the footage again between keys 1 and 7. Does the head slip off the object? If so, you may need to add another key. I found that I had to add another key at frame 5, and then after looking at the motion, another key at frame 4. Notice how I always place keys in the middle between other keys? This helps you get a lot of animation "for free" because the software will try to interpolate the motion between your keys. By examining the halfway points in between existing keys, you are simply checking how well the interpolation works. Sometimes it works perfect; other times, you'll need to make adjustments as we've done here.

 Note: Although my general advice is to minimize the number of keyframes, you may have noticed that you are already adding quite a few for this tutorial. This mainly has to do with the type of movement we are matchamating. Birds tend to move with quick, jerky movements, and that means there are lots of opportunities for the model to misregister. A slower, more gradual type of movement would most likely allow for fewer keyframes.

Frame 1

Frame 3

Frame 7

Figure 9.9 With keyframes set at frames 1 and 7, the object is slipping off at frame 3.

4.   Continue the second pass of your matchamation in a similar fashion to what you've just done for the first seven frames. Go to a frame that is halfway between keys from the first pass and check whether it needs to be adjusted. If it is off, create a new keyframe and move the object to the correct position. Then scrub that section again to see if it's working. Work your way through the entire sequence this way.

The goal of this pass is to have the object correctly aligned at all frames. At the end of this second pass, you may have some frames where the model slips a bit or is slightly misaligned with adjacent keyframes, but you'll address that in the following passes.

Try to keep your keyframes as sparsely placed as possible. Adding too many keyframes can result in a jittery motion that is hard to edit. Sometimes you can make do with one keyframe strategically positioned rather than 10 sloppily chosen keyframes. Figure 9.10 shows the spacing of my keyframes after my second pass.

Figure 9.10 Here's how my timeline looked after the second pass.

Additional Passes

After the second pass, the operative word is "tweak." The goal of any additional passes is to completely nail down the model's fit to the plate. This can be a very tedious process, but it is vital to ensure that the models fit well and that there are no noticeable jumps. It's not uncommon for a matchmover to do six or seven passes to achieve a tight fit.

In these passes, you'll want to start at the beginning again and carefully step through the footage, looking for places where the model comes away from the plate. Go through the sequence again and try to fit the model more accurately.

As you begin tightening up the matchamation, you may be tempted to add more keys. In some cases, it may be necessary, but try to keep them to a minimum. You could also try adjusting the curves in the curve editor to help adjust the ease-in and ease-out motions of certain keyframes. I've personally found it easier to explicitly keyframe the ease-ins/outs.

When you begin working your way through the shot, make sure to preview the animation from time to time. This will help you spot any unforeseen noise or jitter in the motion.

That's about it! The only thing more I can say is to keep tweaking your matchamation until it looks perfect. I recommend that after your third pass, you closely scrutinize the animation. If you're feeling pretty good about it, put a checker-board texture on the proxy bird head and render out a test to see how it's working.

Once you've finished tweaking the animation, the scene is ready to hand over for further work. Now that the position of the bird's real beak is located for every frame, a virtual beak can be animated to do lip sync, as was done in the final shot (Figure 9.11).

Getting a Better View in Maya

Sometimes it is helpful to zoom in on your object during matchamation so that you can accurately see what's going on. The problem is, if you zoom in the camera, you'll break the matchmove. If you're using Maya, there is a way to zoom in the matchmove camera without breaking the matchmove.

Select the camera and open the Attribute Editor. Midway down on the camera's Shape node panel, you'll see the Film Back section. At the bottom of that section are three fields that come in handy: the Film Offset fields and the Overscan field.

These fields allow you to alter the position of the image (actually the film back) without changing the camera's position or focal length. The first Film Offset field moves the film plane on the X-axis (left/right), and the second field moves it on the Y-axis (up/down). These values are expressed in inches relative to the film back size. When the value is at 0.0, the film plane is centered. If you type 0.1 in the first field, the film plane center moves 0.1" to the right. If you type −0.1, the film plane center moves 0.1" to the left. The same applies to the second field, except that it moves the film plane center up and down.

The Overscan field controls how much the film plane is zoomed in or out. When set to 1.0, the image fills the viewport normally. Values over 1.0 zoom the film plane out (technically called over-scan), and values under 1.0 zoom the film plane in.

For this project, I worked on my third pass matchamation with Film Offset values of 0.1 and 0.1 and an Overscan setting of 0.3, which framed up the bird's head nicely and made it easier to see what was going on.

If you use this feature, you need to remember to reset these values to their original settings before turning the scenes over to anyone else. This will affect how the scene renders, so if you leave it zoomed in, the renders will likewise be zoomed in.

Figure 9.11 The matchamation as it looks in the final shot

Object Tracking with Matchmove Software

Most of the commercially available matchmoving programs boast the ability to track objects in addition to cameras. By tracking an object using a matchmove program, you sometimes can bypass all of the painstaking work of matchamating by hand. There are, however, some limits to what can be done with a matchmoving program, and these limits often preclude the use of this approach.

Tracking an object with a matchmoving program is very similar to tracking a camera. The main difference is in what you use for your 2D tracks. When you track a camera, you track features in the scene that do not move relative to one another. When you track an object, you track features on the object only, and those features cannot move relative to one another.

When you export the solution from an object track, you simply specify that it was an object you tracked rather than an environment. The 3D scene that you get will have a static camera with moving locators, rather than the normal way (static locators, moving camera). Object tracking in matchmoving software isn't always a walk in the park, but it's not necessarily the fault of the software. The problem usually lies in the plate itself. Below I've listed some common problems that occur when trying to track an object with matchmoving software.

Not Enough Information to Track

The most common difficulty with object tracking is that there simply aren't enough features to track on the plate to produce a strong calibration. You still need the minimum number of tracks, but object tracking places additional constraints on the 2D tracking.

First, all of the tracks must be on the object only, and second, the tracks cannot move independently from one another.

This last item can be tricky. Imagine you are tracking a person's face. No problem: you can track their mouth, nostrils, the corners of the eyes, eyebrows—the world is your oyster. But usually if you need to track someone's face, something dramatic is happening, and the actor is going to do what most actors do: act. They're screaming, talking, and making all kinds of facial expressions. Their mouth, cheeks, and jaw are moving, as are their eyebrows and forehead. Suddenly your abundance of trackable features becomes extremely limited.

In the case of tracking a highly emotive face, you are usually limited to tracking the upper teeth (not the lower, since the jaw moves independently from the rest of the head), the nostrils (sometimes), the hairline, and the ears. The same problem could show up when trying to track animal's faces (they're more expressive than you'd think).

In many cases, the actor turns their head; if you're tracking one of their ears, it will most likely move behind their head at some point. When there is a lot of movement in the head, you will find yourself bringing in new tracks as the old ones get occluded, and this can complicate the tracking significantly.

At this point, you might be wondering if it's possible to track a person's entire body. Unfortunately, you can't do this with normal, rigid object tracking methods. The different parts of the body all move in different directions, and the software wouldn't be able to solve it. Even something like a forearm would be impossible for the software to calculate, because any points on the surface of the arm would move differently from one another in all three axes (i.e., an arm can twist along its length). More recently, however, the developers of matchmove programs have been creating systems for tracking a person's entire body. The method involves matchmoving multiple image sequences and then using them as a *motion capture* device—that is, motion capture with video cameras. These could not only be used for full body tracking, but also for recording facial deformations and other non-rigid object movement.

Lack of Sufficient Depth

Often when you track an object, the object only comprises a relatively small amount of screen space. Therefore, when you track it, the points are all jammed into a small area of the frame and usually not well spread out. This can make calibration extremely difficult and create weak or flat solutions. Unfortunately, if this is the problem, there is little you can do to improve it, and you will probably have to resort to matchamation.

Camera Moves in Addition to the Object

Usually the matchmove software can track a camera or an object, but doing both can be hit-or-miss at best. The reason is, the matchmove software needs a way to distinguish between the object's movement and the movement caused by the camera. One way to do this is to do two matchmoves for the shot: one for the camera and one for the object.

Some matchmove programs allow you to group tracking markers in the environment independently from markers on the object and generate the appropriate scene. In the programs that do not allow for this, you'll have to solve for each independently and then combine them in your 3D package.

When the Going Gets Tough

Matchamation is one of the tougher jobs a matchmover may be asked to do. I hope the tips in this chapter have provided you with a few new tools that will help make it as painless as possible. In the next chapter, we'll look at some advanced matchmoving techniques as well as ways to troubleshoot problem matchmoves.

Troubleshooting and Advanced Techniques

Each new matchmove will present its own unique set of challenges and issues. Techniques that work for one shot might not work for the next, so knowing how to troubleshoot a matchmove can be an extremely useful skill. Over the years, I've discovered some tricks and techniques that have been helpful in a wide range of situations, and now's my chance to pass them on to you.

This chapter covers a lot of different items related to troubleshooting in a somewhat rapid-fire fashion. You may want to skim through this chapter now and return later when you're having specific problems. The first part of this chapter deals with different methods of troubleshooting, while the second part addresses advanced tools and techniques that can help you conquer tough shots.

Chapter Contents

Effective Troubleshooting

I've always stressed to my students that problem solving is perhaps the greatest asset you can possess as a visual effects artist. Whether you're a matchmover or a high-end TD, you will face many situations where there is a problem and you're the one who must solve it. Many problem-solving strategies are unique to the discipline of matchmoving, and even then they can vary depending on the task at hand. A thorough knowledge of the process helps, but I've found that the best problem solvers tackle a problem with a similar approach (or if you want to use the big art-school words, *methodology*).

The methods I present in this chapter represent a methodology I've found helpful when trying to troubleshoot a bad matchmove, but this approach is not specific to matchmoving. This is by no means the final word on the subject, but I've found it helpful in my everyday work.

Compartmentalize the problem. Okay, so the matchmove isn't working. The first thing you should do is try and isolate exactly where the problem is. Begin with the large generalities and work your way toward more specific causes. For example, does it seem to be a problem with the matchmove camera or the way you've fit the camera into the set? If it's the camera, is the problem in 2D tracking or in the 3D calibration? If it's the 2D tracking, is it a bad track or a track that slips at a particular frame? And so on. As you work your way down the list, you should make observations and test as necessary, in order to rule out the different causes as you go. By starting in broad strokes, you can save yourself time trying to search for problems where there are none. It is also possible that there is more than one problem. Isolating one problem may not completely fix it, but it could improve the problem or at least help you rule out other areas of difficulty.

Categorize your trust level in the data. I generally consider myself lucky if I've received any data about the scene I'm matchmoving, but bad data can often do more harm than good. When I receive data about a camera or scene, I try to categorize how much I trust each piece of information. For example, if I see the same focal length on handwritten set notes and in a type-written camera report, then I give that a high "trustability" rating. However, if I see any inconsistencies, then I tend to trust the data less. The data may be correct, but if I'm having problems, these are the things I look to first as the cause. I don't necessarily write this "trust" list down, I just make a mental note of it and try to keep this in mind as I proceed.

Prioritize the problems. If you determine that you have multiple problems, try to prioritize them in terms of the size of the problem. Tackle the most pronounced problems first, then the less noticeable ones. By doing this, you might fix many of the smaller problems while dealing with the larger ones. For example, if you are troubleshooting a calibration in which some portions are worse than others, try fixing the worst areas first, because they can sometimes bring the rest of the solution together in the process.

Check your iterations. In matchmoving, I tend to iterate my scenes often, that is, I save many new versions of the project as I work. I do this because it's very easy to go down the wrong path when troubleshooting a matchmove. Suddenly you may realize that you've taken a wrong turn a few steps back. By saving versions, you can still access this scene later if necessary. Of course, this can lead to a lot of extra files, so I usually create an "old" folder into which I put files I am no longer using but might want to keep around "just in case."

Troubleshooting Checklist

Now that you have a general framework for troubleshooting, let's see how that applies to matchmoving. Whenever I'm troubleshooting a bad matchmove, I try to be as systematic as possible. I've talked about some troubleshooting techniques in previous chapters, but I want to give you an example of how I proceed through a shot to determine the problem. The following sections are a brief checklist, listed in an order that helps you get to the source of the problem in the quickest and most efficient way:

1. Check the camera's motion.

2. Check set placement and fitting.

3. Scrutinize 2D tracking closely.

4. Check for plate issues.

Check the Camera's Motion

First, I usually try to determine if there is a problem with the camera's motion. The best way to start analyzing this is to look through your 3D camera at your 3D markers or nulls. If the nulls seem to be sticking to the features they are tracking, then it probably is not a camera problem. The exception is if the markers suddenly become larger or smaller, which indicates a fragmented or incorrect motion path for the camera.

Next, I check the camera's motion path in a perspective view and make sure it makes sense relative to what I'm seeing in the plate. Sometimes the path can become broken, inverted (that is, the camera moves in the opposite direction it should), or skewed, which indicates a bad calibration (Figure 10.1).

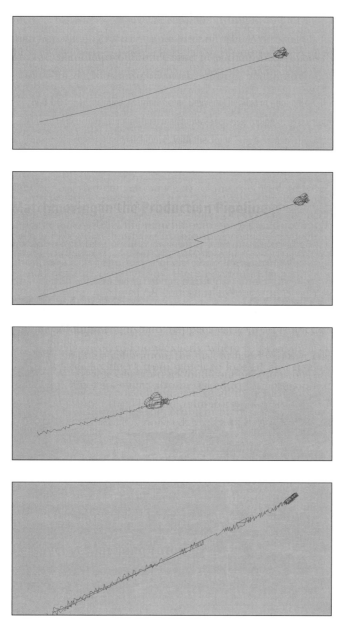

Figure 10.1 A variety of camera paths as seen in a perspective view: a good motion path, a broken motion path, a noisy motion path, and an erratic path

Finally, I examine the camera's motion curves in the motion graph editor (in either the animation program or the matchmoving program). This may highlight problems that are too subtle to see in the perspective view. This also helps identify problems in a pan shot's rotation curves for the same reason. A problem in any of these areas means that more refinement or work is necessary in the matchmove software to get a better solution.

Check Set Placement and Fitting

When you are previewing how the set seems to work with the matchmove, you should be checking for how well it is aligned and how well it stays aligned. If the set or portions of the set seem to drift off from the features they should be sticking to, it could indicate that the camera is not properly fit into the environment. Most often this is because the matchmover or other visual effects artist didn't correctly place the CG element within the scene or else didn't fit the matchmove camera correctly into the scene. Set-fitting problems tend to be subtle drifts rather than sudden jumps, and they may only drift in certain parts of the image, while other parts maintain the correct relationship.

The nulls that import from the matchmove program should correspond to features in the images, so if you use those as starting points for placing your geometry, you should be able to fit the set properly. For example, if the matchmoving program tracked several features on the ground, then when you export the scene to your 3D application, you should have several markers on the ground. These would help you to figure out where ground level is in your shot.

Set-fitting problems generally can be fixed by simply refitting the camera into the environment. If the camera is translating, you may also need to take a closer look at the overall "scale" of the camera move. No, I don't mean simply how large the camera is, but rather how large its move is. For example, if the real-world camera moved 3 meters on the X-axis, then your 3D camera should do the same. This would be particularly true if you were to see anything in the plate that needed to connect directly with a CG element, such as an actor's feet on a CG ground or perhaps a digital set extension (Figure 10.2).

It's also possible for a calibration to be stronger in certain areas of the set and not others. This is usually due to the lack of 2D tracking markers in the weak areas. This shows up as objects that seem to fit in one portion of the set but lose their fit in other parts of the image. The best option here is to add more 2D tracks (if possible) to the weak areas and then recalibrate.

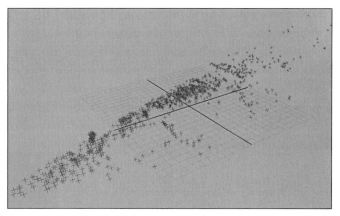

Figure 10.2 The nulls in this solution correspond to the ground. If CG objects need to fit directly onto the ground plane, then it's important that the nulls rest on the ground during the final camera positioning.

Scrutinize 2D Tracking Closely

If you've determined that the camera is the problem, then you need to further subdivide your troubleshooting efforts to determine whether the problem is with the 2D tracks or elsewhere. Tracking problems are often not apparent until you attempt a calibration. The most common problems that point back to a 2D tracking issue are:

- Severe breaks in the camera's motions

- Inability to achieve any solution

- Jitter or noise in the camera movement

- Weak solutions (These often mean that there aren't enough trackers or that the trackers are in the wrong place.)

Of course, if the problem seems to be with the 2D tracking, you'll have no choice but to return to the matchmoving software and retrack or repair the offending trackers. I discuss more detailed techniques for doing this later in this chapter.

Check for Plate Issues

There are times when the problem doesn't have anything to do with what you are doing, but rather what you are trying to matchmove. Problems in this category include:

- Shots that lack parallax

- Excessive film grain

- Readability issues

You can examine the plate for parallax by examining where a foreground object intersects a background object. If parallax is present, you should see a noticeable shift between the two objects. If the shot contains significant amounts of parallax, the matchmove software should have no problem solving it (barring any other non-parallax related problems), and if the shot has no parallax, it should be solved as a nodal pan shot.

Film grain can be a real headache if you are dealing with subtle camera moves, since the grain and noise in the plate often translates to jitter in the camera. One potential solution is to remove grain from the plate, but I'm always hesitant to do this, since that would involve altering the image at the pixel level, potentially causing other problems for the matchmove software. During 2D tracking, the fewer tracks you have, the more likely that film grain will become an issue. I've found that running an automatic tracker on top of any manual tracks will often dampen any jitter in the camera.

If there are problems with the readability of the plate, there is probably little you can do to improve the situation except to manually track around the problem areas. Defects in this category include things like compression artifacts, lens dirt, and lens flares; some of these are demonstrated in Figure 10.3.

Figure 10.3 In this shot, the sunlight and lens flare obscure almost the entire right side of the image as well as a considerable number of trackable features on the road. Also notice how the dirt on the windshield adds to the problem and makes it even more difficult to track.

Diagnosing the Problem

Coaxing a good solution from a bad matchmove can be like a doctor trying to heal a patient. A doctor will analyze the symptoms and make a diagnosis to try and fix the problem. In the following sections, I've described some specific problems that I encounter routinely along with their possible causes and cures:

- No nulls are visible after calibration.
- Nulls are all in a line or a single point.
- The camera path jumps suddenly to another position or is extremely jagged and chaotic.
- Everything lines up on the first frame but quickly slips off.
- Noise or jitter appears in the camera's motion path.
- Objects appear to tear away from plate feature during areas of heavy motion blur.

No nulls are visible after calibration.

Diagnosis: Bad calibration.

Possible causes: Lack of tracking markers; incorrect placement of tracks; lack of parallax; incorrect camera data.

Things to try: Add more tracks. Check placement of tracks. If no parallax is evident, try solving as a nodal pan. Let matchmove software calculate the focal length and internal parameters on its own. (See "Constraints" section later in this chapter.)

Nulls are all in a line or a single point.

Or some nulls are behind the camera, or the motion path is inverted (e.g., left-to-right movement appears as right-to-left).

Diagnosis: Bad or partial calibration.

Possible cause: Same as above.

Things to try: Same as above.

The camera path jumps suddenly to another position or is extremely jagged and chaotic.

Diagnosis: Partial calibration.

Possible causes: Multiple 2D tracks starting or stopping on the same frame; a track that was essential to calibration stopped or started; lack of tracks; something drastically changed in the plate (e.g., a flash of light, a large amount of occlusion).

Things to try: Stairstep all 2D tracks both entering and leaving the shot, even if it means shortening some tracks or lengthening others (Figure 10.4). Add more tracks. Add more keyframes through severe changes in the plate or add more tracks in these areas.

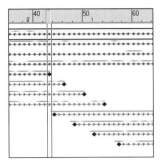

Figure 10.4 Stairstepping tracks

Everything lines up on the first frame but quickly slips off.

Diagnosis: Incorrect frame rate, incorrect starting frame, improper set fitting.

Possible causes: Animation scene was exported from matchmoving software with incorrect frame rate; frame rate was set incorrectly in animation software; camera animation is offset by a frame (e.g., starts at frame 0 instead of 1, or vice versa); camera movement is not scaled properly.

Things to try: Check and reset frame rate. If the problem was in the matchmoving software, you probably don't need to recalibrate, just open up the project, make the changes, and reexport. If you want to make the change in your animation package, you may need to close the scene, change the frame rate, and then reopen the scene. Check that the animation curves for the camera begin on the first frame of your plate. If they don't, just slide the curves forward or back a frame. Rescale camera and check set fitting.

Noise or jitter appears in the camera's motion path.

Diagnosis: Usually a 2D tracking problem.

Possible causes: Heavy film grain; subtle camera shake; digital compression artifacts; plate elements such as rain or smoke; gate weave (film was moving slightly inside the film gate during filming).

Things to try: Track channels with less noise or grain. Run an automatic tracking pass over a manual tracking pass (this can sometimes dampen noise). Slightly blur plate before tracking. Increase pattern size during 2D tracking. If animation curves don't seem overly noisy, check that the camera's animation starts on the right frame. As a last resort this can be fixed by smoothing the animation curves for the camera, although this can sometimes do more harm than good.

Objects appear to tear away from plate feature during areas of heavy motion blur.

Diagnosis: 2D tracking problems, lack of motion blur in CG elements.

Possible causes: 2D tracks not sticking well through motion blur; tracks not consistent in tracking motion blur; lack of motion blur on CG objects is different than that seen on the plate and creates the illusion that they are tearing away.

Things to try: Retrack using a larger search area and possibly a larger pattern. Make sure tracks are following the same "edge" of the motion blur (i.e., front, middle, back of the motion-blurred edge). Render test checkerboards with a level of motion blur that approximates the motion blur seen on the plate.

Advanced Tools and Tricks

Matchmoves can be notoriously difficult to figure out sometimes. Fortunately, there is a wide range of tools designed to help tackle the tougher problems you may encounter. If you can master those tools and use a few of the tricks listed next, it can mean the difference between a long week of tracking a shot by hand and going home early.

Advanced 2D Tracking Tools

Some matchmoving programs have features that enhance or improve the ability of the user to track features that would otherwise be impossible to track. As you've seen above, this is not an uncommon occurrence, and these tools help you get higher quality tracks in such situations.

Most 2D tracking programs use luminance values to track. This is mainly to make the process faster. Some programs (such as MatchMover Pro and SynthEyes) allow you to switch the mode of the tracker so that it analyzes color as well. This is helpful when you're trying to track features that have a similar contrast, but different colors.

Some trackers can also track individual color channels. For example, if you are having trouble tracking green-screen footage, you could switch the tracker so that it only pays attention to the red channel. This usually has the effect of making the markers stand out much more clearly, depending on what color the markers are.

Constraints

Constraints are, as the name suggests, ways of forcing matchmove software to calculate the solution in a particular manner. There are various types of constraints, but they usually define the camera's movement or features in the scene in very specific ways.

Constraints to the camera are done in fairly broad strokes that can help preesti-mate the camera's movement. Perhaps the simplest constraint is the nodal pan con-straint. This constraint lets the matchmoving software know that it can solve the scene using only rotation of the camera.

There are also constraints that restrict the camera to dolly movements on one axis (e.g., dolly on Z only) or to a planar dolly (e.g., moves only on X and Z), as shown in Figure 10.5.

Some constraints are used to help define the relationship of certain features once the solution is finished. One such constraint, survey data, forces an individual track to solve at a particular XYZ coordinate. This can be very helpful, but the survey data needs to be fairly precise.

It is possible to constrain nonsurvey points based on their relationship to the points around them. For example, if you had tracked several markers on a wall that faced the camera, you could place a constraint (all share the same Z value) on the solution that would force the software to create a solution wherein all of those markers are on the same plane. Furthermore, if some of the markers have the same height, you could add a second constraint that forces them to be the same height in the final solution.

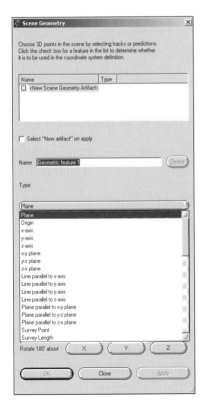

Figure 10.5 Various constraint types in boujou bullet

Constraints can work wonders in helping to solidify a weak solution, but they can sometimes do more harm than good. Adding a constraint to inaccurate 2D tracks can cause the solution to fail. Adding too many constraints can place so many limitations on the calibration engine that it becomes impossible for it to achieve a solution. If you want to use constraints, I recommend adding them one at a time and calibrating as you do so. This way you can see when the solution goes south due to constraints.

One final hazard of using constraints is when you place a false constraint on the solution. A perfect example of this happened to me on a shot in which I assumed two walls were at 90 degrees to each other. The walls actually met at a 75 degree angle. The matchmove solution would consistently fail when constrained. Once I removed the constraints, the camera would solve again.

There are also additional constraints that can be placed on the camera that concern its internal parameters such as focal length. A focal length constraint might seem rather redundant, because you can always "fix" the focal length in the camera panel and force the software to solve as this fixed value. But focal length constraints (in the programs that have this feature) are primarily designed to work for variable lens (zoom) shots. The idea is that if the camera doesn't zoom for the entire duration of the shot, you could specify during which frames the camera is zooming. Given the somewhat unknown nature of the focal length during a zoom (or at least as far as the matchmoving software is concerned), you will most likely use this type of constraint with estimated (sometimes called *initialized*) values that serve as a starting point. The software can change this value if necessary to achieve good results.

I suppose the last word on constraints is this: use them sparingly and cautiously and they can be of great help, but use them too much or with inaccurate data and you might be sorry.

Reference Photos

Some matchmove programs allow you use reference stills in addition to the plate itself in order to solve the matchmove. Conceptually, it's not too different than having a few extra frames of footage. The main reason to do this is to introduce more parallax into the solution where little exists in the plate. If you have a still image of the same scene but from a different angle, it would give the solver a lot of parallax to work with.

MatchMover Pro calls such references "Helper Frames"; I will focus on their implementation of this feature, but you can find similar methods called by other names in other matchmoving applications. Initially, the workflow isn't any different than any other matchmove. First, you import the plate and begin placing 2D tracks. The addition of your Helper Frames is treated as though they were an extra sequence.

Using Helper Frames prohibits using the automatic tracker because the automatic engine will probably fail to track the still image. This means you must use manual tracking (at least for the Helper Frames), and if you track a feature in the plate, then you'll also want to track it in the still image as well. This establishes a correspondence between the plate and the still image that will later be used in the calibration.

Once you have placed all of your tracks in both the plate and the Helper Frame(s), you run a calibration. This calibration may or may not solve correctly the first time out. The reason for this is in the way the calibration engine works. If you remember from earlier chapters, the software first chooses two frames and generates a solution from them. When you are using Helper Frames, you will want at least one of those two main frames to be referencing your still image. If not, the images aren't really doing you any good. If the software doesn't do it for you automatically, you might need to manually specify that the reference images should be used as the two main frames. This can be done by right-clicking the selected frame and choosing Set Frames > First Reference.

A related technique can be more widely used with other software. This technique involves using one sequence to help solve another sequence and vice versa. To do this, you need to be sure that your matchmoving software supports solving multiple sequences at the same time. Basically, you can import both sequences and track them. Since they are being tracked in the same project, the software assumes they belong in the same world-space and tries to integrate them into a single solution with two cameras. This would again probably prohibit the use of automatic tracking.

Forcing a Calibration

Occasionally, the frames that the program is using to create its initial solution (*reference frames*) end up in the wrong place and need to be repositioned. The manipulation of reference frames can also be useful in resolving difficult matchmoves in which a portion of the shot contains parallax, but other parts do not. The technique for doing so is the same as above, but the thing to remember is to choose the new reference frames in an area where there is parallax.

For example, let's say you have a shot in which the camera dollies forward and then, near the end of the shot, stops and pans. After the calibration, the reference frames should be in the part of the shot where the camera is dollying (since that portion contains parallax) rather than the part where the camera is panning (which has no parallax). If this turns out to not be the case, then the reference frames can be moved and the camera recalibrated.

Faking the Focal Length

For times when the calibration is giving you difficulty for one reason or another, I have little trick that sometimes helps the program figure things out. In particular, this is useful in situations when you do not know the focal length of the camera, and the program is giving you a solution that is close but not perfectly solved.

Solving for the focal length of the camera is computationally expensive and can sometimes be a contributing factor when a solution fails. This trick involves giving the program a "false" focal length from which it can then create a better solution. But what focal length do you give it?

The first step is to solve for the camera while letting the program try to solve the focal length on its own. This will produce the weak or bad solution that you've been trying to make work, but that's okay. Once you have the "bad" solution, go to the camera's parameters and see what focal length the program computed. With any luck, it is a reasonable number—that is, a focal length that seems close to what you're viewing in the images. You can then plug this computed value back into the camera settings; this time, however, switch the camera to a fixed value that the program can't change. Then recalibrate the scene.

Many times, this simple step helps the program achieve a good solution—or at least a better solution than before. Since the program doesn't have to worry about computing the focal length the second time, it can instead focus on the task of figuring out the other camera parameters. Occasionally, this is all it takes to help the program along. Of course, this technique can only be used with fixed lenses.

Using Survey Data

On some productions (particularly bigger-budget movies), you might be afforded the luxury of having the set measured by a surveyor. Surveyors can use sophisticated tools to plot out the exact 3D positions of various features in the set. The exact method of survey might differ from job to job, but usually the information is given as a text file containing rows of data, each one corresponding to a particular point on the set and its X, Y, and Z position (Figure 10.6). This is often accompanied by a set of photographs or notes that specify which point represents each feature on the set. Basically, if you were to assign those translation values to a null for each item, you would begin to see how the set was laid out. You could then even build a proxy version of the set using those nulls. This set would be extremely accurate (at least in the parts where survey data exists).

```
Item    X       Y       Z       ID
1       1.749   8.709   8.709   CA1
2       8.708   0.987   9.168   CA2
3       6.080   9.879   8.408   T1
4       9.879   8.454   8.454   M1
5       6.878   0.051   8.974   M2
6       7.019   7.179   7.763   M3
7       0.900   7.921   7.972   M4
8       7.647   9.737   2.170   M5
9       9.423   1.312   6.129   M6
10      4.542   1.000   4.787   M7
11      4.245   7.556   7.154   M8|
```

Figure 10.6 Raw survey data

During set fitting, there are other uses for survey data as well. Since the surveyor's measurements have been converted into nulls, it is possible to make measurements between these markers to help define the scale of the scene in the matchmoving software. Most 3D packages have a way to measure between nulls, so if those features are visible in the plate and you have tracked them, you could use those measurements as a basis for your scale factor in the matchmove software.

Some matchmove programs can actually use the survey data to help solve the scene altogether. The workflow is very similar to a regular matchmove, in that you need to track features in the shot, but in this case, you would want to track the features that have been surveyed. Such programs have a field that allows you to assign the 3D coordinates of the tracked feature as measured by the surveyor. The software is then forced or constrained to use those values during calibration.

When everything goes well, this technique is amazing, because after calibration you simply export your 3D animation scene. When you open that up in your 3D animation package, the set is already fit for you! No creating camera rigs or adjusting the camera's position—it's already in the correct spot because the positioning is based on accurate information about the set.

But there are some problems that can arise when using survey data to help solve the matchmove. Perhaps the biggest restriction is that in order to use the survey data in a solution, you must be able to see it in the shot, and then be able to track it. For normal tracks, you need eight to 12 tracks, but with survey data, you can sometimes get away with as few as four. Since the positions of the survey points are already known, it takes a lot of the load off the solver. The solver really doesn't need to adjust or calculate the positions of the tracks, just the camera. Survey points can be mixed with nonsurvey points, but in that case, you will probably need at least three survey points tracked in addition to five or six non-survey points to get any sort of precise reconstruction of the space of the scene.

When using survey data in a solution, it is implemented as a constraint, and as such, it can help you as much as hurt. On the one hand, it guarantees accuracy, but on the other hand, it demands accuracy as well. Therefore, if the 2D tracks are not well tracked, the survey data might cause your solution to fail. Also, survey-based solutions tend to be highly sensitive to noise. This is because they rely very heavily on the exact positions of a few select tracks, and if those tracks have any noise at all, it can show up in the final camera solution. With normal 2D tracks, the best way to deal with noise is to throw more tracks at it, but since survey is a constraint, adding more survey tracks might actually do more harm than good. About all you can do in these situations is to make the survey tracks you do have as accurate as possible or add more nonsurvey tracks.

Finally, the survey data you receive might not be accurate due to a number of factors. The surveyor might have omitted markers, the photographs or notes about which point is which might be wrong, there might be transposition errors—many such things can sneak up on you. As you work with the data, you may want to monitor the points very closely to make sure that they seem to be accurately laid out (much as you would for nulls in your matchmove solution). If you are having problems solving, try disabling the trackers one at a time and see if you can discover which one is not working right.

All in all, if you are fortunate enough to receive survey data, it can make your job a lot easier, even if you only end up using it in a small percentage of your shots.

Building on the Matchmove

In this chapter, I've covered techniques for getting the right camera, but in the next chapter I'm going to show you another cool thing you can do with the data. I'll cover how to build up geometry based on the matchmove and discuss a related field: image-based modeling.

Modeling from Matchmoves and Image-Based Modeling

Besides cameras, matchmovers can also use their data to create 3D models of an environment. These can be made based on a matchmove or with another technique known as image-based modeling. Both of these techniques involve modeling an object while referencing the original images or image sequence and they are an efficient way to get models that fit correctly.

I've reserved this chapter to discuss various approaches to this process. I'll also discuss image-based modeling, which also uses photogrammetry for the purpose of modeling, rather than camera tracking.

11

Chapter Contents

Making Models from Matchmoves

I was working on a movie once when one of the lead technical directors came to me with a request. We were placing CG cars in an environment with a fairly complex lighting setup. We had plenty of photographic reference of the set and even survey data for much of the environment, from which we had built up a pretty good approximation of the real thing. The problem was that off to one side of the street was a large carousel with hundreds of lights on it, and unfortunately, this was one of the few items that wasn't surveyed or measured in any way.

Since the carousel contained so many lights, it would definitely play a large part in the lighting of the CG cars. The lead TD wanted to know if I could tell him where the carousel was, and if possible, its rough dimensions. Normally, the individual technical directors could simply make a good guess for their shot and run with it. The hope here, however, was to find out the carousel's position once and set up the lighting a single time so that it would be accurate in all of the shots.

To begin with, I looked at the four shots we had already matchmoved that showed the carousel. Two of them were too far away to show much detail, but the other two showed the carousel from slightly different views. I began by combining both cameras into a single scene so that I could look through the different cameras at the same object. I then created a null and tried to position it on a light that represented the middle of the carousel's top. I adjusted this null multiple times while checking it through both cameras until I had a position that worked through both of them.

Once I had the position of the top-center of the carousel, it was a simple matter to create and attach a cylinder to the null and slide it down into the correct position. To take it one step further, I added a little bit more detail to my model so that the TDs would know where various rows of lights were on the carousel, all by comparing my model to the images while looking through the matchmoved cameras.

I found the position and shape of the carousel by taking advantage of certain aspects of matchmove cameras, namely that they represent a known position in space from which to observe the scene. With a little bit of careful examination, you can find fairly precise positions of virtually anything seen in the image.

Modeling from matchmoves is done for a variety of reasons, but most often it's done to:

- Mark the location of an object in the scene

- Create objects for use with dynamics or particle simulations

- Help create a set replacement or extension

As you move down this list, the level of accuracy required for the model becomes more important. For example, marking the location of the object may not require a model quite as accurate as a dynamic object, which in turn may not need to be as accurate as an object being used for set replacement or extension.

The Basic Workflow

Before you begin trying to model from a matchmove, a few things should be in place.

Matchmove the Shot First of all, the shot must have been matchmoved. If you have multiple scenes that feature the same object, it will be easier to find an accurate position by fitting all of the matchmove cameras into the same scene and looking through all of them as you build your geometry. If you are seeing the object in only one shot, then you have the luxury of being able to tailor the geometry to that single camera.

Place 2D Tracks If you know in advance that you will need to do some modeling, it'll be helpful to place 2D tracks in positions that can be used to model key features. These tracks can serve as a framework upon which to hang your geometry and will give you the best accuracy. The exception to this is if you have solved the camera as a nodal pan. In this case, the locators generated by the matchmoving program will not represent actual 3D positions of the features you tracked.

Perform a Set Fitting Once the matchmove camera has been brought into your 3D animation package, you may or may not have to perform a set fitting. It could very well be that since you are building the geometry to the plate, it will simultaneously serve as the fitting. If you are building geometry from scratch, you'll want to make sure you're working in the right scale and orientation in order to make things consistent with the real scene. This is especially true if it is being used for dynamics, where scale differences could radically affect the outcome of a simulation.

Use Your Views When you begin to build the geometry, you look through the matchmove camera(s) with the plate in the background. This ensures the accuracy of the model relative to the plate. You want to keep a perspective view and *orthogonal* views open as well, to verify that your geometry is logical and properly laid out. It's very easy to model only from the matchmove camera only to realize later that the geometry is extremely skewed or warped.

Find the Position The first order of business is to find the position of a feature in the scene, from which you can begin figuring out the positions of other features. It's often easier to do this with a null object initially, because it represents a specific location and can be moved around quickly. Notice how in my earlier example, I began by finding the top-center part of the carousel. It would have been more difficult to find the position of the carousel using a cylinder—mostly because I didn't know the shape or size of the carousel anyway. By finding the center of it, I could then infer at least the center of the cylinder and from this find the scale and proportions of the cylinder.

You might also be able to find the positions of the objects using nulls that you've brought over from the matchmove program. The main limiting factor here would be whether the nulls are as accurate as they need to be. If you can look through the camera at these nulls and they appear to stick, they might work just fine. If not, you may have to create new ones to suit your purposes.

Build Your Geometry After finding the positions of key features with a null or identifying a matchmove null for the same purpose, you can then use a primitive shape, such as a plane or a cube, which approximates the geometry you are trying to create. If necessary, you can move the vertices of the object so that they line up (or snap to) the nulls that have come over from the matchmove (if you have them). It's always best to start with the parts of the model that correspond to nulls from the matchmove, since those are the most accurate points in the scene relative to your matchmoved camera. For areas where there are no locators, you will have to use the plate as your reference.

If the scene you are modeling is fairly geometric, like a group of buildings or an interior scene, you can flesh out quite a bit of the scene by systematically modeling the environment. For example, let's say you've tracked the top corners of a building so that you can position a cube in the right spot. From that you can extend the cube down to the ground (while referencing the plate). Next you can slide another cube along the ground to find out where the next building is and scale it up from there to determine its height and shape, etc. In the next section, we'll do a tutorial that shows exactly how this is done.

Courtesy Greg Downing

Modeling Tutorial

Modeling from a camera's point of view is not too radically different from normal modeling, but the one crucial difference is that you must first try to accurately estimate the camera's position. Whether this is done from still images or a matchmove depends on the project. For this tutorial, we'll use a single still image. The same principles apply to a matchmove, but by using a still image, we can focus on the modeling aspect of the project.

Since we are working with a still image, we need to do a perspective match on the camera. This process is exactly the same as the perspective matching tutorial in Chapter 1. For this tutorial, you'll need the image downtown2.jpg in the Chapter 11 folder on the companion CD. I use Maya for this tutorial, but you can apply these same techniques to virtually any animation program.

1. The first order of business is to create a camera and put the image in its background. To do this in Maya, choose Create > Cameras > Camera. I set the Camera Aperture settings to 0.980 × 0.735 inch and left the focal length at the default 35mm. If you import the plane before changing the Aperture, be sure to click the Fit to Film Gate button in the Placement section of the Image Plane's Attribute Editor.

    You can add the image as an image plane by opening the Attribute Editor for the camera (Ctrl+A), and then opening the Environment section and clicking the Create button next to the Image Plane option. When the imagePlane panel comes up, click the folder next to the Image Name field and select the downtown2.jpg image (Figure 11.1).

Figure 11.1
The original photograph

2. Set the camera height. There aren't any measurements for this camera, but it's reasonably safe to assume that the camera is at eye level. To reproduce this in my scene, I set the camera to 1.82m on the Y-axis.

3. Since this image contains strong lines of perspective on the ground, you can use this to get a first rough positioning of the camera in the scene. But you'll need a ground plane, so create a polygon plane (Create > Polygon Primitives > Plane). For starters, I gave mine 10 subdivisions on the X- and Y-axes and an overall size of 100m (Figure 11.2).

4. Rotate the camera to get the polygon plane to match the perspective you see in the lines on the street. It's more beneficial to restrict yourself to rotating the camera only; don't change the orientation or scale of the polygon plane just yet. The results of this rotation are shown in Figure 11.3. The exact values you use may vary slightly, but the rotation values I ended up with were X: 10.23, Y: –9.184, Z: –0.356.

Figure 11.2 The camera and plane after the initial placement

Figure 11.3 The initial perspective match with the ground plane

These first few steps help to find a starting point for the perspective match. As we place geometry, we will be checking and adjusting the position of the camera at the same time.

Making the Buildings

In our scene, the ground plane seems to match the right perspective, but we need to double-check this by adding in some rough geometry that represents the buildings. Just as we did in Chapter 1, we'll use the corner of a building to zero in on a more exact camera position. For my project, I chose the closest building on the right side.

1. Begin by creating a simple cube (in Maya, Create > Polygon Primitives > Cube). I guessed that the building on the right was about 50 feet tall (15.24m) and relatively square, so my cube was 15.24m on all sides. I also moved the cube so that the bottom of the cube was at ground level.

   Next, you'll try and find the position of the building in the scene. This can be a little bit challenging at this stage, since you're not entirely sure that the camera is correct yet. To help figure this out, you'll use the exact same steps we used in Chapter 1. You'll start by just pushing the cube out there and seeing what it looks like.

2. When modeling to a photograph, I like to "feel" my way around the scene by carefully translating the object. You know that the building rests on the ground and so does your cube, so you don't want to translate the cube on the Y-axis. It's hard to tell the building's exact location relative to the camera because it is off to one side, but there is a way to get a reasonable idea of where it is.

   You can't see where the front edge of the building is since that part is off-screen to the right. But you can see the front edge of the sidewalk, so that will make a good starting point. Slide the cube away from the camera (on the Z-axis) until the front edge of the cube is flush with the front edge of the sidewalk or the front lines of the crosswalk (Figure 11.4).

3. Next, slide the cube over on the X-axis until the left edge is aligned with the left edge of the building, just below the columns (Figure 11.5). If you want to be really accurate here, you could first align the left edge of the cube with the right-side sidewalk, then raise it a bit to account for the height of the sidewalk, then scoot it over and align it with the wall.

   Now that you know where (approximately) the left edge of the building is, you can slide the cube a little farther down the Z-axis so that it lines up at the top corner. But hold on a second—when you do this, it doesn't match the perspective correctly! That means something's wrong.

Figure 11.4 The first building is pushed down the Z-axis until its front edge is flush with the sidewalk.

Figure 11.5 The building is then slid over on the X-axis until its left edge matches up with the left edge of the building.

4. Check the perspective of the objects in your scene and see if any adjustment is necessary. This takes a little bit of experimentation to get the right results. Three factors could cause problems: the focal length of the camera, the rotation of the

camera, or the position of the building. Begin by checking out various areas of the scene by sliding the cube around on the ground and seeing how the perspective looks. In my scene, the perspective of the cube was working fairly well as I pushed the cube away from the camera, but when I scaled up the cube vertically, it seemed to pull away more. This seemed to indicate that the focal length was wrong. If this is the case with your scene as well, you can check this with another test. Duplicate the cube and try roughly aligning your two cubes with the buildings down the right side of the street. If the spacing seems strange and the buildings seem to be elongated along the Z-axis (Figure 11.6), it is another indicator that the focal length is wrong. This stretching effect points to the fact that the focal length is probably wider than what you are currently using.

Knowing this, I began experimenting with wider focal lengths, first a 32mm, then a 30mm, and finally a 28mm lens. Each time I changed the focal length, I had to adjust the rotation of the camera to make the perspective work. By adjusting the focal length and rotation alternately, I found something that seemed to work pretty well. My rotational values ended up being X: 12.789, Y: –9.159, Z: –0.769.

5. Now that the focal length is working better, it's time to massage the camera's position into its final resting place. Move the cube that represents the closest building on the right again (delete the other cubes if necessary), and slide it around until the upper corner lines up with the upper corner of the building just below the cornice. I don't suggest using the corner at the very top of the cornice, because it will be harder to find the position of the lower part of the building later.

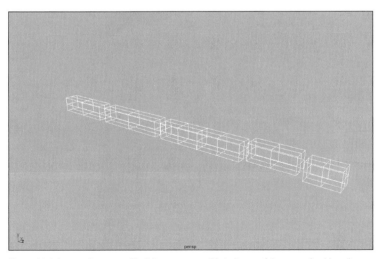

Figure 11.6 Longer-than-normal buildings are a possible indicator of the wrong focal length.

6. Next, you need to create a null or group above the camera that allows you to move it off axis. In Maya, I grouped the camera (Ctrl+G) and then moved its pivot point to the top-right corner of the cube. (Press the Insert key, then hold the v key to snap to the cube's corner vertex.)

 Note: It may be easier in some 3D packages to create a null and snap that to the corner of the cube, then parent the camera under the null. This could be used instead of moving an object's pivot point.

7. From here, you can simply rotate the camera's parent group until the perspective works. I ended up rotating the group mostly on the Y-axis and a little bit on the Z-axis as well (since the camera was slightly tilted to the right).

8. After a bit of tweaking, you should end up with a camera that's fairly close. As a final test, and subsequent tweak, duplicate your cube and slide it across the street to line up with the building on the left. In my scene, I could see some slight misregistration problems, so I continued to adjust the rotation of the camera and the camera's group until both buildings fit (Figure 11.7). You might try this with another building as well. The third building on the right is useful because it is rectangular and therefore easy to compare to your geometry.

9. Name the objects that you have so far in the scene. Let's call the building on the right Bldg_R1 and the one on the left Bldg_L1. Also rename the ground plane polygon to Street.

Figure 11.7 The first two buildings fit into place.

Making the Rest of the Buildings

Fortunately, most of the hard work is already done. Now we need to figure out where the rest of the buildings are in relation to the ones we just placed. We'll start with the right side of the street first.

1. Duplicate the Bldg_R1 object and name it Bldg_R3. Why did we skip R2? The second building on the right looks as though it's set back from the street farther than the first building. The third building seems to be flush with the first building, so it will be easier to fit.

Slide the Bldg_R3 object back on the Z-axis until its front corner matches up to the front corner of the third building on the right. The cube is obviously smaller than it needs to be, so first make sure the cube's pivot is at the bottom-front corner and scale it on the Z- and Y-axes until it is the same shape as the one in the image (Figure 11.8).

Figure 11.8 To place the third building, move it back on the Z-axis, then rescale to fit.

2. Now you're ready to tackle the second building on the right. This time, duplicate the Bldg_R3 object. Rename the duplicated object Bldg_R2 and slide it back on the X-axis until its front corner lines up with the corner of the building farthest away from the camera (Figure 11.9). You are making the assumption here that these two buildings butt up against each other, so by sliding the object back on the X-axis, you are finding out where the corner of the second building meets the wall of the third building.

Since the Bldg_R2 object is now the correct distance back from the street, you can slide it toward the camera on the Z-axis until its front corner closest to the camera lines up with the same corner on the front of the building in the image. For now, just work on the dark part of the building closest to the street. Scale this object until it fits (Figure 11.10).

Figure 11.9 To figure out the location of the second building, you can translate the existing building back on the X-axis.

Figure 11.10 The front part of second building in position

3. You can figure out where the other parts of the second building are located in the same way you figured out where the front of it was. Depending on your modeling skills, you can subdivide the cube and slide the vertices forward until they match the inner corner of where the white part of the building meets the dark part. Then extrude the faces and repeat it for the dark part farthest from the street (Figure 11.11).

A simpler way to do this is to duplicate the Bldg_R2 cube, slide it back until its corner is in the inner corner, slide it forward on the Z-axis until it lines up with the outer corner, and then rescale it. You can repeat this to get the last part of the building. This route is easier, but the model won't be as "clean" geometry-wise.

4. The rest of the buildings on the right side can be made fairly quickly by repeating these steps. Just duplicate the current building, rename it, slide it farther down the Z-axis, and scale it from the bottom corner to fit. As you go down the street, you'll notice that the bottoms of the buildings start to change as they go up the hill. Don't worry about the bottoms just yet. I'll show you how to deal with that later. When you're all done with the right side, you should have something that looks like Figure 11.12.

Figure 11.11 Second building done

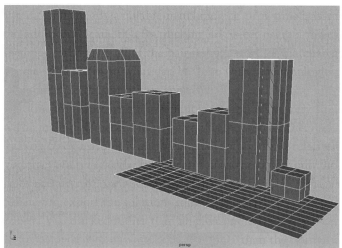

Figure 11.12 Right side of the street done

5. The left side is done exactly as the right. Duplicate the first building and slide it back to fit. You can only really see the first three buildings on the left clearly, but there is another farther down the street. You can find the position of this building by sliding a duplicate farther back until it looks right (Figure 11.13).

Figure 11.13 Left side done

Modeling the Street

The last thing to do is to model the street. The hill in the distance is a little bit challenging, but by careful study of the image, we can work out its slope.

1. The Street object you made at the beginning of this tutorial is probably not big enough to reach all the way back, so the first order of business is to scale it down the Z. You may also want to move it farther down the Z since you can't really see what's behind the camera anyway. Since the hill slopes up, it's a little hard to tell how far back you need to scale it. I scaled mine up by about 10. You can always adjust it later.

2. The best way to tell how high the street is at each distance is to see where the street meets the buildings on the right side. For each building, select the vertices for the bottom of the building and move them up until they are aligned with where the building meets the street. Remember to grab all the vertices on the edge to avoid having just the front of the building move up.

3. Move down the street and do this for each corner of each building on the right. When you're finished, you should be able to look at the buildings in a side view and see the slope of the bottom of the buildings as they go up the hill. You can adjust these as necessary until you have a smooth rise that matches the image.

4. Now that the buildings show you the slope of the hill, select the vertices of the Street object and raise them up until they meet the bottoms of the buildings, and *voilà*! You have a hill (Figure 11.14).

5. Of course, you can model more than just the rough shapes if you want or need to. From here it becomes a simple matter of adding the detail where you want it (Figure 11.15).

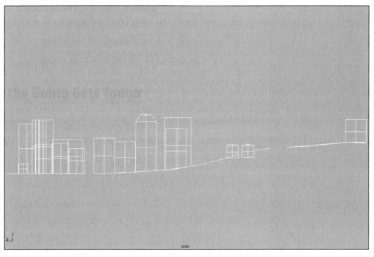

Figure 11.14 Side view of the modeled street, which shows the slope of the street

Figure 11.15 Final model

Image-Based Modeling

Image-based modeling is a kissing cousin of matchmoving. In fact, the two disciplines use the same photogrammetric processes. The main difference between image-based modeling and modeling from matchmoves is twofold: first, image-based modeling is usually done with two or more still images, and second, image-based modeling usually entails more extensive modeling and sometimes texturing of objects.

Courtesy Greg Downing

The Basic Workflow

The workflow for image-based modeling follows a very similar workflow as matchmoving.

Specify Correspondence Points First, the user specifies correspondence points between features in various still images. This is similar in concept to 2D tracking in matchmoving, only the correspondence points don't need to "track" the feature since they are placed by the user (Figure 11.16).

Calibrate the Cameras Once key correspondence points are identified, as in a matchmove, the cameras are calibrated (Figure 11.17). Rather than a single camera for an entire sequence, this calibration generates multiple still cameras. In some respects, the calibration process is simplified because it deals with a smaller number of images. This can also be a bad thing if the corresponding features don't show up in the images.

Most image-based modeling programs have the ability to deal with radically different camera angles and different camera types in one project (you can mix images from a still camera with a frame from a movie camera or with a frame from a video camera). This gives you more flexibility when deciding what types of images you'll want to use.

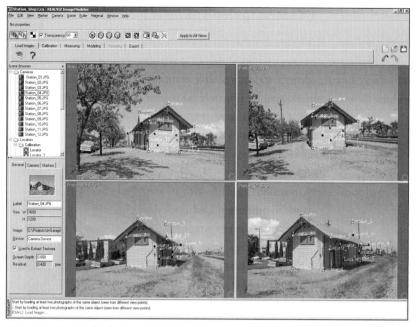

Figure 11.16 The interface for Realviz's ImageModeler, an image-based modeling program

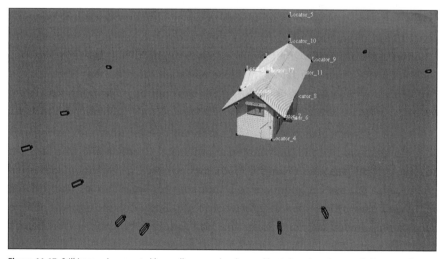

Figure 11.17 Still images (represented by small cameras here) are calibrated much as they are during a matchmove.

Make Your Model Once you've achieved a calibration in an image-based modeler, you get down to what the program was meant to do—model. The modeling tools are very similar to standard modeling tools found in most 3D animation packages, but they usually have been enhanced to work with calibrated cameras. For example, some tools allow you to set the coordinate system and scale. Other tools provide you with multiple ways to snap geometry to locators and to other surfaces (Figure 11.18). It differs significantly from modeling in an animation package, mostly because of the way the cameras are laid out. In an animation program, you work in perspective and orthogonal views to create the model. In image-based modelers, you may not have orthogonal views to work with, but instead have multiple perspective views that are bound to camera positions.

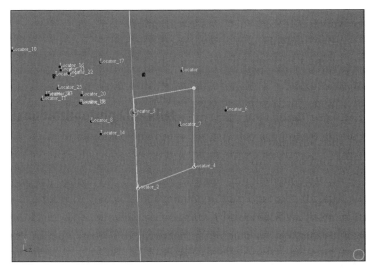

Figure 11.18 Image-based modeling programs have special tools, such as snapping, that help you take advantage of calibration data.

Pull Textures One of the most interesting features of image-based modeling programs is their ability to create or "pull" textures from the images used to photograph the scene. Since the model is built with these images, the fit of the texture is highly accurate and realistic with a minimum amount of fuss. In addition to pulling the texture, they also can perform a process known as *rectification,* which removes the angled distortion from a texture and squares it up with the edges of the objects. In traditional modeling, this is done by the texture artist using paint programs.

The process of pulling textures is not unlike the process for *camera projections.* Camera projections can be done by most 3D animation software; in simple terms, you project the image through the camera onto an object. This is often done to cheat perspective or parallax in still images. There is usually a limit as to how far you can move the camera before the camera projection becomes apparent (Figure 11.19).

a

b

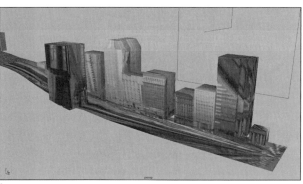

c

Figure 11.19 An example of camera projection: (a) The original image. (b) The image as projected back onto the geometry we just modeled. This camera shows a slightly different point of view than the original. (c) How the projection looks from the side.

Image-based models differ in one other respect, and that is how the textures are created. Since the textures are created from specific images, the lighting information from those images is baked into the model. Many times, this doesn't present a problem because the lighting conditions need to match the plate anyway. But if a TD is planning on enhancing the lighting of the environment, it could be inconsistent with the lighting present on the model. For example, if a harsh shadow was on the object when it was photographed, that shadow will appear on the image-based model (Figure 11.20). When lit from another direction, it looks odd. The best way to avoid this problem is to take images in a neutral lighting environment, such as outside on a cloudy day, or in a studio with multiple lights around the object.

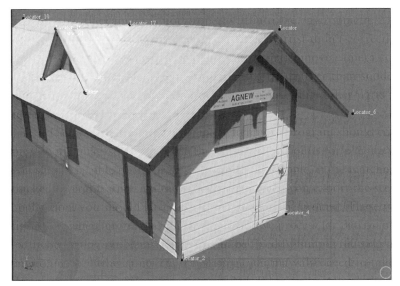

Figure 11.20 The harsh sunlight that was present in the photo will be present in the texture. If we wanted to relight this model from another angle, it might look strange.

Common Problems with Image-Based Modeling

Image-based modeling can have many of the same problems as matchmoving, and a few more on top of that. The most common problem, as in matchmoving, is obtaining a decent calibration. The good news is that most of the matchmoving troubleshooting techniques you've learned in this book can be applied to image-based modeling as well. All the same rules apply: proper spacing, minimum number of tracks, tracking immobile objects, etc. Conceptually, you could look at it as though the series of still images were merely a movie sequence.

Another problem area has to do with textures and their quality. For the most part, the textures you pull will only be as good as the images they were drawn from, so if the images are not of good quality, there's little chance the textures will be any better.

And perhaps the last item that can give you headaches is getting the right photos. There are so many variables that can ruin a photograph, especially for a 3D artist who isn't necessarily a photographer. Problems in this area include bad exposure settings, blurry photos or photos of insufficient resolution, and just not having enough photos from the angles you need to properly model the object.

And That's Not All...

As you can see, creating geometry from matchmoved cameras can be extremely useful. Some proprietary software used by large effects houses can even perform automatic generation of geometry within the matchmove program. Given the utility of this feature, I'm sure it's only a matter of time before this is part of the commercially available matchmove programs.

Of course, modeling isn't the only thing you can do with matchmove data. In the next chapter, I discuss other ways to put all of your hard-earned matchmove information to work.

Multipurposing
Matchmove Data

Matchmovers gather or generate all sorts of data during the matchmove process. We've already seen how that information can be used to mark the key locations of objects within a scene and even to build models from them. In this chapter, I show you some alternate uses for matchmove data and how the data can benefit other artists in the pipeline. You might never need to use these techniques, but I present them here as food for thought.

Chapter Contents
Creating Special Cameras
Matchmoves for Paint Work: Patchmoves
Matchmoves for Compositors
Matchmoves for TD Work

Creating Special Cameras

For the most part, matchmoves involve tracking a camera and then delivering that camera correctly placed into a 3D environment. There are times, however, when the camera you must deliver needs some special treatment to achieve a desired effect, such as adding to or blending a camera move. The bulk of this work happens in the 3D animation program, so the exact procedures will vary, but these techniques are generic enough that you can use them with virtually any program.

Extending or Enhancing Matchmoves

Sometimes the matchmove created from the plate is just the beginning (or end) of a camera move. On occasion, the director may want to begin with the real camera move and then transition to an entirely artificial camera move. There may also be times when you need movement on the matchmove camera in addition to the real camera's movement. Either way, you must take care to avoid creating inconsistent camera moves or breaking the matchmove.

Extending a matchmove camera is a relatively straightforward procedure, much like extending the animation of any animated object. You place new keyframes after the matchmove keyframes (or before the matchmove keyframes if you're adding animation to the front of the shot) and then edit them as you do any other type of animation. The main difficulty you may encounter is that the matchmoved camera is generally keyframed on every frame. This can make it difficult to extend the animation curves properly.

I try to maintain the general flow of all the channels of animation (Figure 12.1). For example, if the X-translation channel is sweeping gently downward, I try to continue the general shape of that curve to help transition it into the artificial camera move. If your curves match the gross movement, then the seam shouldn't be apparent.

If the matchmove camera's animation curves contain a lot of noise or jitter, the transition to the artificial camera may stand out more. This is because the real camera has a lot of high-frequency noise, whereas the artificial camera has none. To remedy this, you simply need to introduce some camera shake into your artificial camera move.

When extending the camera move, you may be tempted to edit some of the matchmove keys or delete them altogether. Whether or not you can do this really depends on the nature of the camera move, plate, etc., but you should be careful. Any time you edit the matchmoved keyframes, you run the risk of breaking the matchmove for those frames. If you do edit them, make sure to check that the matchmove is still working.

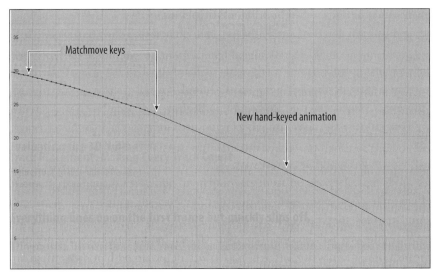

Figure 12.1 In order to get a smooth transition, you should try to match the overall animation curves.

Besides extending matchmoves, you might also be asked to enhance the overall camera move associated with a matchmove. For example, let's say that you matchmoved an actor who was filmed on a stage, and she was supposed to be inside a train car that is moving down the tracks. The stage, of course, is static, and the matchmove is done relative to the stage. In order to get the secondary movement of the train moving down the tracks, the CG train must be animated moving down the tracks, and the CG camera must move with it.

The simplest way to get the camera to move down the tracks is to parent it to the train with the animation on it. This has the same effect as when we parented our camera under a group to fit the camera into the set, except here the parent over the camera is animated. As long as the camera, its associated 3D nulls, and the object it is supposed to be moving with (in this case, the train) all move together, the matchmove shouldn't break (Figure 12.2).

More often than not, an animator, layout artist, or technical director will be performing the secondary animation that the camera needs to inherit. The best thing you can do for them is to parent the camera under a null or group and indicate that they should use that null/group to animate the camera within their scene. This way they can simply parent that null under their moving object or else animate the null directly, and consequently they won't break the matchmove.

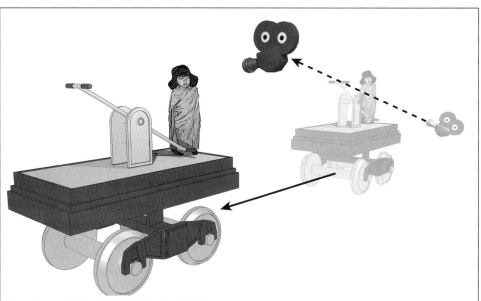

Figure 12.2 Animation can be added to a matchmove camera as long as it is done on a parent object. In this case, the original camera move was straight up. When this camera is parented to the train car, it inherits the forward motion, and therefore the overall camera move is more of a diagonal.

Blending Matchmoves

Blending two separate matchmoves involves a similar process to extending a matchmove but with a few extra twists. The real trick is to make sure that each section of the new matchmove fits together properly and that the transitions remain seamless.

If there needs to be extra frames between the matchmoves, you can begin by performing each camera's set fitting as you normally would, except that you are fitting both cameras into the same set. You can group the camera or parent it under a null and then move that group to the appropriate position within the scene for each camera. Once you are happy with the position of each individual camera, and you have slid their keyframes to the appropriate time range, you can then combine the camera move. How you do this will vary depending on your animation package, but here are a couple of suggestions:

- Bake each individual camera so that its keyframes are in world space, then copy the keys from one camera onto the other.
- Use dynamic parenting or constraints to have one camera follow the other during the frames it is not matchmoved.

When combining the animation of cameras with variable focal lengths, make sure that you transfer the focal length animation as well.

> **N o t e :** This method of blending camera moves isn't only for splicing together two completely different shots; it is also useful for piecing together partial solutions from matchmoving programs. Sometimes difficult shots cannot be solved in their entirety, but you might be able to solve small portions of the shot. If you have multiple partial solutions, you could conceivably blend them together into a full solution.

Things can be much more difficult if you are trying to splice two matchmoves end-to-end, and fortunately this doesn't happen too often. The main reasons this may come up are if the shots are supposed to jump-cut together or if one plate is being blended to another.

If the shot is intended as a jump-cut, you can pretty much follow the same procedure for combining cameras that I just mentioned, except pay particular attention to how each camera is fitted into the set so that the CG elements jump the exact same way as the real cameras do. If the plate has been spliced, you can go a couple of different ways, but this may be one of those rare cases where it's better to matchmove to the modified (i.e., blended) plate. In these cases, pay particular attention to the spliced part of the plate and be aware that it may give the matchmoving programs difficulty. In those situations, you'll often end up manually matching the plate during the transition areas.

Blending Cameras in Maya

Maya has a particularly elegant way of blending motions that I've found extremely useful with cameras, so I think it's worth giving a special mention here. With Maya you can use constraints to help blend the movements of two or more cameras without the headache of copying keys.

Let's say you want to blend two matchmoved cameras together and need a 100-frame transition between them where the camera move is entirely artificial. The following sections show how to do this by creating a camera blending rig in Maya.

Set Up Your Matchmove Cameras

1. Import in your first matchmove camera (let's call this Camera_A). If it's not already grouped under another node, group it. Do the same thing with the second matchmove camera (Camera_B). You should shift the keyframes of the second matchmove so that they start 100 frames after the first matchmove's last keyframe.

2. Fit each matchmove camera into the set or environment as you normally would. Try to keep in mind that they must relate to each other, and the placement should be consistent with that (Figure 12.3).

3. Create a third camera that has the same settings as one of the matchmove cameras, or else duplicate one of the matchmove cameras (this will be Camera_C).

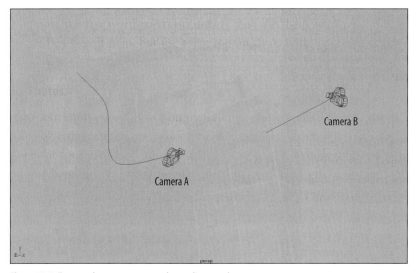

Figure 12.3 Two matchmove cameras ready to splice together

Constrain the Cameras

The next thing to do is to get Camera_C to do Camera_A's movement during the first part and Camera_B's movement during the second part. You'll use constraints to do this, but you need to add another component to your rig first.

1. Create a locator and name it CameraFollower.

2. Select Camera_A, Camera_B, and the CameraFollower locator in that order. Then choose Constrain > Parent and open its options. For those of you unfamiliar with the Parent Constraint, it's like a combination of a Point Constraint and an Orient Constraint. In this case, you'll need to constrain all the channels, and you should make sure that Maintain Offset is not checked. When you've done this, click Add to make the constraint.

The locator should jump to a position halfway between the two matchmoved cameras (Figure 12.4). Furthermore, when either of the cameras moves, the locator moves too. By selecting both of the cameras first, we've constrained the locator to both of them, but since they both have a weight of 1.0, the locator averages the position and rotation of both cameras.

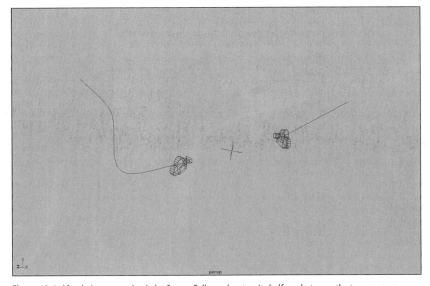

Figure 12.4 After being constrained, the CameraFollower locator sits halfway between the two cameras.

Keyframe the Constraint

The CameraFollower locator will be the base for the camera rig, but it needs to follow each camera's move one at a time in order to do us any good. I'll explain why in a bit, but for now you need to adjust the constraint so that the CameraFollower locator follows Camera_A during the first part of the shot and Camera_B during the second. To do that, you need to keyframe the constraint's weight.

1. Open up the Outliner (Window > Outliner), and you should see the Parent Constraint under the CameraFollower locator. Select this constraint and look in the Channel Box. At the bottom of the attributes list, you should see two items that say something like "Camera_A W0" and "Camera_B W1" (Figure 12.5).

2. These values represent how strongly weighted the constraint is to each camera. A weight of 0 means the locator is not constrained to the camera at all, whereas a weight of 1 means that the locator is entirely constrained to the camera. Since both of the weights are set to 1, the camera splits the difference and finds an average position between them both. Try setting the W1 attribute's value to 0. The locator should snap to the position of Camera_A. This is because now the locator is only fully constrained to Camera_A's position.

3. Next, you'll keyframe the constraint so that the CameraFollower locator follows the appropriate camera at the appropriate time. Go to the last keyframe of Camera_A. If you haven't already done so, set the W0 field to 1 and the W1 field to 0. The locator should snap to Camera_A's position. Set a keyframe for both of the weight attributes. Now go to the first frame of Camera_B and set the values on the constraint weight field to the opposite value so that W0 is 0 and W1 is 1.

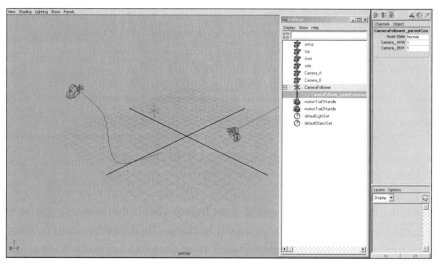

Figure 12.5 The values for the constraint weighting are shown in the Channel Box.

Your locator should now be following Camera_A while it is moving and Camera_B while it is moving, but notice what is happening in between. The locator gradually transitions between the two cameras for the 100-frame gap between them. This is handy because the transition area is interpolated for you so you don't have to guess. Furthermore, you can adjust the curves in the Graph Editor if you want to have it ease in or out as you please (Figure 12.6).

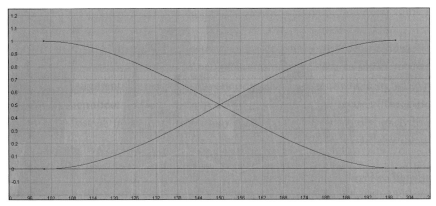

Figure 12.6 The transition of the locator can be controlled by animating the constraint weights. Here the animation has been modified to ease in and ease out the transition movement by flattening the tangents.

Connect the Camera to the Rig

The last thing to do is to hook up Camera_C to the rig to make it follow along as well.

1. Select the CameraFollower locator and then Camera_C in that order. Choose Constrain > Parent. Camera_C should now be following the CameraFollower.

2. Open the Outliner and find the Parent Constraint under Camera_C and delete the constraint. Without changing the current frame, parent the camera to the CameraFollower locator by middle-mouse-dragging Camera_C onto CameraFollower in the Outliner. Scrub the Timeline. Camera_C should now be following both Camera_A and Camera_B at the appropriate times just as the CameraFollower locator does (Figure 12.7).

3. Hook up the focal length of the camera so that it follows along as well. If both of your matchmoves have fixed focal lengths, and the focal lengths are the same, then you could simply change the value of Camera_C to match. If, however, the focal lengths of the two cameras are different, or the cameras have variable focal lengths, you will need to get the focal length data from the two individual cameras onto the new camera. There are a couple of ways to do this. First, you could copy the focal length keyframes from each of the matchmove cameras onto Camera_C.

Another, more flexible way is to write an expression. To do this, select Camera_C and, in the Channel Box, right-click the name of the Focal Length attribute and choose Expressions.

4. This brings up the Expression Editor, where you can create your expression. Make sure that Camera_C is selected and type the following expression in the Expression field near the bottom of the window:

```
$curFrame = `currentTime -q`;
$endCamA = 100; //replace this value with the end frame of the first cam
$begCamB = 200; //replace this value with the beginning frame of the
second cam
if($curFrame <= $endCamA)
    focalLength = Camera_A.focalLength;
if($curFrame >= $begCamB)
    focalLength = Camera_B.focalLength;
```

If you know how to write expressions, this is an admittedly simple expression. If you don't, let me explain what it does.

The first three lines define a few variables for the current frame, as well as what frame the first matchmove camera ends on and what frame the second matchmove starts on. You will need to replace the values I've made in this sample expression with the actual values where your matchmoves end/start.

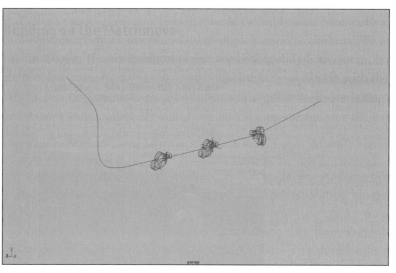

Figure 12.7 Camera_C now follows both of the original cameras, with a smooth transition in between.

The next line says that if the current time is less than or equal to the last frame of the first camera, then do the following line, which says that Camera_C's focal length is the same as Camera_A's. The next two lines say the same thing, except that if the current time is later than the first frame of Camera_B, then the focal length is the same as Camera_B.

When this expression is placed on Camera_C, Camera_C assumes the focal length of Camera_A for the first 100 frames and Camera_B's focal length after frame 200. This expression does have one shortcoming in that it assumes the focal length is the same value at the end of the first matchmove and the beginning of the second matchmove. If the focal length did need to change during the transition, it could be hand-keyed or even done with a more complicated expression, but that's getting well beyond the scope of this book.

That's all there is to it. We've created a pretty nice camera rig for blending cameras. The beautiful thing about this rig is that it allows you total flexibility in case something needs to change. Let's say that you need to fix a problem with Camera_A's matchmove. Any changes you make to Camera_A's keyframes will automatically update on Camera_C. The same thing applies if you move any of the cameras or parts of the rig. You can still move the matchmove camera groups independently, adjust either original camera's keyframes, or adjust either camera's focal length.

In creating this rig, you could have constrained Camera_C directly to Camera_A and Camera_B and achieved the same results. But instead I had you constrain a locator and then parent Camera_C to that locator. The reason for this is to add one more degree of freedom in the rig. If you had constrained Camera_C directly to the other two cameras, then you couldn't animate it during the transition. By inserting the CameraFollower locator, you can animate Camera_C independently of the constrained locator.

To change the animation of the camera during the transition, you can simply keyframe Camera_C. Just remember that you should place a keyframe on Camera_C on the first and last frames of the transition so that you don't accidentally add any animation to Camera_C during the times it should be following either Camera_A or Camera_B (Figure 12.8).

I've found this rig very helpful in trying to piece together matchmoves since it allows me a high degree of control of the entire camera move and it's extremely flexible. It has proved to be an invaluable tool many times.

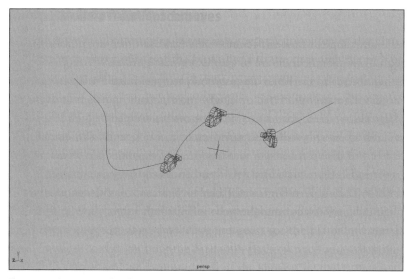

Figure 12.8 By animating directly on Camera_C, we can create virtually any animation we want in the transition area.

Object Track as a Camera Track

Sometimes it is not possible for a director to achieve the camera move they would like using real cameras, and those directors who are technology-savvy know that there are ways to fudge this using CG. Most often this involves items or actors shot on blue screen in which large parts of the final shot will be all CG.

For example, in one of the final scenes of *Sky Captain and the World of Tomorrow*, the actors were supposed to be in a life pod floating in the water while the camera moved in a large 360-degree circle around them as it revealed a fantastic all-CG environment. Since the actors were filmed on a blue-screen stage, it wasn't possible to move the camera in such a manner. Instead, the actors were placed in a small mock version of the pod. The camera stayed stationary while the pod the actors were in spun around in place.

In order to extract the desired camera move from the plate, we matchmoved the scene using markers only on the actor's pod, using a matchmove program in what essentially amounted to an object track. When we were ready to export the camera from the matchmove program, we chose to export the move as a moving camera with a static object rather than vice versa. This gave us a nice circular camera motion around a static pod. When you looked at the scene through the matchmove camera, the actors appeared correctly locked to the CG scene.

Matchmoving programs make this process easy, but if you had to do it by hand, it could be exceedingly difficult. This little trick relies on the fact that the shot is trackable using a matchmove program.

Matchmoves for Paint Work: "Patchmoves"

Sometimes during filming, actors who need to be in precarious or potentially dangerous situations are fitted with safety wires in case they fall. While this is a necessary safety precaution, it can quickly become a headache for postproduction, since wherever the wires appear in front of set elements, they need to be removed by a paint artist in a process known as *wire removal*.

Paint artists usually paint out the wires frame by frame or by combining a single good frame with 2D tracking (done in compositing software) to make the paint work move exactly as the set does in the footage. This process is not easy. It's time-consuming and a real strain on the eyes. In certain cases, the camera move from the matchmove can help solve some difficult painting tasks.

One way to do this is inspired by a method matte painters sometimes use to generate 3D matte paintings. The matte painting technique goes something like this:

1. A 3D model of the environment is rendered through the matchmoved camera.

2. Matte painters use a frame of this render as the starting point for their matte painting.

3. The matte painting is then reprojected through a single frame of the matchmove camera onto the geometry again.

This method allows for more-dynamic matte paintings because it adds an extra dimension to the matte paintings. When the camera is slightly translated, the painting exhibits parallax and depth not possible in a 2D painting.

This technique can be modified to help with paint work. Instead of using the 3D geometry in the scene for a matte painting projection, the artist can use a clean plate to remove the wires. This modified process is a method one of my matchmovers labeled "patchmove," and it goes as follows:

1. The paint artist chooses a frame of the sequence to use when painting out the wires.

2. The paint artist removes the wire for the selected frame and gives the image to a matchmover.

3. The matchmover takes the new wireless image and reprojects it through the matchmove camera at the same frame. The camera-projected objects are rendered using the matchmove camera for the entire shot and given back to the paint artist.

4. The paint artist examines the new camera projection render and makes sure everything works properly against the plate.

Of course, in this example, the matchmover is creating the camera projections, but it also could be done by a TD or animator. The main reason this method works at all is because the scene is already matchmoved and the scene's geometry can be repurposed for wire removal.

There are limitations as to how and when this technique can be used. First of all, it usually works only on fairly geometric surfaces, such as walls and floors. The paint work will potentially replace large sections of the existing plate, and irregular or organic shapes might reveal that paint work is present rather than the real image. Errors of this type usually look like there is an image embedded within the image (which is essentially what we're doing).

Another limitation has to do with how much the camera moves. If the amount of camera translation is too great, the paint work will distort in ways that make it obvious. Sometimes you can project multiple frames at various times throughout the sequence, but then the challenge is to get them to blend smoothly without sudden pops in the texture of the object.

Matchmoves that are being used for "patchmove" purposes need to be exceedingly accurate. In some cases, they need to have the same if not greater accuracy than those required for set extensions. Even a one-pixel jitter can be apparent once the paint work is composited over the footage. In some cases, you might not be able to use this technique with rack focuses or soft focuses because it prevents the matchmovers from achieving a level of accuracy high enough for paint work.

Matchmoves for Compositors

Compositors often need spatial information about the scene they are compositing. Luckily enough, matchmovers have everything they need, and often more. A variety of data generated by matchmovers can be a huge help for problems a compositor may experience.

Compositors, for the most part, work in the 2D world, but it is fairly common to have some 3D capability in the compositing software. While most compositors use 2D tracking, they also may need to access 3D data to achieve certain effects, such as 3D layering, lighting effects, and particle effects. When they do so, they'll need to bring the matchmove into their compositing program.

The good news in this respect is that most of the compositing programs that have a 3D capability also have the ability to import some sort of scene. For example, After Effects can import a Maya ASCII (.ma) file. This is nice because no special scripting is involved, just good old-fashioned import routines. Also, most matchmoving programs these days can export files intended to go directly into compositing packages such as Shake and Inferno.

The 3D scene import will differ with each program, but it goes more or less like this:

1. Track and solve the scene as normal in the matchmoving software.

2. Export the matchmove as a 3D scene (one that can be imported into the compositing software).

3. Import the 3D file into the compositing software and verify that the matchmove is still working against the plate.

When exporting the scene to a compositing program, many of the same techniques apply as when you are delivering a matchmove for a 3D animation package. It will be very helpful to the compositor to know where certain features are, so labeling and organizing the scene is very important.

Matchmoves for TD Work

Matchmovers can provide other visual effects artists with information other than cameras and geometry; they can also provide information about how the scene is lit in certain cases.

In some shots, strong lights from the scene cast strong shadows on the ground or other objects. A good example is in exterior shots when the sun is out. There is a relationship between the light source and the object being lit, and matchmovers can exploit this fact to find the position of the light.

To do this, follow these steps:

1. Track the corner of an object whose shadow you can see on the ground or on another object.

2. Track the shadow of the same object you just tracked. You must track the feature on the shadow that represents the part of the object you tracked. For example, if you track the corner of a building, then you should track the part of the shadow that represents the same corner of the building (Figure 12.9).

3. Track the shot as normal for matchmoving by adding more 2D tracks as necessary.

4. Export the solved scene to your animation program.

Since light travels in a straight line, we know that the light source, the feature on the object, and the shadow of that feature all lie in a straight line as well. When you track the feature and the shadow of that feature, the matchmoving program generates the 3D position of each. If you extend a line from one marker to the next, it will point directly at the light source.

Figure 12.9 By tracking the shadow and the object casting the shadow, we can infer the position of the light source in the scene.

Note: A matchmoving program called SynthEyes actually allows you to calculate this in the program itself using a similar technique. First, you track both the object and the shadow of the object and then you track the shot as normal. Then, using a special feature, the program calculates the position of the light. This light can then be exported with your scene!

Although this is a neat trick, it applies only to certain types of shots. First of all, the light or lights must be strong enough to cast distinct, trackable shadows. Second, you must be able to track the feature as well as its shadow. Sometimes this isn't possible because either the shadow isn't visible or it is too distorted to know what part of the shadow to track. But when this trick does work, it's a great way to accurately re-create the lighting environment.

Not the End of the Road

The tips I've laid out in this chapter are just the beginning of what can be done. It seems that new challenges arise with every project, and as a result I must find new ways to deal with them. Matchmoving will continue to evolve, and new technologies will continue to expand what is possible to achieve. But one thing is for sure: as long as we need to place 3D objects into live-action plates, there will be a need for matchmoving.

Resources

Throughout this book, I've mentioned various forms and images that can be helpful to a matchmover. The forms are included on the companion CD as Adobe Acrobat (.pdf) files so that you can print them out and use them during your matchmoving work. Where applicable, I've also included a Microsoft Excel (.xls) or Word (.doc) version that will allow you to customize them to your needs.

Shot Evaluation Worksheet A checklist you can use as you evaluate matchmoves. To use it, scan down the list and check any applicable item that you see in the live-action plate. A double minus sign (--) means that having that item present in the shot usually makes it more difficult. If the item has double pluses (++), it usually makes the shot is easier. By comparing the number of pluses to minuses, you can get an idea of how difficult the shot is overall.

Scene Delivery Checklist A checklist of things you can do to make your final matchmoved scene easy to use for other visual effects artists. Of course, if you're the only artist working on the shot, it still makes a great reference. This list represents only one way of doing it, and you may find yourself customizing the list quite a bit to fit your needs.

Camera Report A sample camera report that you can use on set to record camera and scene information during filming. An Excel version is also provided in case you need to add additional items.

Set Report The same as the camera report except that it is designed to record information about the set.

X-Sheet A sample X-sheet that you can use to help you lay out your keyframes for matchamation. You can use the frame column to mark which frame the animation takes place on and then use the remaining columns to annotate the type of movement and any notes you may have.

Distortion Grid A grid you can use to record the amount of lens distortion in a camera lens. The grid is scalable so it can be reprinted to virtually any size. To use it, print the file onto paper and then mount it on a rigid substrate (such as foamcore). Take care to mount it as flat as possible so that the lines of the grid remain straight.

Film the grid with any lenses you use during the shoot. The best way to film it is to set up the grid so that it sits directly in front of, and squared up to, the camera. The camera should be mounted on a tripod if possible and be facing directly at the distortion grid. Try to frame up the grid so that it fills up as much of the frame as possible. It's better to have the grid running off the frame than to not reach the edges of the frame.

You only really need one frame for your distortion evaluation, so you don't need to shoot very long. This especially holds true if you are shooting on film, since it is more expensive. If you are using a zoom lens, make sure to shoot at its widest focal length as well as its longest focal length. You might even want to film the grid while you zoom from one to the other.

Matchmoving Software and Useful Links

B

The field of matchmoving has been developing rapidly to the point where there are more tools and more resources available to matchmovers. I've gathered a list of useful programs, books, websites, and other URLs that can be helpful to you.

Matchmoving Software

Many factors come into play when choosing a matchmove program, including price, functionality, and how well it integrates into your workflow. There are a lot of matchmoving programs to choose from, and it can be difficult to know which one is right for you. Below is a list of many of the commercial matchmoving programs currently available.

2d3 boujou and boujou bullet boujou is primarily known for its automatic tracking abilities and ease of use, and it lives up to its reputation. It is a very powerful and popular matchmoving tool that is primarily geared toward automatic tracking. boujou bullet is a lower-priced version without some of the advanced features found in the regular version of boujou.

www.2d3.com

Alias Maya Live The Maya Live module has been a part of Maya for many years. It's somewhat lagging in features compared to other stand-alone matchmoving programs, but nonetheless, it can come in handy for Maya artists since it's integrated directly into the program.

www.alias.com

Andersson Technologies Ltd. SynthEyes SynthEyes is a newcomer on the scene that offers matchmovers an affordable yet full-featured matchmoving program. It has an automatic tracker as well as manual tracking abilities. It also has a lot of tools to facilitate the calibration process.

Perhaps the best thing about SynthEyes is that it has a very low price and yet features that are comparable with other matchmove programs.

www.ssontech.com

Automatic Effects Scene Genie Scene Genie is a matchmoving plug-in for 3ds max. Its tracker is easy to use and has a good solving engine. At the time of this printing, it didn't have an automatic tracker, but it is attractively priced and makes a great option for 3ds max users.

www.scenegenie.com

Pixel Farm PFTrack and PFMatch PFTrack is a matchmoving program that evolved from the Icarus program. Its full-featured tracker has automatic tracking capabilities, nonrigid object tracking (motion capture), and the ability to change the speed of the original footage using optical flow technology. PFMatch is a light version with a lower price.

www.thepixelfarm.co.uk

Realviz MatchMover Pro This program has an excellent 2D tracker but can track automatically as well. It also allows for object tracking, the import of survey data, and refinement of motion control data for advanced matchmove applications.

www.realviz.com

Science D Vision 3D Equalizer 3D Equalizer was one of the first matchmove programs to be commercially available, and it's still going strong. It has a strong following in larger studios because of its excellent 2D tracker and solving capabilities. It boasts a wide range of advanced tools such as motion capture and the ability to track multiple sequences simultaneously. 3D Equalizer is available at different price points and levels of functionality.

www.sci-d-vis.com

Other Useful Programs

In addition to matchmoving programs, there are a few programs that can be added to a matchmover's tool belt. These would include image-based modeling programs and utilities for removing distortion.

Realviz ImageModeler This program, developed by the makers of MatchMover Pro, allows users to model geometry based on still photographs. It uses the same photogrammetry techniques as MatchMover Pro, but has a suite of modeling and texturing tools to allow the creation of photoreal 3D models quickly.

www.realviz.com

Eos Systems Inc. PhotoModeler Another image-based modeler that is easy to use. Eos Systems has geared it more toward the forensics/legal animation market, but it is versatile enough to be used for a variety of other applications as well.

    www.photomodeler.com

Pixel Farm PFBarn This is an image-based modeling tool from the creators of PFTrack. It has all the functionality of other image-based modeling programs, but it also allows you to model from a single image if desired.

    www.thepixelfarm.co.uk

Pixel Farm PFBarrel A distortion removal plug-in that allows the user to remove distortion from images and add distortion to CG elements. PFBarrel not only can automatically solve for barrel and pincushion distortion, but it can do so for complex distortions or distortions that vary over time.

    www.thepixelfarm.co.uk

Imagineer Systems Monet Monet is primarily a 2D tracking program that is designed to help replace elements in a plate, but it's worth mentioning because it has a distortion removal tool built in. It also uses a planar tracker, which is different than any of the trackers we've seen in this book.

    www.mokey.com/products/monet

Books

One of the main reasons I wrote this book is because there aren't currently any books on matchmoving. There are, however, books that are related to matchmoving that deserve mentioning.

Multiple View Geometry in Computer Vision by Richard Hartley and Andrew Zisserman (Cambridge University Press, 2nd ed., 2004). This is an extremely technical book that shows the mathematical principles behind photogrammetry and image-based technology. If you're interested in knowing how the math works (or developing your own matchmove technology), this book's for you. If you're not mathematically inclined, you might not get too much out of it.

The Geometry of Multiple Images by Olivier Faugeras and Quang-Tuan Luong (MIT Press, 2001). This book is similar to the Hartley/Zisserman book in that it is a technical book that shows the math behind the programs. Super technical, but interesting for mathematicians.

American Cinematographer's Manual by Rob Hummel (ASC Holding Corp., 8th ed., 2002). You can never know too much about cameras, and this is a great reference about how film cameras work and are used. It's a technical book full of specifications for various cameras and formats, so it's not exactly light reading, but I've needed to refer to it on many occasions for information about cameras. It's not cheap, so you might consider trying to find a used edition at an online auction. If you do so, try to get the latest edition possible.

The Art and Science of Digital Compositing by Ron Brinkmann (Morgan Kauffman, 1999). Okay, so this is a book on compositing, but it is a great reference to have, and it covers 2D tracking for compositors, which is very similar to 2D tracking for matchmovers.

The Filmmaker's Handbook: A Comprehensive Guide for the Digital Age by Steven Ascher and Edward Pincus (Plume, 1999). This is a great book that provides an overall view of filmmaking and cameras. It's an excellent reference for everything involving cameras, including digital cameras as well as how their images are used in postproduction.

Websites

Greg Downing Greg Downing has always been a strong advocate for image-based techniques. He has worked closely with the Realviz development team, and he continues to push the boundaries in photogrammetry, image-based modeling, and panoramic photography. He is always posting interesting new experiments on his website, and he has created a training DVD on photogrammetry for The Gnomon School which is expected out early in 2005.

www.gregdowning.com

fxguide This is a great site geared toward visual effects. I make mention of it primarily because there is a great article series by Mike Seymour and John Montgomery that covers 2D tracking and 3D matchmoving. They are well-researched articles that include an interesting history of 2D and 3D tracking.

www.fxguide.com

The Letterbox and Widescreen Advocacy Page This site has some good information about the various widescreen formats, including interesting tidbits about their history.

www.widescreen.org

Film Formats

Film formats define, among other things, the size and shape of the image. This information is important to a matchmover, especially if they must solve their matchmoves at a specific focal length. There is an intrinsic relationship between the focal length and the size of the film back (see Chapter 6), and therefore knowing the correct film back measurements for the camera is necessary if you need to have a specific film back.

There are two main factors to consider: type of film used (16mm, 35mm, etc.) and the size of the film aperture. There are usually multiple formats for each type of film used. For example, the Academy format and Full Aperture format both use 35mm film. The difference is in how the image is composed on the film, and this is controlled mainly by the position and size of the film aperture.

When considering the size of the aperture, it is important to take the optical sound track into consideration. No, this isn't the score to the movie! The sound track is a part of the film where the sound can be recorded optically. If the sound track is present on the film, it can mean that less area on the film is available for the image.

In this appendix, I've listed some of the most common formats used, although there are many more available.

16mm Formats

Although you don't run into 16mm very frequently, it's worth listing here.

16mm

Aperture size: 0.404″ × 0.295″ (10.26mm × 7.49mm)

Image aspect ratio: 1.37

Super 16

Aperture size: 0.493″ × 0.292″ (12.52mm × 7.42mm)

Image aspect ratio: 1.69

Super 16 obtains additional space on the film by using the area that is normally reserved for the sound track.

35mm Formats

35mm is the most commonly used film media, and there are a multitude of formats that use it. The main difference is in how much of the film area is exposed.

Academy aperture

Aperture size: 0.864″ × 0.630″ (21.94mm × 16.00mm)

Image aspect ratio: 1.37

Academy aperture allows for a part of the film to be used for the sound track. It's often referred to simply as "Academy."

Full aperture

Aperture size: 0.980″ × 0.735″ (24.89mm × 18.67mm)

Image aspect ratio: 1.33

Full aperture (or "full app," as it's also known) uses the area normally reserved for the sound track.

Super 35 (composed for 2.35)

Aperture size: 0.945″ × 0.394″ (24mm × 10.01mm)

Image aspect ratio: 2.35

Super 35 is similar to full app, but the image can be framed within the full aperture to achieve the desired aspect ratio. It is also possible to compose it at 1:85 or other aspect ratios. Super 35 gives filmmakers the ability to show the film in theaters at widescreen aspect ratios, but it retains the full app image so it can also be transferred to video without having to resort to pan and scan methods.

Cinemascope

Aperture size: 0.864″ × 0.732″ (21.94mm × 18.59mm)

Image aspect ratio: 2.35

Sometimes referred to as "scope," this format uses an anamorphic lens to squeeze the image horizontally at a 2:1 ratio. The image on the film appears to be squashed horizontally, but when it is stretched out to 2.35 aspect ratio, it appears normal. Note that the horizontal aperture is the same as the horizontal aperture size of the Academy format.

VistaVision

Aperture size: 1.485″ × 0.991″ (37.71mm × 25.17mm)

Image aspect ratio: 1.5

VistaVision (also known as "35mm 8-perf") is a format that involves a unique approach. The standard 35mm film is fed through the camera horizontally rather than vertically. This means a larger portion of the film can be exposed. The height is slightly larger than full app, and the width extends across eight perforations.

Large Formats

The number of large formats is considerably less than 35mm, but there are a couple that are used routinely.

65mm

Aperture size: 2.066″ × 0.906″ (52.47mm × 23.01mm)

Image aspect ratio: 2.28

This format uses a larger area of the film for better quality. Theatrical presentations of "70mm" prints are usually filmed with the 65mm format. The 70mm designation refers to the size of the projection print, which includes an area for a magnetic sound track.

IMAX

Aperture size: 2.772″ × 2.072″ (70.39mm × 52.62mm)

Image aspect ratio: 1.33

Digital Formats

It is much harder to determine the correct film back settings for digital cameras because no standard has emerged yet. This can be problematic if you are required to use exact focal lengths.

The most popular CCDs at the writing of this book are the $^1/_3''$ and $^2/_3''$ chips. The size measurement of these chips unfortunately does not indicate their actual size, and that, of course, makes it difficult to come up with a film back measurement for use inside the matchmoving program.

DV cameras often use the $^1/_3''$ CCD chip. Most DV cams have variable lenses, which makes calculating an exact focal length even more difficult. In most cases, it is best to let the matchmove program solve for the focal length. Some DV cameras also allow the user to alter the framing, so the aspect ratio may be varied. For example, the user can use a 16:9 (1.778) aspect ratio, which is cropped from the original 4:3 (1.33) aspect ratio.

HD cameras also come with a variety of film backs and lens types. The aspect ratio of HD is 1.778, but there is no standard for film back measurements. I've had good luck using a film back size of $0.377'' \times 0.212''$ (9.5758mm $\times$ 5.3848mm) for HD cameras such as the Sony F950.

Calculating the Film Back for Cropped Images

In some cases, the image may have been cropped before you receive it. This is not ideal, since the principal point may have been offset during the process. If you are faced with this scenario, you may need to come up with a film back measurement that will work.

If there is some known relationship of the original film back and the crop, you might be able to calculate what the film back should be. For example, let's say you receive an image sequence that was shot at 35mm full app but was cropped to HD proportions during the telecine by chopping off the top and bottom of the original image. The horizontal aperture for full app is 0.980″. To figure what the vertical aperture should be, you can simply divide 0.980″ by 1.778 (HD aspect ratio), which gives a vertical film back dimension of 0.551″.

If it is not known how the image was cropped, you may find clues in the image itself. If you see the edges of the film in the image, you might be able to tell if either the horizontal or vertical is full frame and then deduce the vertical measurement or vice versa. If no edges are visible, it may not be possible to accurately define the film back.

Glossary

anamorphic lens A special lens that optically squeezes the image so that more image will fit on a standard piece of film. Movies made with this type of lens must be projected with a special anamorphic projection lens that reverses the squeeze during playback.

aperture plate The opening on the film gate in a film camera. This opening determines the image aspect ratio of the final image. The meaning here should not be confused with the lens aperture, which is the size of the iris opening.

articulated matte A black-and-white image that separates (or masks) various parts of the image. Specifically, it is a matte that is created by drawing splines by hand.

backface culling A display mode in 3D applications that hides any polygons that do not face the camera.

calibrated camera A camera about which all of the parameters are known, such as position, rotation, and focal length.

calibration The process of computing the camera's position, rotation, and internal parameters. It often involves computing the 3D position of various features seen in the image.

calibration engine The particular algorithms used to calibrate cameras in matchmoving programs.

camera projection A process in 3D animation programs where an image is texture mapped onto an object from the camera's position. This is often used for matte painting and to add slight camera moves to locked-off cameras, among other things.

channels An attribute in 3D animation programs that controls a certain property of an object. For example, the Translate X channel controls the object's left/right position.

charge-coupled device (CCD) A light-sensitive chip in a digital camera that converts light into a digital signal. CCDs are used in digital cameras to replace the film found in traditional cameras.

dailies A meeting where the latest work for a film or television project is viewed and commented on. For visual effects, it is usually attended by the visual effects supervisor, lead artists, and the artists who created the work.

digitization The process of converting film or analog media to digital files.

diopter A supplementary lens used for close-up photography. It is usually placed in front of a lens much like a lens filter would be.

feature A unique part of an image that can be easily identified and tracked.

feed reel/take-up reel On a film camera, these are reels that sit in the film cartridge. One reel feeds the film into the camera, and the other takes it up after it has been exposed.

film aperture The opening in the aperture plate in a film camera. The size of the film aperture usually defines the image aspect ratio.

film back A more generic term for film gate or aperture. Film back is often used to describe the aperture settings in a 3D animation program.

film gate The part of a film camera where the film is exposed. It consists of a pressure plate, aperture plate, and usually a small claw to pull the film through the gate.

focal length The distance between the center of the lens and the film plane, usually expressed in millimeters. Shorter focal lengths show more of the scene and give a sense of depth, while longer focal lengths show less of the scene and tend to make the image look flatter.

forward kinematics (FK) A method in 3D animation packages in which animation of parent objects affects all children objects below them. See also *inverse kinematics (IK)*.

frustum A pyramid-shaped area in front of a camera lens that defines what portion of the scene can be seen by the camera. Its shape is defined by the focal length and the size of the film back.

garbage matte A rough articulated matte. In matchmoving, garbage mattes are often used to define which parts of the image are to be tracked.

image sequence A series of images that when played back produce the footage shot by the camera. These can exist as individual numbered images or as a video file such as AVIs or Quicktime movies.

initialized Given a starting value for calibration as opposed to a completely unknown value.

inverse kinematics (IK) A system used in some 3D animation packages that allows children objects to affect parent objects. This is often used in character animation setups because it allows the character to be controlled much like a puppet. See also *forward kinematics (FK)*.

masks See *articulated matte* and *garbage matte*.

matchamation Also known as *rotomation*. Animating a character or object so that it matches a character or object in the live-action plate.

morph target A modified version of a CG object that is used to change the original object's shape. This is often used for facial animation or to change an object's shape over time seamlessly.

motion capture A system for capturing an actor's performance by tracking markers on their body. Usually this is done with special suits, markers, and motion capture equipment such as infrared cameras or magnetic tracking markers.

nodal, nodal point The optical center of a camera. Generally this is located at the center of the lens, or more specifically, the center of the iris.

nodal pan A camera move in which the camera is rotated around its nodal point.

origin The point in a 3D scene that represents the spatial coordinates X: 0, Y: 0, Z: 0.

orthogonal A method of image projection in which the rays are parallel with the image plane. This type of projection does not produce perspective as with a normal camera; instead, it looks more like a blueprint or technical drawing.

overcranked An method of filming in which the camera is run faster than normal. When played back, it appears to move in slow motion. See also *undercranked*.

parallax The amount of perspective in an image. Generally, it is used to mean the apparent change of perspective from one image to another, although this is technically known as *parallax shift*.

parallax shift See *parallax*.

perspective Characteristics within an image that give the impression of depth. More specifically, objects closer to the camera appear larger, and objects further away seem smaller. Also, parallel lines converge on the horizon at what is known as a vanishing point.

photogrammetry The process of reconstructing the camera and environment in 3D using multiple photographs or a moving sequence.

pipeline The flow of work in film and television production. Often the pipeline is defined in terms of where work goes as each visual effects shot is completed. For example, "further down the pipeline" would mean work that happens later on in the process.

pixel aspect ratio A width/height ratio that defines the shape of the pixels that make up a digital image. Square pixels are represented as a ratio of 1:1, or more simply as a pixel aspect ratio of 1.0. Nonsquare pixels, such as those found on NTSC video, have a pixel aspect ratio of 0.9. That is, they are 10 percent narrower in width than in height. This is not to be confused with the image aspect ratio, which is the width/height ratio of the image overall.

plate The live-action image sequence or video. This is usually the plate before any visual effects, color treatment, etc., have been added.

pose-to-pose A method of animating in which the animator sets key poses first and then works on the poses in between.

pressure plate The back part of the film gate that sits behind the film.

principal point The point on the film plane at which the optical center of the lens projects, usually in the center. If lens distortion is present in the image, it will be less pronounced near the principal point.

projection The process of converting the three-dimensional scene onto a two-dimensional plane such as a piece of film.

projection lines In mathematical terms, it is an imaginary line that intersects a 2D feature on the image, the optical center of the camera lens, and the position of a 3D feature in the scene.

proxy objects, proxy sets Temporary objects that mark position or help the matchmover determine the quality of the matchmove. They are usually low-resolution models and are sometimes textured with checkerboard patterns.

rack focus When the camera is suddenly focused from one subject to another. These are generally more difficult to track.

rectification The process of taking an image that is skewed (such as one that contains strong perspective) and changing its shape to fit another object (such as the shape of a 3D object).

reference frame A frame that is used to define an initial calibration. This term is used specifically in MatchMover Pro.

residual The difference between the two-dimensional position of a feature on an image and the apparent two-dimensional position of a three-dimensional feature when viewed through a calibrated camera. This value is expressed in pixels and it is used as a measure of the success of a calibration during a matchmove. Generally, matchmovers need to keep their overall residual less than 1.0 pixel.

rig Any type of construction in a 3D animation package that facilitates easier manipulation of an object. Matchmovers often create special camera rigs that let them position their cameras within a 3D scene more quickly and accurately.

rotomation See *matchamation*.

rotoscoping The process of defining mattes on an image. This is usually done by creating splines that follow the shapes of features on the image.

shutter The mechanism on a camera that either blocks light or lets light pass through. By blocking the light temporarily, it allows the frame of film to move out of the way without becoming exposed to light as it does so.

solution, solving The process of calibrating a camera and defining the positions of objects in the scene. See also *calibration*.

stereopsis The shift of perspective apparent between two different points of view (as in a pair of human eyes).

stereoscopic A device or method that uses two calibrated cameras to reconstruct a 3D sense of the scene.

stick A small handle that a film camera lens can be mounted onto and looked through. It is often used to let a director or DP get a better sense of how the shot will look without actually mounting a lens or moving the camera.

straight ahead A method of animating in which the animator starts at the beginning frame and sets key poses in a linear fashion for later frames.

symmetrical centering A feature of some 2D trackers that allows the tracker to center on symmetrical features in an image sequence. It's particularly useful for tracking circular features that could change shape during the course of the sequence.

tracks, tracking A marker that follows a 2D feature on an image sequence. The process of placing trackers and making the trackers follow the feature over time is called tracking.

translation Changing position; moving.

uncalibrated camera A camera about which nothing is known, including position, rotation, and internal parameters.

undercranked Footage that was shot slower than normal speed. When played back at normal speed, it appears to have been sped up.

wire removal The process of removing safety wires from a live-action plate.

Index

Lock to Camera option, 79
locking down scenes, 158–159
low-contrast features, **59**, *60*

M

make and model of cameras, 164
manual tracking, **94**
markers
    in 3D calibration, 79, *79*
    circular, 52, *53*
    in matchmove kits, 171–172
    for shoots, **167–168**
masks, **99–100**, *99*
matchamation, **175**
    distances in, **176**
    first passes in, **179–180**,
        189–191, *189, 191*
    imperfect data in, **181–182**
    initial poses in, **177**
    model changes in, **181**
    movements in, **178–179**, 198
    nonlinear animation tech-
        niques in, **178**
    object tracking in, **196–198**
    tutorial, **182–195**, *182–187,*
        189, 191, 193
    tweaks in, 180, **192–195**, *193*
matching characters. *See*
    matchamation
matchmove checking, **135–138**,
    136, 138
matchmove kits, **171–173**, *173*
MatchMover Pro program,
    63, 256
math in photogrammetry,
    30–31, 35
Matte painters, 249
mattes, **99–100**, *99*
Maya, views in, **195**
Maya Live program, 255
measurements
    in perspective matching,
        12–13
    setting, 6
    for shoots, **162–163**,
        163, **166**
measuring tapes and tools, **171**
minimum number of tracks,
    48–49, *49*, 68
misaligned objects, 150

models, **215**
    image-based, **231–233**,
        232–233
        problems with, **235–236**
        pull textures for,
            233–235, *234–235*
    in matchamation, **181**
    from matchmoves,
        216–218, *218*
    tutorial, **219–231**, *219–220,*
        222–230
Monet program, 257
morph targets, 181
motion blur
    in 2D tracking, **56**, *56*
    troubleshooting, 208
motion capture devices, 197
motion control cameras, 25
motion paths, 53
mounts, camera, 164
movements and motion
    camera, **139**, *140*
    2D. *See* 2D tracking
    in 3D calibration, **74–75**,
        75, **83–85**, *84*
    checking, **201–203**, *202*
    in matchamation, **198**
    in matchamation, **178–179**,
        186–187, *187*, 198
multipurposing matchmove
    data, **237**
    blending matchmoves,
        241–242
    camera setup, **242–248**,
        242–246, 248
    for compositors, **250–251**
    extensions and
        enhancements,
        238–239, *239–240*
    object tracks as camera
        tracks, **248**
    patchmoves, **249–250**
    for TD work, **251–252**, *252*

N

natural jitter, 53, *54*
Nodal Pan option, 103
nodal points, 27
nodality of lenses, **118**, *119*

noise
    in 2D tracking, **59**
    in 3D calibration, 81
    automatic tracking for, 100
    troubleshooting, 207
nonlinear animation
    techniques, **178**
Normal to 3 Points option, 89
nulls
    in 3D calibration, 79–80
    for camera rigs, 17, *17*
    in models, 218
    for scaling, 143
    in set fitting, 144, 203, *204*
    in troubleshooting, 206

O

object tracks
    as camera tracks, **248**
    in matchamation, **196–198**
objects
    matching. *See* matchamation
    proxy, 9, **135–138**, *136, 138*
occlusion, **57–58**, *58*
on-set techniques. *See* shoots
optics, **26–27**, *26–27*
optimizing plates, **62**
orientation, coordinate systems
    for, 86
Origin To option, 89
origins, 29, 88
overcranking, 112–113
Overscan field, 195

P

pan shots, 117
    in 3D calibration, 83–84, *84*
    fitting, **139**
    parallax with, 118, *119*
parallax, **35–36**, *36*, 41
    in 3D calibration, 83–84
    checking for, 64, *64*, 205
    with panning, 118, *119*
    in patchmoves, 249
parent objects for camera
    rigs, 17
patchmoves, **249–250**
pattern areas, 46, *46*, 56

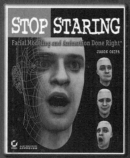